OFF THE BEATEN PATH® SERIES

Rhode Island

THIRD EDITION

Off the Beaten Path®

by Robert Patrick Curley

The Globe Pequot Press

Guilford, Connecticut

Copyright © 1996, 1998, 2000 by The Globe Pequot Press

Off the Beaten Path is a registered trademark of The Globe Pequot Press.

Illustrations by Carole Drong
Maps created by Equator Graphics © The Globe Pequot Press
Cover and text design by Laura Augustine
Cover photo by Paul Rocheleau/Index Stock Imagery

Library of Congress Cataloging-in-Publication Data

Curley, Robert Patrick.
   Rhode Island : off the beaten path : a guide to unique places / by Robert Patrick Curley.—3rd ed.
     p. cm. — (Off the beaten path series)
   Includes index.
   ISBN 0-7627-0645-7
   1. Rhode Island—Guidebooks. I. Title. II. Series.

F77.3 .C87 2000
917.4504'43—dc21   00-029391

Manufactured in the United States of America
Third Edition/First Printing

*To my wife, Christine, who is always there for me,
especially during deadline; and to Christopher and Shannon,
for being the best children anyone could ever hope to have.*

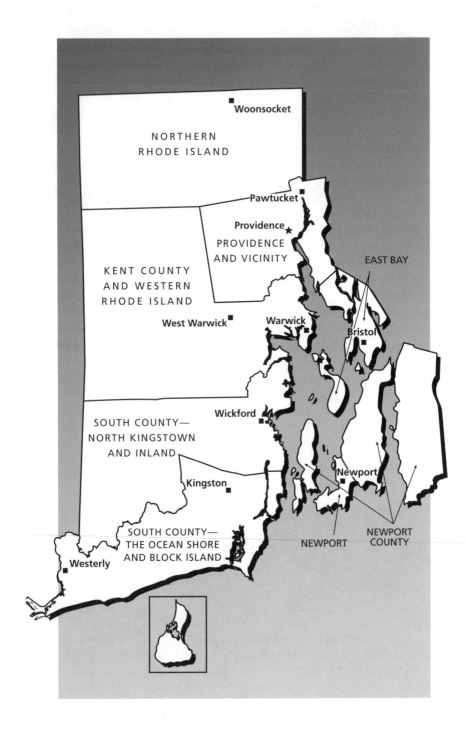

Woonsocket

NORTHERN
RHODE ISLAND

Pawtucket

Providence ★
PROVIDENCE
AND VICINITY

EAST BAY

KENT COUNTY
AND WESTERN
RHODE ISLAND

Warwick

Bristol

West Warwick

Wickford

SOUTH COUNTY—
NORTH KINGSTOWN
AND INLAND

Newport

Kingston

SOUTH COUNTY—
THE OCEAN SHORE
AND BLOCK ISLAND

NEWPORT
COUNTY

NEWPORT

Westerly

Contents

Acknowledgments vi

Introduction vii

Providence and Vicinity 1

Kent County and Western Rhode Island 31

Northern Rhode Island 53

The East Bay 79

Newport 101

Newport County 125

South County—North Kingstown and Inland 153

South County—The Ocean Shore and Block Island 173

Index 206

Acknowledgments

Special thanks to the idea people: Frank Singer, Gary Enos, Melissa DeMeo, Mary Grady, Marie Kapsales, Cindy DeMaio, Karin Welt, Kerri Hicks, Jennifer Mooney, Bill Kanapaux, Eleyne Austen Sharp, Simone Joyaux, Lisa Starr, Loren Spears, Darlene Dame, Evan Smith, Officer Parker (the one-man police force of Prudence Island), Maryellen Cicione, and Kerry Molloy. For their time and courteousness, thanks to all the people at all the sites in this book, and a special acknowledgment must go out to those who keep the fire of knowledge and history burning: the wonderful folks at Rhode Island's historical societies, libraries, visitors centers, and tourism agencies. Finally, thanks to Paula Bodah for thinking of me, to Mace Lewis for his blind faith in my ability to get this book done, and to Justine Rathbun and Christina Lester for picking up the ball.

Introduction

Rhode Island may be the smallest state, but it has the biggest heart. And it definitely has the longest name.

Officially the State of Rhode Island and Providence Plantations, Rhode Island was founded on the principles that Americans hold most dear, such as freedom of speech, assembly, and religion—freedoms that were in short supply in the New World settlements of the seventeenth century. Sometimes known as "Rogue's Island" for its insider politics and past habit of harboring privateers and other free spirits, the colony (and later, state) of Rhode Island was more beloved as a haven for dissidents of every stripe. The state remains a place where self-expression is encouraged and strangers welcome—in short, the perfect place to spend a holiday.

With the exception of Newport, which unquestionably is one of the nation's most famous cities, it can be argued that all of Rhode Island is off the beaten path. Sure, television has thrust Providence into the spotlight recently, but many tourists, assuming that nothing so small can be very interesting, still know Rhode Island mostly as a speed bump on the interstate between New York and Boston. Closer examination, however, reveals a state of great contrasts, rich history, and quirks aplenty, as the following chapters will demonstrate.

A frequent problem when visiting an unfamiliar place is the nagging question of whether, amidst the tourist attractions, you are experiencing the real people and places—seeing what makes the area tick, not just the pretty face put on for visitors. So here are some suggestions if you want a taste of the real Rhode Island:

1. Stay off Interstate 95. Instead, drive at a leisurely pace on the uncongested back roads that make the state a joy to explore. Route 102, for example, begins in South County's seaside town of Wickford and courses through the rural and wooded western part of the state, turning north for an enchanting drive that avoids all the big towns and cities, crosses over the beautiful Scituate Reservoir and through the quaint village of Chepachet, and doesn't end until it reaches the state's northern border near Woonsocket. A drive on Route 102 is a great way to spend a day.

2. Avoid fast food franchises. Rhode Island has some of the best seafood restaurants anywhere—try them! In places like East Providence and Bristol, fine Portuguese fare is on the menu. Providence's ethnic diversity is reflected in the city's wide array of eateries, from the Italian cuisine on Federal Hill to the Indian, vegetarian, and other offerings on Wickenden Street and Thayer Street, to the fine continental dining featured downtown.

If you see a Del's Lemonade stand—and the state is full of them—stop and order a cup. This mix of slush ice, sugar, and real lemon juice and lemon chunks is quite possibly the best drink ever invented for a hot summer day. If you are daring, try the little hot dogs served up at any store proclaiming the availability of NEW YORK SYSTEM WIENERS. Rhode Island legend has it that these spicy red wieners are best eaten after a night of revelry, and that the best purveyors are the places where the grillman lines the dogs up on his arm as he cooks.

Real Rhode Island jonnycakes—flint-corn pancakes spooned onto a hot grill—are found at many restaurants and also at traditional May breakfasts, sponsored each spring by local churches, grange halls, and other civic groups. Instead of clam chowder, look for quahog chowder, made from Rhode Island's indigenous breed of bivalve.

3. Meet the people. Despite the caricature of the laconic, reserved Yankee, most Rhode Islanders you meet are friendly and fiercely proud of their home state—even if they do bad-mouth their politicians. Perhaps this easygoing nature is the result of living in a state where the total population is under one million people, and everyone seems to know everyone else—and everyone else's business. Whatever the reason, Ocean State residents always seem happy to talk to visitors who show an interest in the state's great natural and historical heritage. This advice extends to those attractions in this book that are open by appointment only: Don't be afraid to call and ask for a showing—it's a great way to meet "real" Rhode Islanders.

So come along: "The Biggest Little State" is waiting to be explored.

The prices and rates listed in this guidebook were confirmed at press time. We recommend, however, that you call establishments to obtain current information before traveling. The area code for the entire state of Rhode Island is 401.

Providence and Vicinity

ike all great cities, Providence draws its strength from its distinct, diverse neighborhoods, many of which center on a single, thriving street that serves as both business district and social center for the community.

Thayer Street is Providence's answer to Greenwich Village, an arty, multicultural pastiche that feeds on the energy of the students and faculty of nearby Brown University and the Rhode Island School of Design (RISD). Just a few blocks up College Hill from the historic homes lining Benefit Street, Thayer Street on the East Side of Providence moves to the beat of multiple *record stores, bookstores, and cafes* featuring Indian, Greek, and Southwestern cuisine. Shops peddling vintage clothing, New Age trinkets, and sportswear are a magnet for a young, hip crowd, as are the handful of bars that thrive here.

OOP! (297 Thayer Street, 455–0844) is a typically eclectic shop, where you can spend a few bucks or a few thousand on original works of art by over one hundred local and regional craftspeople. The **Avon Cinema** (260 Thayer Street, 421–3315) is the local art house, showing obscure foreign films and independent releases that the big theater chains won't touch. There are midnight screenings, too. The street comes alive at night—in the summer and on weekends when school is in session—when, between the sidewalk cafes, skateboarders, and throngs of strollers, Thayer Street resembles its New York counterpart even more.

Wickenden Street, located at the southern end of the East Side, is more sedate than Thayer Street but also offers an array of interesting places to shop and eat. Start your walk from the south end of the street. For thin-crust pizza served with a variety of imaginative toppings, **Fellini Pizzeria** (166 Wickenden Street, 751–6737) is the place to go; fresh-squeezed juices and pastas are also served. Across the street at number 207 is the spiritual center of Wickenden Street, the **Coffee Exchange** (273–1198), which is so popular that it outgrew its former storefront location and now occupies a large house and outdoor deck. Stick

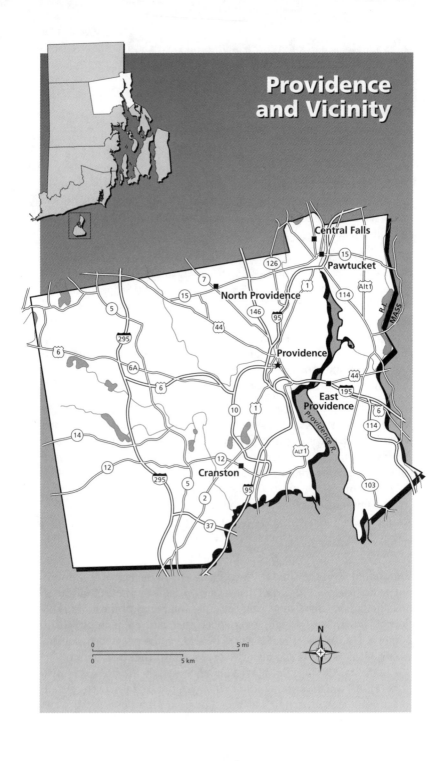

Providence
and Vicinity

PROVIDENCE AND VICINITY

Waterplace Park

McCoy Stadium

Slater Mill

Federal Hill

The Culinary Archives and Museum

Feast of St. Joseph, Federal Hill; May

Keep Providence Beautiful Pasta Challenge, Providence; September

Providence Waterfront Festival, Providence; September

First Night, Providence; December 31

Armory Acts Festival, Providence; September

Convergence Arts Festival, Providence; June

around for a few weeks, and you might be able to sample their more than two dozen varieties of coffee, espresso, and cappuccino. For each pound of coffee sold, the Coffee Exchange donates 25 cents to help impoverished children working in coffee fields around the world. Open Monday to Thursday 6:30 A.M. to 10:00 P.M., Friday 6:30 A.M. to 11:00 P.M., Saturday 7:00 A.M. to 11:00 P.M., and Sunday 7:00 A.M. to 10:00 P.M.

The *O-Cha Cafe* (221 Wickenden Street, 421–4699) serves up an adventurous mix of Thai and Japanese cuisine; they'll make your meal as spicy as you like.

Back when this was a much tougher street, 244 Wickenden was the address for Manny Almeida's Ringside Cafe, where the mealtime entertainment was provided by boxers swapping leather. Today the spot is occupied by the more sedate *Z Bar and Grille* (831–1566). For fascinating photographs of old Providence, framed prints, and old posters, check out the *Alaimo Gallery* at 301 Wickenden Street (421–5360).

Near the top of the hill, where Wickenden Street ends at Governor Street, a cluster of antiques shops have sprung up, including the *Providence Antique Center* (442 Wickenden Street, 274–5820) and *Antiques and Artifacts* (436 Wickenden Street, 421–8334).

Providence long has been a center for jewelry manufacturing, but at first blush there is nothing too entrancing about the city's *Jewelry District.* Amid the industrial sites and old warehouse buildings, though, a few gems shine. Part coffeehouse, part restaurant, part antiques store and gift shop, *CAV* (14 Imperial Place, 751–9164) is a Rhode Island original, much like owner Sylvia Moubayed. Located in an old factory building, CAV (the acronym stands for Coffee, Antiques, and Victuals) is consistent in its eclecticism. Mediterranean, Middle Eastern, Greek . . . you'll find all sorts of interesting cuisine at CAV, in addition to a variety of vegetarian dishes. The lobster ravioli remains a personal favorite. Dinner specials vary from day to day.

CAV's decor is a reflection of Sylvia's passion for collecting unusual antiques and artifacts from around the world, and the rambling, brick-walled restaurant is filled with African tribal masks, Finnish

Armory Acting and "Armory Acts"

Providence's Armory District is a diverse ethnic neighborhood centered on its namesake, a massive, turreted armory built in 1914 that is one of the city's great landmarks.

Until recently, the armory was the home for the Rhode Island National Guard. Today, the armory's future is uncertain, but in 1997 director Michael Corrente (Federal Hill, American Buffalo) used the building's main hall as a sound stage for his latest movie, Outside Providence. *The city hopes that other Hollywood types will follow suit.*

The big stone building also provides an attractive backdrop for the annual Armory Acts Festival, a multicultural blend of Hispanic, African-American, and Asian food and music that's representative of the local community. Sponsored by the West Broadway Neighborhood Association (831–9344), the festival is held every September.

folk art dolls, and pre-Columbian artifacts. One corner of the building is used as a gift shop, selling unusual jewelry, scarves, and rugs. CAV also frequently features live music, including blues and jazz artists. To get to CAV, take exit 2 off Interstate 195 east, make a right at the end of the ramp onto Wickenden Street, and proceed $1/2$ mile to Hoppin Street and make another right. Pass the Harvard Pilgrim Health Care building and park in the large parking lot in front of Imperial Place. The door to CAV is located in the courtyard between the two brick buildings facing the lot. CAV is open daily (except Sunday) for lunch and dinner (lunch only on Monday) and stays open late; live music starts at 9:30 P.M.

Also worth a visit in the Jewelry District is **Snookers** (145 Clifford Street, 351–7665), a huge billiards hall with twenty pool tables; the Green Room lounge, where live bands perform on weekends; and a bar that has numerous beers on tap. Snookers also serves food and runs eight-ball and nine-ball tournaments; expect to wait for a table on weekends. It's open until 1:00 A.M. on weeknights, 2:00 A.M. on weekends. Another place to hear live music while you eat is the **Atomic Grill** (99 Chestnut Street, 621–8888), where the menu is written on giant chalkboards and atom mobiles spin overhead.

Located in an alleyway off Elbow Street, the entrance to the **Sandra Feinstein-Gamm Theatre** is unpretentious. But the intimate space occupied by SFGT (31 Elbow Street, 831–2919; www.sfgt.org) is warm and welcoming, and artistic directors Nigel Gore and Kate Lohman produce works that seem worthier of a larger stage. From a contemporary take on Shakespeare's *King Lear* to Ronald Harwood's *The Dresser*—a backstage look at a British theater troupe of the 1940s—the SFGT's established company of actors tackles the classics, new works, and even holiday musicals with equal aplomb.

The Call (15 Elbow Street, 751–2255) is the Jewelry District's prime spot for live music, featuring blues bands and local rockers with a softer edge. For more cutting-edge live performances, the adjoining **Century Lounge** (150 Chestnut Street, 751–2255) has a stage in a cozy basement setting with open-beamed ceilings, oversized couches for lounging, and a copper-trimmed bar for imbibing.

Depasquale Square

The **Providence Children's Museum** (100 South Street, 273–5437) provides preteens with a hands-on, interactive experience that mixes play and learning. Whether your children like to climb on a bulldozer or sit at a computer, they'll have a great time here. Exhibits include Water Ways, where kids and parents can experiment with wave and bubble machines, and Little-woods, an indoor forest of the imagination. The museum is open Tuesday through Sunday 9:30 A.M. to 5:00 P.M.; Monday during the summer and on holidays. Admission is $4.50; free the first Sunday of each month.

Federal Hill is Providence's Little Italy, and it has the food to prove it. At one time most of the New England Mafia operated out of a storefront on the Hill, but these days the area is known more for its cannoli and cal-zones than its crime figures.

To get to Federal Hill from downtown Providence, pick up Atwells Avenue from where it intersects with Broadway just west of the Provi-dence Civic Center. Take Atwells Avenue across Interstate 95, and you'll be greeted by a greenish *arch* (pronounced locally as "the Aahch") hung with an Italian pinecone—a traditional symbol of welcome much like the pineapples decorating stores and homes elsewhere in the state.

The Old World feel of Federal Hill is evident everywhere, from the umbrella-covered cafe tables surrounding the fountain in *Depasquale Square,* to the chickens hanging in the window of the local poultry shop and the bread stacked high in bakery display cases.

From the simplest pizza joint to the most elegant dining room, Fed-eral Hill is the place to go in Providence for Italian food. For sand-wiches made with imported Italian ingredients, exquisite desserts including tiramisu and delicate sorbets, and great coffee and cappuc-cino taken alfresco, pull up a chair at *Cafe Dolce Vita* (59 Depasquale Avenue, 331–8240). In fact, most of the restaurants on Depasquale

Square have outside seating, but one you'll want to go inside for—if only to marvel at the bright, elegant decor—is **Walter's La Locanda del Coccio** (265 Atwells Avenue, 273–2652), where fine Italian dishes are prepared using an ancient Etruscan method of terra-cotta cooking. It also has chairs and tables on Depasquale Square. For a quick, inexpensive meal served in a lively, noisy communal setting, **Angelo's Civita Farnese** (141 Atwells Avenue, 621–8171) is your destination. A trio of upscale, black-tie restaurants vie for the attention of diners looking for a romantic, elegant meal with a good bottle of wine: **The Blue Grotto** (210 Atwells Avenue, 272–9030), the **Old Canteen** (120 Atwells Avenue, 751–5544), and **Camille's Roman Garden** (71 Bradford Street, 751–4812).

One short block north of Atwells Avenue is Spruce Street, home of **Caserta's** (121 Spruce Street, 272–3618, 621–3618, or 621–9190), acclaimed as the best pizza place in the state. Don't leave Providence without trying one of their huge, square, cheesy pizzas. **Casa Christine** (145 Spruce Street, 453–6255) is a small, quiet restaurant where you can bring your own wine.

If you really want to step back into the Old World, drop in at **Scialo Bros. Bakery** (257 Atwells Avenue, 421–0986) and indulge in some fresh and imported Italian baked goods and delicacies. Opened in 1916, Scialo Bros. retains its traditional charms, with rounded candy bins and antique display cases; and the biscotti, amaretti, cannoli, and tiramisu are as delicious as ever. A free cup of coffee makes everything taste that much sweeter.

Providence's Spicy Mayor Cianci

*I*t's uncertain whether there's a key to the city of Providence, but there's one thing every visiting dignitary can be sure of receiving: a jar of the mayor's marinara sauce.

Providence Mayor Buddy Cianci is what you might call a "character." Critics blast him for his imperious control of city government, while supporters love his quick wit and penchant for showing up at almost any event, big or small—even if he's always late.

Buddy also has more than a bit of salesman in him, which explains his success in promoting Providence—and the tomato sauce. "The Mayor's Own Marinara Sauce" is from an old family recipe and is available at most local supermarkets or by calling 453–0333. Proceeds benefit a scholarship fund for Providence students.

Finally, for a change of pace, a bit farther west on Atwells Avenue are **Mexico** (948 Atwells Avenue, 331–4985), a tiny restaurant that has won high praise for its authentic south-of-the-border cuisine, and **Montego Bay on the Hill** (422 Atwells Avenue, 751–3040), where jerk pork and "rasta pasta" provide a taste of the Caribbean. **Mi Guatemala** (1049 Atwells Avenue, 621–9147) starts you off with homemade nacho chips with three kinds of sauces for dipping then serves up huge portions of grilled pork steak—the Central American nation's national dish—on fresh, hot corn tortillas. For an appetizer try the Tostados Chapinas, black beans on a flat tortilla garnished with onions and stewed tomatoes. You can wash it all down with a Mexican beer or choose from a selection of specialty juices, such as tamarind or cashew. Open Monday to Thursday 9:30 A.M. to 10:00 P.M.; Friday to Sunday 8:00 A.M. to 11:00 P.M.

Don't miss Federal Hill's raucous **Feast of Saint Joseph** celebration if you're in town in May; there's a red, white, and green stripe painted down the middle of Atwells Avenue to remind you of this annual party celebrating the patron saint of Italy.

Providence once had a place in the record books as home to the world's widest bridge, but the distinction was dubious: The bridge was part of an ill-conceived plan to enclose the polluted rivers that flow through the city's downtown. In recent years, however, the rivers have been cleaned up, and the city has embarked on an ambitious plan to revitalize the waterways and the whole downtown area. The plan has been a huge success, and no more so than with the construction of **Waterplace Park** and the **Providence Riverwalk.**

Where once railroad tracks ran along a weedy right-of-way, a beautiful riverwalk today allows pedestrians to stroll both sides of the Woonasquatucket River. A round basin features a fountain and a small **amphitheater** for live outdoor performances. Near a tunnel that allows

The revival of downtown Providence has come a long way, but it's still a work in progress. Future plans include the creation of an arts and entertainment district in the Downcity area. The riverwalk is being extended south toward Narragansett Bay. The city recently opened an ice skating rink in the center of Providence, at Kennedy Plaza, and developers have agreed to build a new movie theater downtown, as well.

But perhaps the most anticipated change to the downtown landscape is the new Providence Place Mall, built on a former parking lot across the street from the Westin Hotel. The 150-store upscale mall spans the Woonasqua-tucket River with a graceful glass atrium bridge and is connected to the Westin and the Rhode Island Convention Center by a pedestrian skyway. Stores include Nordstrom, Filene's, and Lord & Taylor, and plans also call for a state-of-the-art, twenty-screen cinema. Strollers have direct access from the mall to the Riverwalk, as well as a series of outside restaurants and entertainment venues.

access from the river walk to **Kennedy Plaza**—the heart of downtown Providence—is a plaque describing the history of this area and its transformation from a natural cove, to a place of landfill and concrete, and back to an oasis of beauty.

From many spots on the Riverwalk you can look up to admire the brilliant white marble dome of the **State House** (222–2357), just a short walk away and worth a visit to check out its architectural grandeur and an original painting of George Washington by native son Gilbert Stuart. Open free of charge Monday through Friday 8:30 A.M. to 4:30 P.M., with guided tours at 10:00 and 11:00 A.M.

Abutting the Riverwalk is Citizen's Plaza, usually the site of the annual **Keep Providence Beautiful Pasta Challenge,** which brings out the best in the state's restaurants each September (typically the second weekend of the month) as they compete for the votes of the people wandering from booth to booth sampling the entries. Also at Citizen's Plaza is the popular **Cafe Nuovo** (1 Citizen's Plaza, 421–2525), which has outdoor seating along the river and serves nouvelle cuisine with a multicultural twist, along with some spectacular desserts.

From Citizen's Plaza, which sits at the confluence of the Woonasquatucket, Moshassuck, and Providence Rivers, you can see the series of elegant arched bridges linking downtown Providence to the East Side, home of Brown University. Under these bridges passes an increasingly diverse array of watercraft, partly thanks to **Paddle Providence** (located on the Riverwalk at Memorial Park, 453–1633). From May to October you can rent a canoe or kayak for a unique perspective on the city and its renaissance. Downtown skyscrapers, the historic homes of the East Side, old brick warehouses, and the capitol building are all on display as you paddle along this urban waterway. Open noon till nightfall on weekends May and June and September and October; daily during July and August.

Perhaps the most unusual watercraft in New England can be found on the rivers of Providence: a pair of authentic Italian gondolas. From May to October, gondoliers Marco and Marcello push **La Gondola** (421–8877) along on a sedate, forty-minute ride down the length of the Riverwalk to Waterplace Park. The gondola can accommodate groups of up to six people (although it's much more romantic with just two!). As you glide through the quiet city, you'll be serenaded by Italian love songs, and guests are welcome to bring a bottle of their favorite wine aboard.

If you cross any of the bridges spanning the river to the East Side and walk 1 block, you'll come to **South Main Street,** popular with the local lunchtime crowd but not well known to out-of-town visitors. A stroll south along this broad thoroughfare will take you past the historic buildings housing the Rhode Island Supreme Court and Superior Court to an area where old warehouses and office buildings have been converted to retail space and storefronts now are home to trendy restaurants and art galleries. If you're looking for that unique gift for the person who has everything, check out the goods at **Comina** (245 South Main Street, 273–4522). For vintage, estate, and designer jewelry and antique accessories and furniture, pay a visit to **Camden Passage** (359 South Main Street, 453–0770). Along the way, be sure to pause at **Gardiner-Jackson Park** between Westminster and Pine Streets, the latest addition to the Riverwalk. At the center of the park is a 75-foot-tall World War I monument, topped by a statue of the Greek goddess Athena. The statue once stood at the focal point of a horrendous downtown traffic rotary known locally as "Suicide Circle"; it seems much more at home here.

The sleek modern building housing **Hemenway's** (One Old Stone Square, 351–8570) may clash with the nineteenth-century buildings across South Main Street, but the floor-to-ceiling windows provide a great view from any seat in this atrium restaurant. Founded by local culinary legend Ned Grace, Hemenway's is renowned for its fresh seafood and raw bar; come for lunch or dinner. After dinner you can stroll down to **L'Elizabeth** (285 South Main Street, 621–9113) to order dessert, coffee, or a drink at the bar; indulge while relaxing on a couch or easy chair.

WaterFire Stokes the Senses

*O*n special nights throughout the year, Providence plays host to an amazing fusion of fire, water, and music known as WaterFire. The work of artist Barnaby Evans, the WaterFire display acts simultaneously on a variety of senses. A dozen cauldrons filled with firewood and perched above the Providence River are set ablaze to the strains of classical music. Watch the flames reflected off the dark water and casting shadowy forms on the stones of the Riverwalk while the smell of burning wood tickles your nose and the music echoes hauntingly off the quiet buildings of downtown.

Evans says that the close proximity of the fire and water symbolizes the fragility of life—either is capable of destroying the other, yet they exist, at least for a time, in harmony. We say that WaterFire is an experience worth harmonizing your schedule for. For information on upcoming performances, call 272-3111, or visit www.waterfire.org.

If you've had dinner and dessert and still are looking for something to do, see what's playing at the **Cable Car Cinema** (204 South Main Street, 272–3970), where you and that special someone can curl up together on a couch (again!) and take in a movie. At night the theater plays offbeat, arty films; during the week, the Cable Car operates primarily as a cafe, with indoor and outdoor seating. On Saturday mornings puppeteer Mark Kohler takes the stage ($5.00 for adults; $3.00 for children).

At any point along South Main Street it's a quick walk down to the river or uphill to the "mile of history" of **Benefit Street.**

Besides the East Bay Bike Path, which begins at India Point Park on the East Side, the best place for a walk or jog is on the path running down the wide, tree-lined median of **Blackstone Boulevard,** a street that also has some of Providence's finest homes. For a more serene pastime, you should take a stroll through **Swan Point Cemetery,** a beautiful place where you can walk along to the edge of the cliffs overlooking the Seekonk River. While you're here, look for the headstone marking the final resting place of macabre author H. P. Lovecraft and Civil War General Ambrose Burnside. To cool off after a brisk walk, go to **Maxmillian's** (1074 Hope Street, 273–7230) for some top-notch homemade ice cream.

Also along the river on the East Side is one of Providence's more out-of-the-way restaurants that's nonetheless earned a reputation for great food and atmosphere. The cuisine at the **Gatehouse Restaurant**

Hoofing It Around Providence

*T*he ability to experience Providence on foot has always been one of the city's chief virtues: You can easily walk to the State House on Smith Hill, explore Downcity, and cross the Providence River to check out the East Side—all in a single day, if you're feeling ambitious.

Still, it helps to have a little guidance as you make your way from place to place, and Providence's new Banner Trail is just the thing for those who want to ramble at their own pace. Bright, color-coded banners mark the city's best sites, most of which are within a mile of one another. Along the way you'll find great museums, historical sites, and superb examples of classic urban architecture. Beginning and ending at Waterplace Park, the Banner Trail also incorporates various events and exhibitions throughout the year. You can pick up a map at 30 Exchange Terrace, at the northeast corner of Kennedy Plaza, or by calling 274–1636.

If you crave a little more structure, organized walking tours are conducted by the Providence Walking Company. Call 751–6643 for reservations and information.

Sullivan Ballou's Grave

*A*mong the graves in Providence's Swan Point Cemetery is that of Major Sullivan Ballou, a member of the Second Regiment, Rhode Island Volunteers, during the Civil War. The monument over Ballou's grave is inscribed with a poignant passage from a letter he wrote to his wife, Sarah, on July 14, 1861, as his unit was preparing to move toward the front. In the letter, Ballou wrote passionately to Sarah of his love of country and sense of duty, yet he also expressed the anguish of knowing he might never see her or his children again.

Ballou ended his letter with a promise that, if he should fall in battle, his family would be reunited in the hereafter: "I wait for you there. Come to me and lead thither my children." Just two weeks later, on July 29, 1861, Ballou was killed in the first major clash of the war, the First Battle of Bull Run, also known as First Manassas.

If you want to read the full text of Ballou's letter, you can find it on the Web site of Rhode Island photographer Don LaVange: http://users.ids.net/~tandem/sullivan.htm.

(4 Richmond Square, 521–9229) is a mix of New England, Mediterranean, and New Orleans styles. The Gatehouse shares a great view of the Seekonk River with the adjoining River Deck Pub, where lighter fare is served to the beat of live singers and musicians. Located in the former gatehouse of the Red Bridge connecting Providence and Seekonk, Massachusetts, the Gatehouse Restaurant is well worth the drive across the East Side (follow the signs for Richmond Square).

Providence's other off-the-beaten-path attractions are scattered throughout the city. To literally get an overview of downtown, find **Prospect Terrace,** a small park on the East Side, at the corner of Cushing and Congdon Streets. To get to the park from Benefit Street, take Meeting Street 2 blocks east to Congdon Street and make a left. In this small patch of green is a statue of Roger Williams, the founder of Rhode Island, who is buried here. From this spot you have a great view of the capitol as well as the tall buildings of the financial district. For a broad look at what Roger Williams created, pay a visit to the **Museum of Rhode Island History** (331–8575), also on the East Side at 110 Benevolent Street (off Hope Street). Located at Aldrich House, an 1822 Federal-style mansion, the museum's galleries feature a changing series of exhibits on Rhode Island history, art, and architecture. Admission is $2.00 for adults, $1.50 for seniors and students, and $1.00 for children. Open Tuesday through Friday 9:00 A.M. to 5:00 P.M., and Sunday noon to 4:00 P.M.; the museum is closed between exhibits, so call ahead.

The arts are alive and well in Providence—the city is working on creating

Rhode Island's Black Heritage

The first black people in Rhode Island came unwillingly, imported as slaves as early as the mid-seventeenth century. Many of the early fortunes of Providence, Newport, and Bristol were built on the back of the slave trade. Yet black Rhode Islanders began making a mark for themselves even before slavery was abolished in the state: The famous First Black Regiment of Rhode Island fought with distinction during the Battle of Rhode Island in 1778.

The trials and triumphs of black Rhode Islanders is chronicled at the Rhode Island Black Heritage Society Museum (46 Aborn Street, 751–3490). A permanent exhibit, entitled "Creative Survival," documents black history in the state and includes manumission documents, old photographs, and a dress that belonged to Sisseretta Jones, an early black opera singer. The society also presents lectures and special exhibits, such as a recent examination of the Amistad *story. The downtown museum is open Monday to Friday 9:00 A.M. to 4:30 P.M.*

an arts and entertainment district in the Downcity area—and no more so than at *AS220* (115 Empire Street, 831–9327), the city's own special breeding ground for innovative and unusual theater and fine arts. At the large AS220 complex on Empire Street, you can find something happening just about any day of the week, thanks in part to the fact that roughly two dozen artists are in residence and a major theater company (the *Perishable Theatre*, 331–2695) and a dance troupe (*Groundwerx,* 454–4564) also call AS220 home.

In the galleries upstairs and in the *AS220 Cafe* (831–9190) are a variety of daily free showings by local, usually unknown, artists. The bohemian atmosphere carries over into the cafe, where you can choose from a daily menu of sandwiches, vegetarian dishes, and assorted fruit juices. In the evenings there are musical performances ranging from Irish folk songs to jazz to intense rock and roll, with a cover charge that rarely exceeds $5.00. Film festivals and poetry slams also are part of the AS220 scene. You can even take a dance class or learn to act.

AS220's galleries are open Monday through Friday 10:00 A.M. to 4:00 P.M. and Saturday 1:00 to 4:00 P.M. The cafe is open weekdays 10:00 A.M. to 1:00 A.M. and weekends 7:00 A.M. to 1:00 A.M.

While you're downtown and in the mood to be entertained, don't overlook Providence's excellent live music scene. Clubs like *Lupo's Heartbreak Hotel* (239 Westminster Street, 272–5876) and the *Met Cafe* (130 Union Street, 861–2142) bring in up-and-coming national acts as well as second-tier established stars and groups. You can catch a good show any weekend and on most weeknights. For top-shelf local bands, try the *Living Room* (23 Rathbone Street, 521–5200), a landmark on the local club scene that recently relocated to new digs.

If the band you're watching goes into a third or fourth encore, you may find your late-night dining choices somewhat limited once you exit the concert hall for the darkened city streets. Fortunately, there's a strange but satisfying diner within walking distance of the Downcity clubs. Late nights, find the trailer housing the **Haven Bros. Diner** (861–7777), open 5:00 P.M. to 3:00 A.M., parked next to Kennedy Plaza by City Hall. It's not unusual to find businesspeople and bikers mingling at the cramped counter there. Mainly for night owls—their hours are midnight to 5:00 A.M daily, plus daytime hours on weekends—is the **Silvertop Diner** (13 Harris Avenue, 272–2890), an original 1939 dining car that specializes in omelettes, burgers, and steak sandwiches. It's a little hard to find (especially at this time of night); from downtown, take Francis Street (heading right toward the State House) to the end, make a left on Hayes Street, a left on Park Street, cross the river, and make a right on Kinsley Street, then bear left onto Harris Avenue to the diner. Or call for directions.

Wes's Rib House (38 Dike Street, 421–9090) might just be the perfect out-of-the-way restaurant. It has great food (barbecued ribs, chicken, and chopped meats) in a genre that's a rarity in New England; the restaurant is open late; and it's located in a desolate part of town that's hard to find.

Wes's implores you to "put some South in your mouth" and has a wood-fired open grill serving up awesome Missouri-style barbecue. You can order ribs by the piece—two to forty—or choose from a number of dinner platters. Try the Show-Me Platter so that you can sample four of the tasty meats; dinners also come with moist corn bread and excellent barbecued beans. If you're really hungry, start with a bowl of Wes's

Thursday Night Brings the Arts to Life

*L*ooking for something to do in Providence on a Thursday night? It's not as hard as it might sound, especially if you're here on the third Thursday of the month. That's the night that the Providence Artrolley makes its rounds between the city's art galleries, antiques stores, and performance venues. The free trolley runs continuously from 5:00 to 9:00 P.M. in a loop from Citizen's Plaza (along the Riverwalk) through downtown, up College Hill and down Wickenden Street and Benefit Street. Along the way you can hop off at more than fifteen galleries plus events like poetry slams, dance performances, and plays.

To pass the time on board the trolley, members of the Providence Preservation Society are on hand to provide a narrated tour of the city. Free parking is available at Citizen's Plaza on the nights when the trolley is running. For more information on the Artrolley, call 274–9120 or 751–2628.

chili—made with meat, of course. Friends from Texas, where they know barbecue, say this is the best they've tasted up North.

To find Wes's Rib House from downtown Providence, take Westminster Street west, passing under Route 10 and over the railroad tracks, then make the second left onto a service road leading into a forbidding industrial park. The road ends at a parking lot, which belongs to Wes's. The restaurant is in an old factory building. From Interstate 195, take the Route 6 exit (Olneyville), then exit onto Hartford Avenue. Follow Hartford Avenue until it merges with Westminster Street. Take Westminster Street east to Bough Street, make a right, then make a left onto Dike Street. Wes's is 2 blocks down, on your right. Open Monday through Thursday 11:30 A.M. to 2:00 A.M., Friday and Saturday 11:30 A.M. to 4:00 A.M., and Sunday 11:30 A.M. to 2:00 A.M.

The *Culinary Archives and Museum* at Johnson and Wales University (315 Harborside Boulevard, 598–2805) is a feast for the eyes. The answers to all of your questions about the preparation and consumption of food probably can be found here. One of Rhode Island's best-kept secrets, the Culinary Archives contains more than 400,000 items related to food and hospitality, which incidentally are the major course offerings at Johnson and Wales University.

If a president of the United States ever jotted down a note asking an aide to send out for pizza, the Culinary Archives probably has that note in its collection. Archival documents include a dinner invitation from Thomas Jefferson, vintage postcards featuring restaurants and other food purveyors, and more than 40,000 menus from around the world. Displays feature 4,000-year-old Native American cooking stones, ancient Egyptian and Roman spoons, a bread ring from Pompeii, and a collection of stoves from the nineteenth and twentieth centuries.

In all, the museum—the only one of its type in the world—presents a virtual banquet of more than 300,000 items that any fan of food will enjoy. To get there, take I–95 to exit 18 (Thurbers Avenue). If coming from the north, take a left on Allens Avenue (Route 1A) when you get off the exit; if approaching from the south, take a right at the end of the exit ramp. Proceed on Allens Avenue until you see a Shell gas station on your left, and make a left turn on Northup Street, which becomes Harborside Boulevard. At the bottom of the hill, make a left into the first parking lot; the museum is located in the large warehouse building with an Art Deco arch. The Culinary Archives and Museum is open Tuesday through Saturday 10:00 A.M. to 5:00 P.M. (last tour at 4:00 P.M.). Admission is $5.00 for adults, $4.00 for seniors, $2.00 for students, and $1.00 for children ages five to eighteen.

With the recent opening of the beautiful **Westin Hotel** downtown (One West Exchange Street, 598–8000), Providence finally has a selection of hotels worthy of a city on the rise. However, if you want to be immersed in the history of Rhode Island, there's no better place to stay than *The Old Court Bed and Breakfast* (751–2002). Located at 144 Benefit Street (perhaps the best-preserved original Colonial street in America), The Old Court was built in 1863 as a rectory and sits next to the historic Rhode Island Courthouse. Rooms at this rather austere Italianate inn feature private baths and include a full breakfast at rates that are competitive with the big hotels.

For an even more private place to stay on Benefit Street, ring up innkeeper *C.C. Ledbetter* and book a room at her eponymous bed-and-breakfast (326 Benefit Street, 351–4699). Unassuming from the outside—there's not even a sign—the interior of this circa 1780 Colonial is brightened with dhurrie rugs, maps (the innkeeper is a professional cartographer), handmade quilts, contemporary paintings, and C.C.'s engaging personality. Start your day with your choice of four kinds of juice, gourmet coffee, fresh fruit, warm bread, and coffee cake, and you'll be ready to take on the sights of the East Side and nearby downtown Providence.

The neighborhood behind the state capitol won't be written up in travel brochures anytime soon, but there is at least one nice street in the area, and on this street is the *State House Inn* (43 Jewett Street, 351–6111). Located in the shadow of the capitol building, the State House Inn is a well-kept, three-story Colonial Revival building with ten guest rooms dressed in a country folk art style—not at all what you would expect in the heart of a busy city. But it works, thanks in no small part to the inn's friendly staff, led by innkeepers Frank and Monica Hopton. The inn is fully equipped with air-conditioning, cable televisions, phones, and fax machines, and a full breakfast is included in the room rates, which range from $109 to $159. That's a steal considering you're just steps from the capitol and a brisk walk from beautiful Waterplace Park and the rest of downtown Providence.

East Providence

Just over the Providence/East Providence city line is the best place in Rhode Island to see live comedy. The *Comedy Connection* (39 Warren Avenue, 438–8383) is located in a former bank building, but there's no mistaking the place's intention to make you laugh—the giant rubber duckie on the roof gives it away. Inside, you can loosen up with a few drinks from the bar, warm up with some local talent onstage, then laugh it up with top regional and national comedians every Wednesday through Sunday night. Showtime is 8:15 P.M., and reservations are required. On Friday and Saturday there is also a 10:15 P.M. show.

Take I–195 to exit 4 (the first exit after the Washington Bridge), and you'll find *Veterans Memorial Parkway,* one of the most pleasant drives in the Providence area. The road begins in a residential area but quickly reaches the Providence Harbor shoreline, where it parallels the route of the defunct Old Colony Railroad line, now the *East Bay Bike Path.* In fact, if you want to take a bike ride on the path, the lot just off Veterans Memorial Parkway is one of the best places to park your car. (For more on the bike path, see the East Bay chapter.)

The road continues on a narrow causeway on the Watchemoket Cove, near the Metacom Country Club, then affords a quick glimpse of the *Fuller Rock Lighthouse* off Kettle Point before reaching the access road for *Squantum Woods State Park,* also traversed by the bike path. Soon Veterans Memorial Parkway merges with Pawtucket Avenue (Route 103); continue south on Route 103.

The road splits and you'll want to bear right onto Bullock's Point Avenue, which will take you through the middle of the village of *Riverside.* Crossing the bike path at the old railroad right-of-way, you'll see on your left an old train station. Until 1948, trains making this stop on the Old Colony Railroad disgorged hordes of summer visitors onto the streets of Riverside. Today, however, the building is home to *Callegaro's Old Depot Deli* (250 Bullock's Point Avenue, 433–2647), which caters not only to local residents but also to people using the adjacent bike path. The Old Depot has good deli sandwiches, and the chili, although somewhat on the mild side, has won local awards. If you want to spice it up, order a bowl topped with fresh jalapeños. They also will sell you a big stuffed quahog for $1.25.

Sharing the parking lot with the Old Depot is the *Dari-Bee Soft Serve* ice cream stand (240 Bullock's Point Avenue), a Riverside fixture for the past thirty-five years that boasts the best milkshakes anywhere. Open May 1 until the weather turns chilly.

At one time Riverside was a resort community with grand old hotels that catered to visitors to the Crescent Amusement Park, located near the end of Bullock's Point Avenue by Bullock's Neck. Alas, the once sprawling park was closed and demolished some years ago, and condominiums now stand in the place of the old roller coaster and midway. Just one vestige of the old park remains, but it is worth seeing: the 1895 *Crescent Park Looff Carousel.*

Charles I. D. Looff is acknowledged as having been the preeminent master of carousel design, and he favored elaborate, ornate designs in constructing his wooden masterpieces. Rhode Island is fortunate to have a number of Looff-designed carousels, but the best is in East Providence. The Crescent Park Carousel was designed as a showpiece for prospective carousel buyers, so Looff pulled out all the stops in building it. So personal to Looff was this carousel that he carved his own likeness in the decorative panels around the rim. Besides the magnificently carved wooden horses, the carousel is decorated with beveled mirrors, colored glass and jewels, and dainty lights. Organ music plays as the carousel whirls around.

The Crescent Park Carousel is open noon to 8:00 P.M. on weekends from Easter Sunday to Memorial Day, then adds Friday evening hours (3:00 P.M. to 8:00 P.M.) from Memorial Day through mid-June. From mid-June to Labor Day, the carousel is open Wednesday through Sunday from noon to 9:00 P.M. From Labor Day to Columbus Day, the schedule reverts back to weekends only from noon to 8:00 P.M. Closed the rest of the year. Rides are 75 cents or three for $2.00; there's also a snack bar and gift shop on the premises. Call 433–2828 for information.

East Providence, by the way, is home to a substantial Portuguese population, one of the more plentiful ingredients in Providence's melting pot. For a taste of spicy chourico and other zesty Portuguese-style dishes, drop by *Madiera* (288 Warren Avenue, 431–1322), the king of East Providence's Portuguese restaurants.

North Providence

*H*ere's another restaurant that proves that Providence doesn't have a monopoly on fine dining: North Providence's *Florentine Grille* (1195 Douglas Avenue, 354–8411) exudes ambience from its classy, wood-paneled bar to the open wood grill where your dinner is prepared before your eyes. Speaking of eyes, yours will widen at the selection of antipasti displayed on a center table as you make your way to your seat. Starters include a delectable assortment of bruschettas, topped with fresh mozzarella, grilled red peppers, and other palate teasers. After all this, the main course may seem an afterthought, but save room for the Florentine Grille's excellent entrees, including grilled meats, pizzas, fresh fish, and pasta. Open for dinner Tuesday to Sunday.

Pawtucket

I t may be Pawtucket's top tourist attraction, but relatively few people come to see the **Slater Mill National Historic Site** (725–8638). Don't make the same mistake, because Slater Mill occupies a key place in the history of the United States.

After conceding defeat in the Revolutionary War, Great Britain was determined to prevent the upstart United States from obtaining the technology needed to join the Industrial Revolution. But the British didn't count on Samuel Slater, an independent-minded man who came to America after managing one of the most progressive mills in England.

Financed by Moses Brown and William Almy, Slater founded the first successful cotton mill in the United States in 1793. The rest, as they say, is history: Building on Slater's success, over the next century American industry grew to such strength that it eventually dwarfed even that of the mighty British Empire.

The Slater Mill complex includes the original **Slater Mill,** a yellow, wooden Colonial building sitting over a raceway by the falls in downtown Pawtucket, and the **Sylvanius-Brown House,** built in 1758. Slater Mill contains all of the carding, drawing, spinning, and weaving equipment needed to turn raw cotton into cloth, and museum tours include demonstrations of how each item worked. If the process seems primitive by today's standards, take a look at the spinning wheels and other hand-operated tools in the Sylvanius-Brown House. The rise of the mills soon caused the extinction of such cottage industries.

The **Wilkinson Mill,** the other major structure in the park, is a stone mill built in 1810 by Oziel Wilkinson and considered the birthplace of the American machine tool industry. The mill contains a working nineteenth-century machine shop that is still powered by a 16,000-pound waterwheel.

The Slater Mill complex, which also includes walkways and benches overlooking the powerful **waterfall** that powered the mills, is located on Roosevelt Avenue in downtown Pawtucket, just north of the intersection with Main Street (take exit 27 off I–95 south, or exit 28 if coming north on I–95). Buildings are open for tours Tuesday through

Saturday 10:00 A.M. to 5:00 P.M. and Sunday 1:00 to 5:00 P.M., May 1 through December 1, and on Saturday and Sunday 1:00 to 5:00 P.M., March 1 to April 30. December 1 through March 1, 1:00 P.M. tours *only* on Saturday and Sunday. Admission is $6.50 for adults, $5.50 for seniors, and $5.00 for children ages six to twelve.

Downtown Pawtucket is a little hard to navigate; the city fathers, in their wisdom, decided to make the major city artery into a giant, one-way street. All well and good if you're a local who knows where you're headed; not so good if you're a visitor searching for an unfamiliar shop or restaurant. Still, it's worth the effort to seek out Pawtucket's *Morris Novelty* (523 Main Street, 728–3810), a 50,000-square-foot store crammed with endless strange and unusual supplies for the theme party of your wildest dreams. From Mardi Gras to a Cinderella wedding, Morris Novelty has the accessories you need to make your party a hit, and the place is just a hoot to walk around in. Morris Novelty really shines from October to December—Rhode Island's largest assortment of Halloween decorations, masks, and costumes gets pushed aside in November for a huge display of Christmas trees, ornaments, Santa costumes, and more. Open Monday through Saturday 9:00 A.M. to 5:00 P.M.

Contrary to naysayers from down the river, Pawtucket is not bereft of culture. In fact, as the *monument* at the corner of Exchange, Goff, and Broad Streets can attest, Pawtucket was featured in the movie *American Buffalo,* starring Dustin Hoffman and Dennis Franz and directed by favorite son Michael Corrente. The arts continue to thrive at the nearby *City Nights Dinner Theatre* (27 Exchange Street, 723–6060), which serves up live comedies and musicals along with a family-style roast beef, turkey, or pork dinner. The troupe's nine-show annual run is held at the landmark Elks Building, once an ornate ballroom.

Ribbons mark your route to the roof at the *Rhode Island Rock Gym* (210 Weeden Street, 727–1704; www.rhodeislandrockgym.com), an indoor climbing facility where people of all ages and abilities can challenge themselves on a variety of surfaces, from simple vertical walls studded with hand and footholds to a padded, artificial cave with a 70-degree angled ceiling. A total of 3,500 square feet of terrain offer plenty of options for top-roped climbing, lead climbing, and low-level bouldering, including a number of challenging overhangs. A day pass costing just $10 lets you climb from 11:00 A.M. to midnight on weekdays and noon to midnight on Saturday and Sunday; individual and group lessons are also available (call for appointment). The on-site shop offers both equipment rentals and sales.

Modern Diner

Good, cheap food you expect from a diner—but ambience and history? Not usually, but the **Modern Diner** (364 East Avenue, 726–8390) is a major exception. From the outside, the Modern Diner resembles a big, tan, diesel train engine of the 1940s. Inside, the padded booths and long, polished counter fronting the grill look much the same as they did half a century ago. The Sterling Streamliner–model diner, a local landmark, also was the first diner in the country to be listed on the National Register.

Did we mention good and inexpensive eats? A delicious burger can be yours for $2.55, while the priciest item on the menu, the Steak Delmonico, will set you back a grand $7.95. The diner is open Monday through Saturday 6:00 A.M. to 3:00 P.M. and Sunday 7:00 A.M. to 2:00 P.M.

For a polar-opposite experience on the same street, check out the **Garden Grille** (727 East Avenue, 726–2826), which claims to be the region's only full-service vegetarian restaurant. Wood-grilled veggie burgers and other healthy delights are served up in a cheerful setting, where patrons can sidle up to a fresh juice bar for a healthy alternative to the blue-plate special. Dinner entrees include honey maple-smoked tofu, vegetable pad Thai, and stuffed butternut squash. Open Monday through Saturday 10:00 A.M. to 9:00 P.M.; Sunday noon to 8:00 P.M.

Pawtucket's **McCoy Stadium** is home to Rhode Island's beloved Pawtucket Red Sox (www.pawsox.com), better known as the Pawsox. If you've given up trying to explain to your kids why baseball is so important, bypass the major league millionaires and bring them to McCoy. This is baseball like it used to be, and still oughta be.

The AAA International League farm club of the Boston Red Sox, the Pawsox are a Rhode Island success story writ large. Bankrupt when current owner Ben Mondor bought the team in 1977, the Pawsox drew more than 596,000 fans to McCoy Stadium (capacity 10,031) in 1997. Like the franchise, the team on the field has been a success during the past few years, finishing first in their division in 1994 and 1996. Players like Roger Clemens, Jim Rice, Mo Vaughn, Wade Boggs, and Nomar Garciaparra all have had stints at McCoy before moving on to fame and fortune in the majors.

The high-quality play of young hitters and pitchers aiming for a shot at the big leagues is one attraction; another is the family atmosphere at McCoy. Despite a recent expansion, the stadium is small enough to be called intimate, and there are no bad seats in the house. In fact, the 1999 remodeling now gives fans new vantage points from a left-field tower and a grass berm and bleachers beyond the outfield fence. During batting practice, youngsters "fish" for players' autographs by tying string to cut-up plastic milk containers and lowering programs and baseballs down to the dugouts. Most players happily oblige. The outfield fence is lined with billboards, just like in the old days, and the ramps leading into the stadium are adorned with murals of the Pawsox stars of the past. A tent down the right-field line marks a picnic area where groups can enjoy the game along with a barbecue.

A Pawsox game is a great value, appealing directly to the Yankee heart (that's Yankee as in long-term New Englanders, not the hated Bronx

The Longest Game

*T*he longest game in professional baseball history was played right here at McCoy Stadium beginning (but not ending) on April 18, 1981. Thirty-three innings long, and taking more than sixty-five days to complete, the game ended on a single to left on July 23, 1981, that gave the Pawtucket Red Sox a 3–2 win over the Rochester Red Wings.

The game had gotten off to a rocky start when the stadium lights failed to work properly, but neither fans nor players had an inkling of what they were in for. A Rochester run in the top of the seventh inning was matched by a Pawsox run to tie the game in the bottom of the ninth. The two teams then went another eleven innings without scoring.

An RBI double by Rochester's Dave Huppert put the Red Wings ahead in the top of the twenty-first, but to the chagrin of the Rochester squad and perhaps even some of his own teammates and fans, future All-Star first baseman Wade Boggs tied the game up in the bottom of the inning with an RBI double of his own.

Another eleven scoreless innings passed before, mercifully, the game was suspended at 2–2. The time: 4:09 A.M. on April 19. Pawsox owner Ben Mondor gave season tickets to all nineteen diehard fans who remained in the stands.

More than two months later, the game was resumed at McCoy, and the end came quickly: future big-leaguer Marty Barrett singled with the bases loaded in the bottom of the thirty-third inning for a 3–2 Pawsox win. The game had taken eight hours and twenty-five minutes to play and earned Pawtucket a place in the Baseball Hall of Fame in Cooperstown.

Bombers). Reserved box seats are just $7.00, and general admission tickets are $5.00 for adults and $4.00 for kids and seniors. Hot dogs are just $1.50, and if you come early enough, you can even park for free in the stadium's small parking lot or on neighborhood streets.

The Pawsox play seventy-two home games between April and early September, and you generally can get tickets right up until game time. McCoy Stadium is located on Columbus Avenue; easiest access is from Newport Avenue/Route 1A or from School Street/Route 114 via Pond Street. Call 724–7300 for ticket information, game schedule, or directions.

Pawtucket's **Slater Memorial Park** is the center of the city's recreational life, featuring baseball fields, tennis courts, pony rides, and paddleboats. It also is the site of **Daggett House,** where eight generations of the Daggett family lived between 1685 and 1894, when the family farm was sold to the city to create the park.

Colonel John Daggett and Nathan Daggett both fought in the Revolutionary War, and the Daughters of the American Revolution have restored the house with eighteenth- and nineteenth-century furniture and antiques. Among the items in use or on display are a dress worn by Catherine Littlefield Greene (wife of General Nathaniel Greene) when she danced with Lafayette and a bedspread and quilt owned by Esther Slater. The house is open for tours June through September on most Saturdays and Sundays from 2:00 to 5:00 P.M.; tours by appointment April through December. Admission is $2.00 for adults and 50 cents for children under age twelve. Call 724–5748.

Also in Slater Park is Pawtucket's beautiful **Looff Carousel,** built in 1894. One of the nation's oldest carousels, the Slater Park merry-go-round is of the "stander" variety—the horses go round and round, but not up and down. The admission charge will remind you of the nineteenth century, too: It's just 25 cents a ride. Open daily from Memorial Day to Labor Day 11:00 A.M. to 5:00 P.M.; call 728–0500, extension 252 for information.

Entrances to Slater Park are on Newport Avenue (Route 1A) and Armistice Boulevard (Route 15).

Cranston

The story of the Sprague family is one that a lot of Rhode Islanders, familiar with decades of entrenched political cronyism in state and local government, can relate to. William Sprague turned an old gristmill into a multimillion-dollar cotton manufacturing company in the early eighteenth century and used his wealth as a springboard to the governorship. Following in his namesake's footsteps, William Sprague III spent $125,000 of the family's money to get himself elected governor in 1860 and moved from there to a seat in the U.S. Senate after the Civil War. By the mid-1870s, however, Sprague's lavish spending and financial speculation caused the loss of the family fortune and control of the A & W Sprague Manufacturing Company.

At the height of the Spragues' power, however, the family was worth an estimated $19 million, and their company was the largest in the state and one of the nation's most important firms. The **Governor Sprague Mansion** (944–9226) at 1351 Cranston Street in Cranston, built in 1790 and expanded in 1864, contains many examples of fine period furniture, especially in the restored parlor. There also is a collection of Oriental art donated by the Carrington family and a carriage house and stable filled with old carriages, sleighs, wagons, and carts. Tours are available by appointment; call for information.

In the same part of Cranston is perhaps the state's most popular in-the-know restaurant: *Twin Oaks* (100 Sabra Street, 781–9693). Just across the city line from Providence on Spectacle Pond, Twin Oaks is a local legend, pulling in big, hungry crowds all day long for its huge portions

Central Falls

*E*very state has a community that seems to be the butt of all the local jokes, and the sad fact is that in Rhode Island that place is Central Falls, a heavily industrialized town that has weathered some hard economic times.

Such criticism is more than a little unfair, in my opinion. For example, although Central Falls' main artery, Broad Street, is no Rodeo Drive, it does feature one of the more interesting historic sites in Rhode Island: the Cogswell Tower (727–7474) in Jenks Park.

Built in 1890, the imposing tower was constructed on Dexter's Ledge, a site that played an important role in King Philip's War. From this spot in 1676, a local Indian tribe spotted a Colonial raiding party approaching their village and ambushed the attackers along the Blackstone River. Pierce's Fight (named after the commander of the raiding party) ended in a rout, with the doomed colonists fleeing upriver to Cumberland followed by the natives in hot pursuit.

Climb the tower and you'll discover a panoramic view of hardworking Central Falls—not an idyllic landscape, perhaps, but interesting, nonetheless. Afterward, be sure to enjoy one of the authentic ethnic restaurants that dot Broad Street.

of delicious steaks, chops, and Italian favorites, all at reasonable prices. Unless you're a Rhode Island "somebody," the challenge here is to get a table, so coming at off-hours is recommended. If you love the tomato sauce—and most diners do—you can take home a jar as a tasty remembrance of your visit. Open daily for lunch and dinner, 11:30 A.M. to 12:30 A.M. From I–95 north or south, take Route 10 to Reservoir Avenue (Route 2) exit, bear right, then make a right onto Pleasant Street, then follow signs to Sabra Street.

OK, let's get this straight right off the bat: There are no real, live cows at *Nature's Best Dairy World* (2032 Plainfield Pike/Route 14, 888–315–TOUR). But the kids will get over that minor disappointment once the interesting and informative tour of one of the area's biggest dairies begins. Visitors get a peek at the processing plant and can relax in a small theater for a video presentation, followed by interactive displays showing how cows turn grass into milk and detailing A Day in the Life of a Cow. In warm weather the children can ride the historic carousel salvaged from the Rocky Point Amusement Park midway and indulge in one of the dairy's best products—ice cream. Open year-round, 9:30 A.M. to 2:00 P.M. Monday through Friday and 10:00 A.M. to 4:00 P.M. Saturday; hours vary, so call ahead. Tours are offered every half hour. Admission $1.00; children under three admitted free.

Cranston's *Wein-O-Rama,* located at 1009 Oaklawn Avenue/Route 5 (943–4990), is another one of those great old roadside attractions that locals love. A big neon sign promises a good, cheap meal, and this restaurant delivers. With a name like Wein-O-Rama, it's no surprise that hot wieners are a staple here, and a flavorful dog is just $1.00. (By the way, these are regular hot dogs, not the miniature, spicy wieners of the New York System shops found throughout Rhode Island.) Also on the menu are inexpensive sandwiches, burgers, and dinners; for instance, a breaded veal cutlet platter, which includes fries and coleslaw, will run you the princely sum of $4.10.

Like the food, the decor at the Wein-O-Rama is simple, with a few booths along the windows and a lunch counter with revolving stools.

If the Wein-O-Rama isn't exactly your idea of a fine repast, there's an excellent nearby alternative off Route 5, also just south of the interchange with Routes 2 and 33. *The Sunflower Cafe* (162 Mayfield Avenue, 463–6444) imparts its baked pastas, braised stews, and roasted vegetables with a unique flavor, owing to the same ancient Etruscan clay-pot cooking method used at Providence's La Locanda del Coccio restaurant. Not only are the meals here delicious but they're also low in fat. Open for lunch and dinner; lunch is served noon to 2:00 P.M. Monday through Friday, dinner 5:00 to 9:00 P.M. Tuesday through Friday and 5:00 to 9:30 P.M. on Saturday.

Edgewood Manor is a fabulously ornate, 1905 Greek Revival mansion that innkeeper Andrew Lombardi has transformed into a richly appointed bed-and-breakfast (232 Norwood Avenue, 781–0099). From the moment you walk into the lobby with its coiffured ceiling and stylish wood stove, every room at Edgewood Manor is a unique visual treat, with decor ranging from Art Nouveau to Louis XIV. Breakfast is served in an Italian-style dining room with hand-carved walls, and Victorian guest rooms are individually decorated with rare antiques and include Jacuzzi baths and/or working fireplaces. Room rates, including breakfast, range from $110 to $225 nightly.

Located on the border of Providence and the section of Cranston closest to Narragansett Bay, it's a short walk from Edgewood Manor to Roger Williams Park and Zoo. A bit farther south is *Pawtuxet village,* founded in 1638. A small cluster of historic homes and public buildings, the village is located at the point where the Pawtuxet River meets the bay. Although this part of Cranston is heavily developed, you can get a glimpse of its natural past along the *Pawtuxet Reservation Riverwalk,* a 3-mile hiking trail that explores the wetlands, forests, and fields surrounding the river. The best trail access is from the parking lot of the Rhodes on the Pawtuxet banquet hall, located off Park Avenue in Cranston (you can't miss the sign) on Broad Street. For more information contact the Pawtuxet River Authority at 461–2618 or 467–8271.

Johnston

Dame Farm* (949–3516) is a reminder of an agrarian lifestyle that, while it flourished until the middle of the twentieth century, largely has been obscured and forgotten in this part of the state. Just 8 miles from the heart of downtown Providence, Dame Farm's mission is to help visitors understand how the food at their local supermarket is grown and harvested.

Owned by the state and operated by four generations of the Dame family, who still live here, Dame Farm raises tomatoes, peppers, eggplant, squash, and some of the state's best corn. Fall is the time for apple picking and, in October, Halloween pumpkins.

Not only can you buy fine produce at reasonable prices (the corn goes for about $4.00 a dozen), but if you ask them the Dames will take you out into the fields and demonstrate the planting, tilling, tending, and picking that such a harvest demands.

The eighteenth-century farm is part of **Snake Den State Park,** a large wooded preserve that lies beyond the fields of corn and vegetables. Trails starting at the farmhouse lead through the cultivated fields and into the oak/hickory forest, skirting two historic cemeteries, ponds, and a swamp.

Dame Farm is located on Brown Avenue, about halfway between Route 6/Hartford Avenue and Route 5/Greenville Avenue. The property is open year-round; the farm stand is open July through October. Open sunrise to sunset.

If you like sports that really get your adrenaline flowing, give paintball a try. At **Boston Paintball South** (351–2255), you can engage in friendly combat armed with gas-powered guns that shoot pellets filled with paint. Your mission: Attack the other team's fort and steal their flag; an alternative game is to attack the bad guys until everyone is "dead"—meaning hit by a splatter of paint and thus eliminated from the competition.

Boston Paintball South (www.bostonpaintballsupply.com/ fields. htm#RI) has a 10,000-square-foot indoor playing field with a medieval theme; players start behind the walls of opposing castles and attack across a no-man's-land filled with barriers and hiding places. Individuals can call in advance to join in an open game, or groups of ten or more can call to rent the field for three hours, with equipment and 200 rounds of ammunition included, for $35 per person, $30 under age 18. A new, outdoor playing field offers an environment where players can do battle; prices are the same.

The indoor paintball field, as well as a shop selling paintball equipment and supplies, is located at 1428 Hartford Avenue/Route 6A in the basement of the Bond Plaza shopping center. The entrance is around the back of the building. The field is open Wednesday through Sunday; call for hours and open game times.

Amid the body shops and modest homes lining Route 128/George Waterman Avenue in Johnston is a house that stands in sharp contrast to its surroundings. On a small, green patch along the busy road is the **Clemence-Irons House** (617–227–3956), an example of seventeenth-century stone-ender architecture that is unique to Rhode Island.

Taken from a style of home building developed in western England, the Clemence-Irons House was constructed by erecting a massive limestone wall and chimney that anchors the rest of the wooden house. Built circa 1680, the house is one of fewer than half a dozen examples of this style left in Rhode Island. The unpainted exterior of the Clemence-Irons House is a real eye-grabber, while the interior is modestly furnished with a period bed and other pieces.

Listed on the National Register, the house is maintained by the Society for the Preservation of New England Antiquities and is open for tours by appointment. The house is located on Route 128 about 1 mile south of Route 44/Putnam Pike.

While you're in Johnston, don't overlook *Il Piccolo* (1450 Atwood Avenue, 421–9843), an acclaimed Italian restaurant where style and fine cuisine belie the pedestrian, strip-mall locale. Open for dinner Monday to Thursday 5:00 to 9:00 P.M. and Friday and Saturday 5:00 to 10:00 P.M.; Monday to Friday 11:30 A.M. to 2:30 P.M. for lunch.

PLACES TO STAY IN PROVIDENCE AND VICINITY

(ALL AREA CODES 401)

PROVIDENCE
Days Hotel on the Harbor, 200 India Street, 272–5577

Holiday Inn Downtown, 21 Atwells Avenue, 831–3900

C.C. Ledbetter Bed & Breakfast, 326 Benefit Street, 351–4699

The Old Court Bed and Breakfast, 144 Benefit Street, 751–2002

The Providence Biltmore, Kennedy Plaza, 421–0700

The Providence Marriott, Charles and Orms Streets, 937–7768 or (800) 937–PROV

The State House Inn, 43 Jewett Street, 351–6111

Westin Hotel, One West Exchange Street, 598–8000

PAWTUCKET
Comfort Inn, 2 George Street, 723–6700

The James Brown House B&B, 33 South Street, 724–6482

CRANSTON
Days Inn Cranston, 101 New London Avenue, 942–4200

JOHNSTON
Sky-View Motor Inn, 2880 Hartford Avenue, 934–1188

PLACES TO EAT IN PROVIDENCE AND VICINITY

(ALL AREA CODES 401)

PROVIDENCE
Al Forno, 577 South Main Street, 273–9760

Angelo's Civita Farnese, 141 Atwells Avenue, 621–8171

AS220 Cafe, 115 Empire Street, 831–9190

Atomic Grill, 99 Chestnut Street, 621–8888

The Blue Grotto, 210 Atwells Avenue, 272–9030

The Boathouse Restaurant, Waterplace Park, 1 American Express Way, 272–1040

Cafe Dolce Vita, 59 Depasquale Place, 331–8240

Cafe Nuovo, One Citizen's Plaza, 421–2525

Camille's Roman Garden, 71 Bradford Street, 751–4812

The Capital Grille, 1 Cookson Place, 521–5600

Casa Christine,
145 Spruce Street,
453-6255

Caserta's Pizzeria,
21 Spruce Street,
272-3618

CAV, 14 Imperial Place,
751-9164

Coffee Exchange,
207 Wickenden Street,
273-1198

Downcity Diner,
151 Weybosset Street,
331-9217

Fellini's Pizzeria,
166 Wickenden Street,
751-6737

Finnegan's Wake,
397 Westminster Street,
751-0290

The Gatehouse Restaurant,
4 Richmond Square,
521-9229

Haven Bros. Diner,
Kennedy Plaza, 861-7777

Hemenway's,
One Old Stone Square,
351-8570

L'Elizabeth,
285 South Main Street,
621-9113

Maxmillian's,
1074 Hope Street,
273-7230

Mexico,
948 Atwells Avenue,
331-4985

Montego Bay on the Hill,
422 Atwells Avenue,
751-3040

New Rivers,
7 Steeple Street, 751-0350

O-Cha Cafe,
221 Wickenden Street,
421-4699

The Old Canteen,
120 Atwells Avenue,
751-5544

Plaza Grille,
64 Depasquale Avenue,
274-8684

The Pot Au Feu,
44 Custom House Street,
273-8953

Rue de L'Espoir,
99 Hope Street, 751-8890

Scialo Bros. Bakery,
257 Atwells Avenue,
421-0986

Silvertop Diner,
13 Harris Avenue,
272-2890

Walter's La Locanda del
Coccio, 265 Atwells Avenue,
273-2652

Wes's Rib House,
38 Dike Street, 421-9090

Z Bar and Grille,
244 Wickenden Street,
831-1566

EAST PROVIDENCE
Callegaro's Old Depot Deli,
250 Bullock's Point Avenue,
433-2647

Madiera,
288 Warren Avenue,
431-1322

NORTH PROVIDENCE
Florentine Grille,
1195 Douglas Avenue,
354-8411

PAWTUCKET
City Nights Dinner Theatre,
27 Exchange Street,
723-6060

Lisboa-A-Noite,
17 Exchange Street,
723-2030

Modern Diner,
364 East Avenue,
726-8390

Selected Chambers of Commerce in Providence and Vicinity

Greater Providence Chamber of Commerce,
30 Exchange Terrace, Providence 02903; 521-5000

East Providence Chamber of Commerce,
148 Taunton Avenue, East Providence, 438-1212

Cranston Chamber of Commerce,
48 Rolfe Street, Cranston, 785-3780

North Central Chamber of Commerce,
1126 Hartford Avenue, Johnston, 273-1310

CRANSTON
Caffe Itri,
1686 Cranston Street,
942–1970

Chelo's Beef Hearth,
1275 Reservoir Avenue,
942–7666

The Sunflower Cafe,
162 Mayfield Avenue,
463–6444

Twin Oaks,
100 Sabra Street, 781–9693

Wein-O-Rama,
1009 Oaklawn Avenue,
943–4990

JOHNSTON
Il Piccolo,
1450 Atwood Avenue,
421–9843

OTHER ATTRACTIONS WORTH SEEING IN PROVIDENCE AND VICINITY

John Brown House,
Providence

Cathedral of St. John,
Providence

First Baptist Meeting House in America,
Providence

Old State House,
Providence

The State House,
Providence

The Providence Atheneum,
Providence

The Rhode Island School of Design Museum of Art,
Providence

Roger Williams National Memorial, *Providence*

Roger Williams Park Zoo,
Providence

HELPFUL WEB SITES ABOUT PROVIDENCE AND VICINITY

Providence/Warwick Convention and Visitor's Bureau, www.providence cvb.com/

City of Providence,
www.providenceri.com/

City of East Providence,
www.eastprovidence. com/

Providence Chamber of Commerce, www. provchamber.com

Providence Preservation Society,
www.cs.brown.edu/ fun/pps/home.html

Town of Johnston,
www.johnston-ri.com

Cranston Historic District Commission,
www.cranstonri.com

Kent County and Western Rhode Island

Warwick

Warwick founder Samuel Gorton was an outcast among outcasts, whose belief in individualism apparently so bordered on anarchy that the notably tolerant Roger Williams—himself exiled from Massachusetts—ordered Gorton out of Providence. Gorton and his followers moved south during the 1640s and established their own settlement by the shores of Pawtuxet Cove, naming it after Gorton's protector, the Earl of Warwick.

Warwick's independent spirit once again was on display during the period immediately preceding the American Revolution, when local residents helped attack the grounded British revenue schooner HMS *Gaspee* in 1772. Stuck on a sandbar off present-day Gaspee Point, the ship was set upon by eight longboats full of men furious about the crown's tax collecting practices. On June 9, 1772, in the first armed conflict of the war, the colonials attacked and captured the ship, offloaded her crew, and burned the *Gaspee* to the waterline. Each May and June, the village of **Pawtuxet** celebrates the first blow for freedom with the **Gaspee Days Celebration,** with displays by colonial militia units, craft fairs, dances, and a colonial muster along the Narragansett Parkway (access from Route 117). For information contact the *Gaspee* Days Committee at 781–1772, or visit their Web site: www.gaspee.com.

Like most of Rhode Island, Warwick enjoyed a period of prosperity during the Industrial Revolution. Some coastal areas of the town became popular summer destinations during the latter half of the nineteenth century, only to be devastated by the great hurricane of 1938. During the latter half of the twentieth century, Warwick has settled into its role as a pleasant suburban community, home to Rhode Island's airport and its major shopping malls.

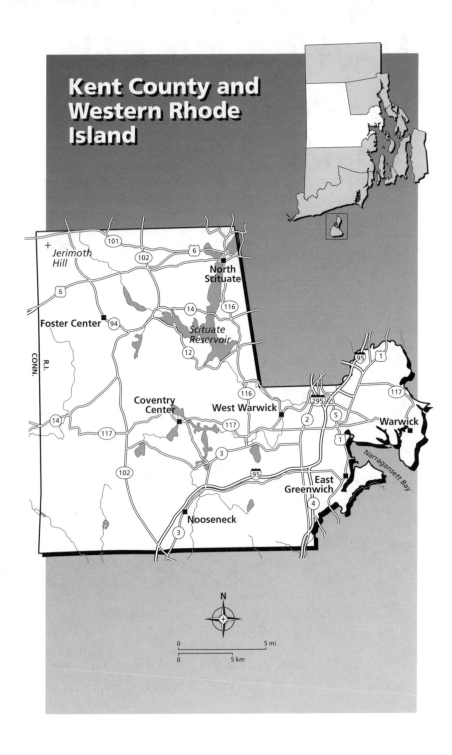

Kent County and Western Rhode Island

Jerimoth Hill

North Scituate

Foster Center

Scituate Reservoir

CONN.

R.I.

Coventry Center

West Warwick

Warwick

Narragansett Bay

East Greenwich

Nooseneck

N

0   5 mi
0   5 km

That said, many of Warwick's best places are along its Narragansett Bay coastline. *Conimicut Point Park,* located near the historic villages of *Conimicut* and *Shawomet,* offers a breathtaking panoramic view of the bay. The park has a beach and playground but otherwise is relatively small and ordinary, except for one spot. At the very tip of Conimicut Point is a sandbar that curves out into the bay, reaching for the offshore *Conimicut Point Lighthouse.* Parking your car at the end of the lot, you can walk out on the sandbar until it narrows to a thin, wet line of sand washed by waves from both sides. (A word of caution: The sandbar is relatively safe for adults in good weather, but storms and even passing ships can cause waves to inundate this fragile spit of land. Nonswimmers and children should not venture too far out.)

Looking straight ahead, you'll see that the sandbar continues, barely submerged, for a few hundred feet more, beyond where even the seagulls can stand. The tide surging madly over the barrier is impressive, and you now understand the need for the small lighthouse that stands watch a little farther out.

From this vantage point, you can look across to the homes lining the western shoreline of Warren and Bristol, down the bay to the wooded outline of Prudence Island and up toward the city of Providence, where the oil tanks of India Point and the skyscrapers of downtown are clearly visible.

The park is free and open from dawn until sunset. To get there, take West Shore Road/Route 117 to Conimicut village; look for Economy Road on the east side of the street. Turn onto Economy Road, then bear left onto Symonds Avenue. When you come to Point Avenue, make a right; this will take you directly to the park entrance.

If you plan to linger by the seaside, your best bet for local lodging is the *Enchanted Cottage B&B Inn,* a three-story Cape Anne with a big porch that offers glimpses of Narragansett Bay. Run by the Sandford family, this bed-and-breakfast is just north of Conimicut Point, off Route 117 on Beach Avenue (16 Beach Avenue, 732–0439). Rates range from $85 to $125.

Warwick's Rocky Point Amusement Park was one of the oldest seaside fun parks in America until its sad demise in 1996. The midway has been silenced and the Shore Dining Hall closed down, but a few vestiges of the grand old park remain. One of these is the *Rocky Point Chowder House* (1759 Post Road, 739–4222), which carries on the tradition of serving hot, greasy bags full of Rocky Point's famous clam cakes, along with steaming bowls of chowder. The restaurant is open seven days, 11:00 A.M. to 9:00 P.M.

Farther north on Post Road is, in our opinion, one of Rhode Island's most underrated restaurants. While Providence earns its reputation as one of the premier dining cities in the country, don't overlook Warwick's **Portofino** (897 Post Road, 461–8920). Located in a simple storefront in humble surroundings, Portofino conjures up images of Italy that will quickly make you forget you're on a busy commercial strip. Try the Chicken Sorrentina, sautéed with mushrooms, artichoke hearts, and roasted red peppers covered with melted mozzarella, or indulge in the grilled portobello mushroom—a vegetable entree that even the most ardent meat eater must respect. Open for dinner Monday through Saturday, 5:00 to 9:00 P.M. weekdays and 5:00 to 10:00 P.M. on Friday and Saturday.

Once Samuel Gorton's westernmost settlement, **Apponaug** grew up to become a shipping port involved in manufacturing and molasses-for-rum-for-slaves commerce of the triangle trade, thanks to the protected cove that snakes its way into the center of town. Although Apponaug has become a busy crossroads in a congested part of Warwick, vestiges of the past remain along Post Road. Next to Warwick's 1894 Town Hall is the **Warwick Museum, of Art,** 3259 Post Road (737–0010), located in the historic Kentish Artillery Armory. Rotating exhibits feature works by local artists as well as dramatic and musical performances. The museum is open weekdays 9:00 A.M. to 1:00 P.M., plus 4:00 to 8:00 P.M. on Wednesday evening and weekends from 1:00 to 3:00 P.M. during exhibitions.

Sauce Is the Secret to Bakery Pizza

*Y*ou need to be careful with your Rhode Island pizza, and that doesn't just mean avoiding spilling sauce on your shirt. Being a native of New York, where we like our pizza thin and cheesy, I was horrified to discover that some Ocean State natives considered thick-crusted, cheeseless pizza a delicacy. Rhode Island's bakery pizza soon won me over, however.

The secret, as you might imagine, is in the sauce, which should be slightly tart and oily enough to impart the proper sensation. As the name implies, you'll primarily find sheets of bakery pizza at neighborhood Italian bakeries, not pizza parlors, although there's no hard-and-fast rule. Bakery pizza is available throughout Rhode Island, but Warwick has more than its share of popular pizza purveyors. For an unexpected treat, call Antonio's Home Bakery (2448 West Shore Road, 738–3727), Sweet Temptations (2792 Post Road, 732–2516), or the Italian Bread Box (745 West Shore Road, 737–9842).

KENT COUNTY AND WESTERN RHODE ISLAND

AUTHOR'S FAVORITE ATTRACTIONS / EVENTS

East Greenwich

Nathaniel Greene Homestead

Historic Pontiac Mills

George B. Parker Woodland

Warwick City Park

Portuguese Holy Ghost Festival, West Warwick September

Gaspee Days Celebration, Warwick; late May/early June

Scituate Arts Festival, Scituate; October

St. Patricks Day Parade, West Warwick; March

Steam Up, East Greenwich; September

Also in Apponaug is *The Crow's Nest,* 288 Arnolds Neck Drive (off Post Road/Route 1 just south of Route 117, 732–6575) an out-of-the-way restaurant that attracts fans of fresh seafood and budget-conscious diners alike. Voted best cheap eats by the readers of *Rhode Island Monthly,* The Crow's Nest also can boast of a nice view of Apponaug Cove and excellent, if straightforward, seafood dishes such as fried clams, stuffed shrimp, baked fish, and broiled lobster. Best of all, you can get a generous portion of fish and chips along with a bowl of creamy, meaty chowder served with three fat, round clam cakes for under $12.

Understandably, The Crow's Nest is a local favorite, and it tends to be busy even on weeknights during the summer. Seniors flock here, as do sailing families coming off boats docked at the Ponaug Marina across the street. Free popcorn at the bar helps pass the time, or you can cross Arnolds Neck Drive and admire the boats and the bay from a small, unmarked boardwalk with built-in wooden tables and seats. The Crow's Nest is open 11:30 A.M. to 10:30 P.M. weekdays, 11:30 A.M. to 11:00 P.M. on Friday and Saturday, and 11:30 A.M. to 10:00 P.M. on Sunday. The restaurant is closed during the month of January.

Next, take Route 117 east from Apponaug and bear right onto Long Street just after you pass under the railroad bridge. Follow Long Street until it intersects with Buttonwoods Avenue, then continue straight onto Asylum Road. At the end of Asylum Road you'll find one of Warwick's true hidden treasures: *Warwick City Park.* Almost unknown except to locals, City Park is a beautiful, wooded thumb of land thrust between Buttonwoods Cove and Break Neck Cove. Some of the land is given over to ball fields and the like, but much of it remains wooded. Tracing the perimeter of the park is a serpentine jogging and biking path, which affords frequent views of the water as it meanders through forest and up and down some challenging hills (the path makes some sharp turns and can be narrow in spots, so watch your speed).

Rhode Island's two largest shopping malls are the center of activity in the western part of Warwick, but hidden off a side street across from the Warwick Mall is a shopping experience about as far from your average trip to the mall as you're likely to find. The **Historic Pontiac Mills** (737–2700) complex has seventy-five diverse tenants ranging from a theater group to an archery center to a host of wholesale and retail merchants.

Built in 1863, Pontiac Mills was the original home of the Fruit of the Loom Company, and it was considered such an important part of the national economy and war effort (the company made uniforms for Union soldiers) that President Abraham Lincoln was on hand to dedicate the mill and, as local legend has it, be the first to ring the bell in the mill tower.

Manufacturing firms still occupy some of the mill complex, but increasingly the buildings are being filled by artists' shops and antiques stores that welcome customers from off the street. The best shops, like **Diva's Palace,** Building S–1, second floor (739– 0918), make the most of surroundings that are still very mill-like, with massive stone walls, steel girders, and painted wooden floors.

To say that Diva's Palace owner Michael Turner has dressed up this

Oakland Beach

*L*ike many seaside communities of the nineteenth century, Warwick was blessed to have its share of amusement parks and grand shore hotels—places where people could escape the summer heat in the days when air-conditioning was a distant dream.

One of these icons of a bygone era was Rocky Point Amusement Park, which survived for more than a century before succumbing to bankruptcy in 1996. For the time being, Rocky Point's cavernous Shore Dining Hall still stands watch over Narragansett Bay, but the old park's rides have been sold off. You can still ride the park's classic carousel if you visit Nature's Best Dairy World in Cranston; see the listing in the Providence and Vicinity chapter in this book.

The smaller amusement park at Warwick's Oakland Beach came to a similar end years ago. Once the site of the grand Oakland Beach Hotel, today this peninsula off Route 117 (take 117 east from Apponaug, past the intersections with Buttonwoods Avenue and Route 113; make a right on Oakland Beach Avenue) still has a small public beach (better for strolling than swimming) and a cluster of seaside restaurants, including the redoubtable Iggy's Doughboys (887 Oakland Beach Avenue). While Iggy's does a booming business on summer nights selling fried dough covered in powdered sugar, more traditional fare, particularly seafood, is on the menu at Cherrystone's (898 Oakland Beach Avenue, 732–2532). By the way, actor Brad Pitt ate at Cherrystone's during the filming of Meet Joe Black in Warwick.

If you happen to be in town for the Fourth of July, Oakland Beach is one of the best places to view the fireworks around the bay.

vintage clothing and costume jewelry store is not just a play on words. From a drab hallway or elevator you step into a magical world of mannequins and gaily painted chairs and settees, where everything from the floors to the walls to the columns supporting the ceiling have been beautified to create the illusion of luxury. In addition to

Historic Pontiac Mills

gilded pins, lockets, picture frames, and sequined and feathered hats, Turner and his staff bring plain wool and velvet jackets back to life by adding artistic trim and jewels.

Diva's Palace is open Monday to Saturday from 10:00 A.M. TO 5:00 P.M. and Sunday from noon to 5:00 P.M.

On the main floor of Building S–1, a life-size statue of a pig welcomes you to **Castique, Inc.** (738–8866). The personal gallery of artist Marion Manning-Lovett, Castique is a menagerie of indoor and outdoor statues cast in concrete and gypsum. The statues range from the oddball (the aforementioned swine, which is actually a big piggy bank) to the elegant, such as a nymphlike statue of a woman surrounded by chestnuts. Manning-Lovett also casts pedestals, which would be the perfect platform for a potted ivy or creeper, and an assortment of smaller items that complement tabletops and walls. Castique is open 7:00 A.M. to 5:00 P.M. Monday to Friday; call ahead for weekend hours.

You've heard of dinner theater, right? Well, at **Pontiac Mills' Young Actor's Theatre Company,** (734–9554) they do things a bit differently. The price of a ticket to a production such as Neil Simon's *The Sunshine Boys* or *Murder at the Howard Johnsons* includes not your choice of chicken or fish, but rather a dessert buffet. The company also puts on seasonal productions that feature young actors (thus, the name) from its theater classes. Tickets are $15 general admission, $12 for seniors and students. Located in Building S–1.

Entering the main building through the bell tower, you can take the elevator to the second floor, where the **New England Architectural Center** has filled 18,000 square feet of space with artifacts salvaged from the demolition of old buildings. These urban archaeologists offer for sale such items as stained-glass windows and vintage chandeliers that might otherwise have fallen victim to the wrecking ball. If an old movie theater box office would be just the thing to make your home complete, this is the place to find it.

On the third floor of Building 1 is **Decorum,** a high-end interior design shop that also features unique furniture and accessories. Decorum is open Tuesday to Saturday, 10:00 A.M. to 5:00 P.M.; call 732–8898. **Copper Wave** (ground floor, Building 1; 736–8342) manufactures and sells decorative copper fountains and other copper accessories. A walk through the showroom, surrounded by the soft sound of running water, is relaxation itself. Copper Wave is open 10:00 A.M. to 5:00 P.M. Tuesday to Saturday; noon to 5:00 P.M. on Sunday. Nearby is **Houle Pianos** (739–8510), where you can tinkle the ivories in a showroom full of new and used pianos. The store is open 11:00 A.M. to 4:45 P.M. weekdays, 10:00 A.M. to 5:00 P.M. on Saturday, and 3:30 to 6:30 P.M. Sunday.

Between the main mill building and the east building, a narrow alley called the Pontiac Mews takes you under wooden walkways and past chutes and arched doorways and windows into the heart of the **old mill complex.** Although this part of the mill is rather gritty and overgrown in spots, it still presents some unexpected delights, like a glimpse of the **Pawtuxet River** through a fence and a peek at the **prop warehouse** belonging to Matunuck's Theatre by the Sea.

Most of the second floor of the east building belongs to **Tangy's Indoor Archery Lanes** (737–8193), which has fourteen lanes open to beginners and experienced bowhunters alike. The front of the shop is divided between a 60-foot target range and a shop selling compound and recurve bows, arrows, and custom strings, while a back room has a 105-foot wildlife target range where archers can take aim at plastic pheasants, bobcats, deer, and other woodland creatures hiding in an artificial forest.

Lane rentals are $7.00 per hour for adults and $5.00 per hour for children. Beginners are welcome, and owner Jim Dean recommends either a $10, fifteen-minute lesson plus fifteen minutes on the lane to get the basics of archery down or a $40, one-hour private lesson ($30 for youths) that allows time to work on bow skills and techniques. Equipment can be rented for $11.00 per hour ($8.00 for youths). Tangy's also runs youth and adult leagues and tournaments. Open weekdays from 6:00 to 10:00 P.M. and Saturday and Sunday from 1:00 to 5:00 P.M.

On your way back downstairs, stop to look out the window on the staircase landing for a great view of the waterfall on the Pawtuxet River. Keep an eye out for the geese and snapping turtles that inhabit this quiet stretch of water. Grab some gospel and a cup of Joe at the **Crossroads Coffeehouse,** part of the Amazing Grace Church. Stop in on Friday and Saturday nights for live music (some Christian, some not); call 732–5335 for information.

If all this shopping has made you crave some biscotti or a nice cup of homemade soup, drop by the **Renaissance Cafe.** From her tiny kitchen, owner Bernadette Cicione produces some amazing European pastries, pasta, pizza, and cookies—all washed down with specialty teas, espresso, latte, or cappuccino. Located in the small building in the Pontiac Mills parking lot. Open Monday to Saturday, 8:00 A.M. to 5:00 P.M.; special European brunch served 10:00 A.M. to 2:00 P.M. on Saturday (738–5566).

The Historic Pontiac Mills complex is located at 334 Knight Street; from Route 2 north make a right on West Natick Street after passing the Warwick Mall, then go two lights and make a right on Knight Street. The mill will be on your right, and it is open Tuesday through Sunday from 10:00 A.M. to 7:00 P.M., although individual shop hours vary.

Warwick's Route 2: A Mixed Blessing for Shoppers

*W*arwick's Route 2 (aka Quaker Lane) is both a blessing and a curse for shoppers. The good news is that the Warwick Mall and the Rhode Island Mall are located on Route 2, both near the junction with Route 113. Numerous major retail giants, from the Sports Authority to K-Mart to CompUSA, also have stores located along the stretch of Route 2 running roughly from Route 113 south to Route 3. Between Route 117 and Route 3 is the Christmas Tree Shoppes, a year-round mecca for bargain shoppers from across the state. Still farther south is the state's largest movie theater, the Showcase Cinemas, at the interchange with Interstate 95.

The bad news? Traffic—lots of traffic. Especially on weekends, Route 2 can resemble a parking lot, and conditions can be particularly bad where the road narrows just south of Route 113. Best advice for avoiding problems on busy days: To get to the malls, take Interstate 95 south to the Route 113 exit or I-95 to Interstate 295 to the appropriate mall exit. If you then want to visit the stores farther south, jump back on I-95 south one exit to Route 117 west, which soon intersects back with Route 2, or go one more exit to the Route 2 off-ramp, which is where the movie theater and restaurants like Outback Steakhouse, Ruby Tuesday's, and McDonald's are located.

West Warwick

West Warwick is a small, densely populated former mill town whose downtown is most familiar to Rhode Islanders for its motor vehicle registry office. But West Warwick also has plenty of history: The town is home to the state's first stone cotton mill and Rhode Island's oldest Catholic church (**St. Mary's** on Church Street was built in 1844 and is listed on the National Register).

West Warwick's unassuming **Mr. Taco** (49 Providence Street, 828–7573) is helping make West Warwick known more for plates of delicious Mexican food and less for license plates. Although its ads boast of "Mexican Food American Style," Mr. Taco has won food lovers over with its more traditional dishes, such as Arroz Yucatan, a seafood dish that includes whitefish and shrimp sautéed in red wine with peas and red peppers and served over rice.

Of course, if you want chips smothered in cheese with salsa for dipping, they have that, too, along with chilled margaritas to wash it down and cut the spice. For dessert, try the fried ice cream covered with honey, whipped cream, and cherries. Open Sunday to Thursday, 11:00 A.M. to 10:00 P.M. (11:00 P.M. in summer); Friday and Saturday, 11:00 A.M. to midnight.

West Warwick also is home to **The Station,** a pool joint, bar, and concert venue best known for bringing in hard-rock headliners whose arena days are behind them (211 Cowesett Avenue, 823–4660).

Scituate

The story of the **Scituate Reservoir** is, in some ways, the story of the town of Scituate. Needing a stable supply of drinking water for the city of Providence, the state in 1915 claimed 13,000 acres in the heart of Scituate (whose name comes from a Native American word meaning cold running water) and built a huge dam on the Pawtuxet River. The subsequent filling of the river valley created the largest body of fresh water in the state, but under the waters of the reservoir are the remains of six villages that were condemned in the process. (The residents, happily, were moved out first.)

If you look at a map of Scituate, the reservoir sprawls across town like a giant, crooked letter V. At the right tip of the V is the town of **North Scituate,** located at the crossroads of the Danielson Pike (Route 6) and Route 116. Although it is the largest community in this rural town, North Scituate is a sleepy little place for most of the year. It's always a pleasant place to stroll, and you can easily walk to the picturesque **Horseshoe Dam** from the village center.

The town really comes alive in the first week of October, however, for the annual **Scituate Arts Festival.** Whereas the more famous Wickford Art Festival primarily attracts painters and sculptors, the Scituate festival includes more craftspeople, making for an eclectic group of displays spread around street corners, churchyards, and lawns up and down the streets of town. A drive to the festival also is a good excuse to go leaf-peeping as the local forests explode with color when cool fall weather approaches. Contact the Scituate Arts Festival, Inc. at 647–0057.

About a mile north of the town of North Scituate is the **Seagrave Memorial Observatory,** 47 Peep Toad Road, a half-minute west of Route 116 on the right side of the road (934–0980). Here astronomers gather on cloudless nights to gaze at the stars and other heavenly bodies. The observatory, built in 1914 by amateur astronomer Frank Evans Seagrave on the grounds of his Scituate estate, was later purchased by the Amateur Astronomy Society of Rhode Island, now known as Skyscrapers, Inc. (http://chandra.cis.brown.edu/astro/skyscrapers).

The observatory contains three telescopes, including a 12-inch Meade

A Fall Stroll in Scituate

*O*n a picture-perfect New England fall afternoon my family took a drive up to Scituate to enjoy the fall foliage, which typically peaks by early to mid-October. Unsatisfied with the view from the car window, we pulled off Route 116 just south of Scituate Avenue (Route 12) into a small parking lot on the west side of the road. Leaving our car, we followed a few small groups of people headed down a well-trodden path under a leafy canopy of gold, red, and orange.

One of the few places around the Scituate Reservoir where human intrusion is permitted (access is otherwise restricted in order to maintain the purity of the state's drinking-water supply), this wooded road is a pretty easy hike for all but the youngest and frailest travelers, although by the end I was carrying my three-year-old daughter on my shoulders. From the parking lot, you follow a main trail that proceeds west into the woods and then offers you the choice of turning north toward the dam. Taking this northerly jog will bring you swiftly to Route 12, where you'll exit the woods just at the eastern end of the huge dam that holds back the reservoir waters. There's a cutout on the north side of the road where you can linger for a quick snack or for pictures (my son found a snakeskin on a rock here) before retracing your steps back to your car.

Schmidt-Cassegrain–type scope with computer-controlled tracking. On a cloudless night these telescopes are powerful enough to give you a clear view of the rings of Saturn and atmospheric storms on Jupiter, as well as deep-sky objects like nebulae and distant galaxies. Since the club is composed of astronomy buffs, there's always somebody around to tell you what you're looking at.

Skyscrapers is a membership organization that holds regular meetings and outings, but it also opens the observatory to visitors on the first Friday and the third Saturday of each month. The observatory opens at dusk and stays open for as long as someone wants to use the telescope, sometimes as late as 11:30 P.M. There also are other special public events throughout the year, and children are always welcome. Tours can be arranged by appointment.

Route 116 heading south of North Scituate is a great drive, with the silver glint of sun on water a constant companion as you skirt the edge of the reservoir. For breathtaking vistas of the reservoir, you can take the right turn at the Plainfield Pike (Route 14) to the **Ashland Causeway,** a narrow half-mile berm with water on both sides; or keep driving south on Route 116 to Route 12, where a right turn takes you to the mile-long **Ganier Memorial Dam,** whose construction created the reservoir. A spillway a little farther east feeds the Pawtuxet River, which meanders south from the reservoir through West Warwick before emptying into Narragansett Bay near the Warwick village of Pawtuxet.

East Greenwich

ast Greenwich is a great little town for shopping, dining, or just walking around. Route 1 is Main Street in East Greenwich, yet despite such a central location the town appears in few tourist guides, which tend to focus on nearby Wickford. Don't you make the same mistake, because downtown **East Greenwich** definitely is worth a visit.

If you want history, East Greenwich has it on Pierce Street (which runs parallel to Main Street) in the form of the **General James Mitchell Varnum House** (57 Pierce Street, 884–1776). Built in 1773, this mansion belonged to another Rhode Islander who, like the better-known Nathaniel Greene, became a general in George Washington's continental army. Varnum was the first commander of the Kentish Guards, an elite unit that later was headquartered at the **Armory of the Kentish Guards,** built in 1842 at 80 Pierce Street. Early weapons and other items pertaining to the unit's history can be found at the **Varnum Military Museum,** open by appointment at 6 Main Street (884–4110).

The Varnum mansion is fully furnished with period items and is open from Memorial Day to Labor Day, Thursday through Saturday from 10:00 A.M. to 2:00 P.M. and in September on Saturday from 10:00 A.M. to 2:00 P.M. and by appointment.

Walking the streets of town, you also will pass many fine antiques stores and bridal shops as well as some interesting specialty stores. **The Robin's Nest Gift Shoppe** (885–7717), at 36 Main Street, has a selection of hand-dipped candles and crafts and a huge assortment of Boyd's collectibles (open Tuesday and Wednesday 10:00 A.M. to 5:00 P.M., Thursday and Friday 10:00 A.M. to 8:00 P.M., Saturday 10:00 A.M. to 5:00 P.M., and Sundays noon to 5:00 p.m.), while **The Chocolate Delicacy** (149 Main Street, 884–4949) threatens your waistline with homemade chocolates, fudge, and truffles. Open Monday 10:30 A.M. to 6:00 P.M. and Tuesday to Saturday 10:00 A.M. to 6:00 P.M.; closed Sunday.

The Green Door (130 Main Street, 885–0510) lives up to its billing as "a unique shopping experience"—everything in the store seems to be a one-of-a-kind treasure, from hand-painted bowls from Key West to vintage tablecloths and owner Susan Swanson's own floral arrangements. The store's eclectic offerings are highlighted by a display case full of hand-painted porcelain boxes, called Limoges after their birthplace in France.

Also worth checking out is **Grace-fully Yours** (442 Main Street, 885–1010), especially if your taste runs to country furnishings. Grace Platter's shop is full of lovely handmade solid-wood furniture, lamps with hand-painted shades, and a nice selection of decorative clocks and afghans. Open Tuesday and Wednesday 10:00 A.M. to 5:00 P.M., Thursday and Friday from 10:00 A.M. to 7:00 P.M., Saturday from 10:00 A.M. to 5:00 P.M., and Sunday from noon to 4:00 P.M. If you prefer the beauty of the American Southwest, however, be sure to drop by **Tailored Crafts** (232 Main Street, 885–1756), which features Native American gallery crafts, silver jewelry, blown glass, metalwork, and more.

Jigger's Diner (145 Main Street, 884–5388) is a labor of love by Carol Shriner, the owner and operator who also works behind the counter of this East Greenwich institution. As early as 1917 there was a diner at this address, and the Worcester Dining Car Company diner that presently houses Jigger's was moved here in 1950. For nearly a decade, however, the diner sat stripped and vacant until Shriner renovated it and reopened for business in 1992.

On any given day you're likely to find Carol working the grill in this quaint little spot that is very popular for breakfast and lunch among locals, who will gladly stand and wait for a precious booth or a seat on one of the red stools lining the counter.

Jigger's has excellent omelettes, pancakes, and waffles for breakfast, but the house specialty is their authentic, hot-off-the-griddle Rhode Island jonnycakes. State law allows Jigger's to use the traditional spelling to refer to their jonnycakes (no "h") because they are made from rare white flint corn grown in Exeter and stone-ground at Carpenters Grist Mill in Matunuck. Open Monday through Wednesday 6:00 A.M. to 2:00 P.M., Thursday through Saturday 6:00 A.M. to 8:00 P.M., and Sunday 6:00 A.M. to 1:00 P.M.

Altogether, East Greenwich has more than a dozen restaurants to choose from, ranging from the pizza-and-a-cola offerings at **Frank and John From Italy** (186 Main Street, 884–9751) to the small-town atmosphere of the **Kent Restaurant** (223 Main Street, 884–9855). Downtown also has an abundance of lunch and breakfast joints like **Audra's Cafe** (315 Main Street, 884–4411), where everything on the menu—from American Chop Suey to Chicken Marsala—rings in under $5.00. Open Monday to Saturday 6:00 A.M. to 2:00 P.M.; Sunday 6:00 A.M. to 1:00 P.M. But perhaps the town's most intriguing restaurant is located at the very north end of downtown. The **Post Office Cafe** (11 Main Street, 885–4444) is just what it sounds like: a restaurant in a former post office. In this case, the former post office is a grand brick building built in 1934, and the owners have tried to retain as many vestiges of its original function as possible. The acoustics provided by the 20-foot ceiling in the foyer complement the music of a baby grand piano, which is surrounded by tables and chairs. Along the walls are the old tellers' cages, their cherrywood finish buffed to a warm glow.

The dining room, in a refurbished mail-sorting room, features an innovative menu emphasizing Northern Italian veal and seafood dishes. Open Tuesday through Thursday 4:30 to 9:00 P.M.; Friday and Saturday 4:30 to 10:00 P.M. The owners of the Post Office Cafe also run **The Grille on Main,** a less tony alternative located across the street (80 Main Street, 885–2200). The publike interior, dominated by wood paneling and large mirrors, is warm and inviting. The menu features sandwiches, pizza, pastas, and seafood entrees. Open Monday to Saturday 11:30 A.M. to 1:00 A.M.; Sundays 11:00 A.M. to 4:00 P.M.

As you walk toward the south end of downtown East Greenwich, you're liable to notice the aromatic signature of the **Indian Club** (455 Main

Street, 884–7100, www.theindianclub.com) before you spy the restauranty itself. The large, popular dining room of this relative newcomer to Main Street features fine Indian cuisine, including a large selection of breads, rice specialties, tandoori dishes, and entrees featuring curried chicken, lamb, beef and vegetables, as well as more exotic offerings.

Open daily 11:30 A.M. to 2:30 P.M. for lunch, and 5:00 to 10:00 P.M. for dinner.

On a chilly afternoon—or any afternoon, for that matter—there's no better way to warm your tummy than with one of Peter Charlebois' homemade soups, the main attraction at *Julia's* (250 Main Street, 886–5282). Chicken and sausage gumbo, split pea, and sweet potato soup are among the half-dozen or so hearty broths served daily in big, handled bowls. Soups are accompanied by freshly baked bread, including a crusty, gluteous Italian loaf. Also on the menu are chili, salads, and sandwiches. If you're feeling a bit under the weather, ask Peter to prepare his "flu soup" for you—chicken and vegetable infused with Chinese astragalus root, an immune-system booster. Open Monday through Thursday 11:30 A.M. to 5:00 P.M., Friday and Saturday 11:00 A.M. to 4:30 P.M.

Completely renovated in 1995, the **East Greenwich Town Hall** (125 Main Street) was built in 1804 and formerly served as the Kent County Courthouse, one of the five original State Houses built in Rhode Island. Two other recent projects have added even more spark and diversity to East Greenwich. For years the once-popular **Greenwich Odeum** movie theater (59 Main Street, 885–9119) was shuttered, killed off by competition from the multiplex that opened just down the road on the corner of Route 401 and Route 2. However, a group of preservationists has brought the old house back to life as a nonprofit theater featuring performances by national as well as local performers.

Owner Steve Erinakes, whose family ran the Odeum for more than forty years, describes the present enterprise as total theater, with fare running the gamut from plays to ballet, opera, and live jazz and country music. Recent performances included concerts by folk singers Janis Ian and Patty Larkin and a two-show stint by the National Shakespeare Company. Built in 1926, the 410-seat theater holds performances year-round during the week and on weekends; call for times and ticket prices.

For lodging that's convenient to downtown, it's hard to beat the *1873 House,* a bed-and-breakfast in a historic home located on the next block up the hill from Main Street (162 Pierce Street, 884–9955). One three-room suite is available for $55 to $75 per night, depending on the season. The **Allen House** (71 Verndale Drive, 885–7979) is another small bed-

and-breakfast, located within walking distance of most shops and restaurants, and features two great rooms with private baths for $80 to $125 nightly. The nearby **Vincent House** (170 Cedar Avenue, 885–2864; www.vincenthouse.com) has a deck overlooking a former cranberry bog and provides guests with a private living room with a fireplace, a billiards room, and a private dining room where you can enjoy an unhurried continental breakfast. Rooms go for $80 to $105 and include private baths and computer dataports. The **Silverwood B&B** (133 Silverwood Drive, 884–8217) is farther away from town, but it has the advantage of a quiet residential setting and amenities that will appeal to active guests, including a swimming pool and a private tennis court.

Turning the corner from Main Street onto Queen Street, you'll pass under a railroad bridge and come out on Water Street, which hugs the shoreline of Greenwich Cove and is lined with marinas and restaurants. For fine dockside dining try **20 Water Street** (885–3700), which has a nice deck that's open during the summertime. Open 6:00 to 10:00 P.M. Monday to Saturday. Nearby **Harbourside Lobstermania** (884–6363) specializes in lobsters, seafood, and steaks and also has drinking and dancing till the wee hours in the summer. Open Monday to Saturday 11:30 A.M. to 1:00 A.M.; Sunday noon to 1:00 A.M.

Like moths drawn to a candle, area residents flock to the neon glow of the **Hilltop Creamery** (5720 Post Road, 884–8753) on warm summer nights. Once, the Hilltop Creamery was a mandatory stop for ice cream before catching a movie at the Hilltop Drive-In across the street. Sadly, the drive-in is now just a memory, but the Creamery lives on. The soft-serve is particularly good here; for a treat try Kay's Famous Torch, a cone-inside-a-cone creation topped with a little American flag. The prices are right, too. You can still get a cone for under a buck.

Despite its industrial theme, the **New England Wireless and Steam Museum** (885–0545) sits on a peaceful country lane at Place's Corner, an otherwise obscure crossroads. Devoted to the science of engineering, the museum features exhibits on early radio, telegraph, and television equipment, as well as engines powered by other means, including steam, gas, and oil. There's a collection of telegraph machines that were used from the mid-nineteenth century to the early twentieth century and George H. Corliss steam engines with giant flywheels, built right here in Rhode Island in the 1880s. Each fall the annual Steam Up sees the giant engines hissing and spinning as they are turned on in an impressive display of power. The museum is located at 1300 Frenchtown Road and is open by appointment. Admission is $6.00 per person.

Although East Greenwich has experienced a building boom in recent years, with developments of large executive homes springing up across the landscape, many parts of town retain their rural character. One such place is *Davisville Memorial Wildlife Refuge,* where you can follow a path along the Hunt River to a small pond popular for fishing in season. To get to the park, take Route 4 south to the exit for Route 402 and Route 403, then bear left onto Route 403 (Devils Foot Road). After you come off the highway ramp, the park will be on your right.

Coventry

R hode Island native General Nathaniel Greene was a Revolution-ary War hero of the first rank, but his name is not one you auto-matically associate with Rhode Island. Greene was George Washington's second in command and played crucial roles in both the Battle of Trenton and the Battle of Yorktown, two decisive victories of the war. After the war the Georgia legislature—grateful to Greene for driving the British out of the state—gave the general a plantation in Savannah, where he moved from his home in Coventry in 1785. Greene died soon afterward and was buried in Georgia, and the Peach State held onto the bulk of Greene's legacy.

Fortunately, Rhode Island got to keep the house where Greene lived for many years and entertained such visitors as Lafayette and General Rochambeau and his French army. The *Nathaniel Greene Homestead* (50 Taft Street, 821–8630) strives to educate visitors about Greene's place in Rhode Island history. The Greenes were Rhode Island pioneers: The general's father and brother built and operated one of the first trip-hammer forges in the country, making iron products such as the door-knobs, hinges, and tools used in colonial homes. The remains of the forge are still visible if you walk down a quiet path behind the Greene house to the banks of the Pawtuxet River. Historians believe the cannon sitting on the lawn of the homestead also was cast in the Greene forge.

Inside the circa 1770 house, period furniture—some passed down from the Greene family—is used to approximate how the rooms might have been furnished in General Greene's time. Some of the artifacts in the house actually belonged to the general and his wife, Catherine Littlefield Greene. After General Greene's death, Catherine, who spent most of the war raising the couple's four children while her husband was off fighting, used the government pension money she was granted to support Eli Whitney's successful development of the cotton gin.

Also on the homestead property is a historic cemetery marking the final resting place of many generations of Greenes, their servants, and their slaves. The Nathaniel Greene Homestead is open from April to October 31 Wednesday through Saturday 10:00 A.M. to 5:00 P.M. and Sunday 1:00 to 5:00 P.M. To get to the site, take Route 95 to Route 117 west; just after crossing the town line into Coventry, make a left on Laurel Avenue, cross a small bridge, and make the second left onto Green Street. Take Green Street to Taft Street, make a right, and the homestead will be on your left.

As you continue west on Route 117, the congestion that bedevils this narrow road in the more populous part of Coventry finally yields to open country driving. Apart from some old homes and churches and a series of reservoirs, there's not much to see other than some nice scenery along this stretch of road. You drive for 8 or 9 miles before reaching the intersection with Route 102, but your patience will be rewarded.

Take the right onto Route 102 north and proceed about 2 miles to Maple Valley Road. Turn right here, and a short drive brings you to the *George B. Parker Woodland* (102 Maple Valley Road, 397–4472), yet another excellent Audubon Society nature preserve. Seven miles of trails begin near the historic Issac Bowen House, built between 1755 and 1795 and now a private residence.

Conquering Jerimoth Hill

*P*eople who have climbed Washington's Mount Rainier (14,410 ft.) and Alaska's Mount McKinley (20,320 ft.) to pursue the claim of having stood at the highest point of every U.S. state have been stymied in their quest by dinky Jerimoth Hill.

Rhode Island's highest point, Jerimoth Hill, stands a grand 812 feet above sea level—and in testament to man's ability to put up barriers more insurmountable than those of the natural world. The summit of Jerimoth Hill is just 100 feet south of Route 101 in Foster, but access to the spot is blocked by private property, and the owner has adamantly refused to allow hikers to cross his land. The actual summit is owned by Brown University, but the school has refused to cooperate with groups like the Highpointers Club in allowing hikers access to the state's highest spot.

In frustration, the Highpointers (www.highpointers.com) recently decided to allow members to claim to have conquered Rhode Island's top peak simply by standing next to the Jerimoth Hill sign alongside Route 101.

As you follow the trails through this rugged, 600-acre forest, you will notice that the park has an unusual number of artifacts signaling the past presence of man. Back in the 1700s this area was Coventry Center, a small farm community that also boasted a sawmill on the Turkey Meadow Brook. In

Nathaniel Greene Homestead

time, however, the town was largely abandoned, and Coventry Center was reestablished a few miles to the east near a large pond.

Scattered throughout these woods are old cellar holes, the remains of the mill and a charcoal processing site, and rock walls. There's also something rather mysterious: a series of stone cairns that might have been built by local Native American tribes, although that's just a guess. In truth, nobody is really sure who made these curious stone monuments or why. The Parker Woodland is open dawn to dusk.

If you return to the intersection of Route 102 and Route 117, you'll notice a small side street, Old Summit Road. This road leads into the tiny hamlet of *Summit,* once a stop on the New York, New Haven, and Hartford Railroad line. You can still see the right-of-way for the railroad, along with a few historic buildings (the *Summit Baptist Church,* built in 1862, and the *Summit Free Library,* built in 1891) and the *Summit General Store* (25 Old Summit Road, 397–3366), which claims to be Rhode Island's only real general store. Supporting this assertion is the fact that not only does the store sell groceries, hardware, hay, and feed, but it also serves as the town's post office and video rental store.

Foster

Rhode Island seemed to have everything it took to make up the quintessential New England state: great ocean beaches, rolling farmland and deep forests, old mill towns and quaint village greens. Only one thing was missing: a covered bridge.

So residents of rural Foster decided to put their town on the map by building Rhode Island's only covered bridge. Alas, no sooner was the bridge finished and dedicated than some teenage vandals came along and burned it down.

The story has a happy ending, though. Seemingly the whole town (including at least one repentant young firebug) pitched in and, with donated lumber and countless volunteer hours, rebuilt the bridge in 1994. A replica of an early-nineteenth-century span, the **Swamp Meadow Covered Bridge** crosses Hemlock Brook on a quiet, wooded road near an old mill. To see the bridge, take Route 102 north from the intersection with Route 117 to Route 94, then make a left and proceed north until you reach the Central Pike. Turn left on this dirt road and the bridge is $1/4$ mile ahead.

Popular with truckers and families alike, the **Shady Acres Restaurant and Dairy Bar** (164 Danielson Pike, 647–7019) is the best place to stop along Route 6 for a quick meal or ice cream. Located between the Route 94 intersection and the Connecticut border, Shady Acres is an oasis on this sparsely developed road that runs between Hartford and Providence. Inside there are booths and counter service for patrons who take a seat on the diner stools, while outside there is a screened-in porch and a picnic grove among the shade trees that give the restaurant its name. There's even a small playhouse and swings for the kids to play on while you're waiting for your order from the window. Open Monday through

The Moosup River Railroad Trestle

*T*he railbed of the former New York, New Haven, and Hartford Railroad, cutting across rural Coventry, today serves as the foundation for the Trestle Trail, a hiking and mountain biking path that offers glimpses of railroad history amid lush wilderness.

While diehard hikers may want to walk the trail from Carbuncle Pond (parking off Route 14) to the Coventry Reservoir (parking off Hill Farm Road near Coventry Center on Route 117), you can take a short hike from the Carbuncle Pond end of the trail to view one of the highlights: the 50-foot-high former railroad trestle that crosses the Moosup River. On a hot summer afternoon this is a great spot to kick back, soak up the sun, and enjoy the beautiful view of the river and forest below, enveloped in near-total quiet and solitude.

It's perfectly OK to come this far and then turn back to your car, or, if you're in the mood, keep going east and you'll pass the small village of Greene and then Summit, where you can get a cold drink at the Summit General Store before heading back.

Saturday 6:00 A.M. to 9:00 P.M. and Sunday 7:00 A.M. to 9:00 P.M. during the summer; closes at 8:00 P.M. during the winter.

PLACES TO STAY IN KENT COUNTY AND WESTERN RHODE ISLAND

(ALL AREA CODES 401)

WARWICK

Comfort Inn Airport,
1940 Post Road, 732–0470

The Enchanted Cottage B&B Inn, 16 Beach Avenue,
732–0439

Crowne Plaza at the Crossings,
801 Greenwich Avenue,
732–6000

MainStay Suites,
268 Metro Center Boulevard, 732–6667

Motel 6,
20 Jefferson Boulevard,
467–9800

Radisson Airport Hotel,
2081 Post Road, 739–3000

Residence Inn by Marriott,
500 Kilvert Street,
737–7100

Sheraton Providence Airport Hotel, 1850 Post Road, 738–4000

Suisse Chalet Warwick,
36 Jefferson Boulevard,
941–6600

WEST WARWICK
Spring Hall by Marriott, 14 J.P. Murphy Highway, 822–1244

EAST GREENWICH
The Allen House B&B,
71 Verndale Drive,
885–7979

The 1873 House B&B, 162 Pierce Street, 884–9955

Silverwood B&B,
133 Silverwood Drive,
884–9217

Vincent House B&B,
170 Cedar Avenue,
884–2864

FOSTER
Stone House Motor Inn,
152 Danielson Pike,
Route 6, 647–5850

PLACES TO EAT IN KENT COUNTY AND WESTERN RHODE ISLAND

(ALL AREA CODES 401)

WARWICK

Bugaboo Creek Steak House, 30 Jefferson Boulevard, 781–1400

The Crow's Nest Restaurant, 288 Arnolds Neck Drive, 732–6575

The Greenwich Tavern,
195 Forge Road, 885–4999

Iggy's Doughboys, 889 Oakland Beach Avenue,
737–9459

Legal Seafoods,
2099 Post Road, 732–3663

Portofino, 897 Post Road,
461–8920

Rocky Point Chowder House, 1759 Post Road,
739–4222

Selected Chambers of Commerce in Kent County and Western Rhode Island

Central Rhode Island Chamber of Commerce—
3288 Post Road, Warwick 02886, 732–1100;
www.centralrichamber.com/

East Greenwich Chamber of Commerce—
5853 Post Road, East Greenwich 02818, 885–0020;
www.eastgreenwichchamber.com

Solis Japanese Steak House,
1599 Post Road, 738–8336

WEST WARWICK

Cowesett Inn,
226 Cowesett Avenue,
828–4726

Mr. Taco,
49 Providence Street,
828–7573

Stephens Backyard,
11 Curson Street,
821–0030

EAST GREENWICH

Harbourside
Lobstermania,
Water Street, 884–6363

Hilltop Creamery,
5720 Post Road, 884–8753

Jason's Food & Spirits,
1149 Division Road,
885–3900

Jigger's Diner,
145 Main Street, 884–5388

The Post Office Cafe,
11 Main Street, 885-4444

Richard's Pub,
3347 South County Trail,
884–2880

Twenty Water Street Warehouse Tavern,
20 Water Street, 885–3703

FOSTER

Shady Acres Restaurant &
Dairy Bar, Danielson Pike,
647–7019

**OTHER ATTRACTIONS
WORTH SEEING IN
KENT COUNTY AND
WESTERN RHODE ISLAND**

John Waterman Arnold
House, *Warwick*

Lakeview Amusements,
Coventry

Goddard Memorial State
Park, *Warwick*

**HELPFUL WEB SITES ABOUT
KENT COUNTY AND
WESTERN RHODE ISLAND**

Providence/Warwick
Convention and
Visitors Bureau,
www.providencecvb.com

Warwick Online,
www.warwickonline.com

Northern Rhode Island

The six towns lying north of Providence are linked to the capital city in that they are all part of Providence County. In attitude and atmosphere, however, the northern part of the state is a different world.

The Blackstone River dominates the eastern part of Northern Rhode Island, and mill villages dot the riverbanks. If town names like Arnold Mills and Grant Mills point to the region's industrial past, then the French names on mailboxes and storefronts evidence the area's large Acadian population. The river, on the other hand, is named after William Blackstone, a renegade cleric who rode into the area on the back of a bull around 1630 and became the first European to settle here. You won't find any trace of Blackstone's home in Cumberland, however, because the entire hill it once sat upon was leveled and removed in 1886 to make way for the construction of the Ann & Hope Mill.

The western half of this region is largely rural, with large tracts of forest dotted with lakes, ponds, and reservoirs fed by rivers and streams, some of which were significant enough to support small mill towns of their own. Even native Rhode Islanders rarely venture into the hilly northwestern part of the state except to fish, hike, or hunt. Thanks to the cooler temperatures in the region's valleys and hollows, towns like Gloucester are famous for declaring school snow days when the rest of the state is getting rain.

One of the best ways to gain an appreciation of this area's place in history is to take a river tour. The ***Blackstone Valley Explorer*** departs from a variety of points and offers a unique perspective of the mills, towns, railroads, and grand homes that embraced the river's power during the Industrial Revolution. And although the Blackstone has long been a working river, in many places it still retains its natural beauty.

Among the excursions offered by the Blackstone Valley Tourism Council, which operates the forty-nine-passenger riverboat, are the Woonsocket Falls Tour, which covers the mill-dotted riverbank from Woonsocket to Blackstone, Massachusetts, and the Valley Falls and Wilderness Tour, which explores less-developed sections of the river in Central Falls,

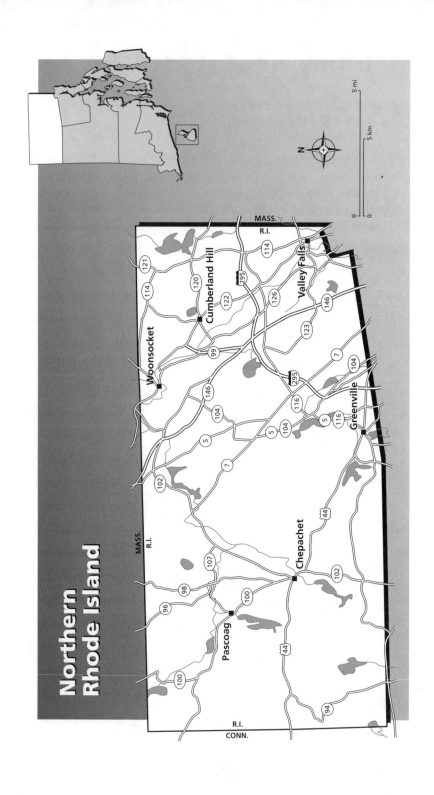

Northern
Rhode Island

MASS.
R.I.

Woonsocket

Cumberland Hill

Valley Falls

Greenville

Chepachet

Pascoag

MASS.
R.I.

R.I.
CONN.

N

5 mi

5 km

Cumberland, and Lincoln. There also are special fall foliage tours and Haunted River cruises around Halloween. Regularly scheduled tours operate from April through October on weekends and holidays, 1:00 to 4:00 P.M. The forty-five-minute tours are $5.00 per person. Call the Blackstone Valley Tourism Council (800) 454–BVTC.

A footnote on Blackstone River attractions: Under the banner of the Blackstone River Valley National Heritage Corridor Commission, efforts currently are under way to expand and link parkland along the river all the way from Worcester, Massachusetts, to Providence. The Corridor comprises twenty-five communities lying along 46 miles of Blackstone River watershed and is intended as a living museum of the industrialization of America. At many of the historical sites in this chapter, as well as elsewhere in this book, you'll notice new signs designating the location as part of the Corridor. In many cases you'll find interpretive information posted as well. Plans call for a bike path and right-of-way linking many of the places mentioned in this book, including Slater Mill in Pawtucket, the Blackstone River State Park in Lincoln, the Blackstone Gorge Bi-State Park in North Smithfield, and Valley Falls Heritage Park in Cumberland. The Lincoln section of the bike path is already open, with a 3-mile ribbon of pavement starting at Front Street. For more information contact the Commission at 762–0250.

Woonsocket

The city of Woonsocket shares Providence's urban setting but is much more firmly tied to the Industrial Revolution than her southern sister. The river waters surging through the Blackstone Gorge made Woonsocket a center for mill industry during the nineteenth century, and the city—actually a melding of five smaller mill villages—remains largely wedded to its industrial heritage. The Providence and Worcester Railroad cuts through the heart of downtown, and unlike many other Rhode Island locales, where the mills have either been abandoned or turned into shops or condos, Woonsocket still has many factories and plants in operation. A recent restoration project, still in progress, has spruced up downtown's business district. The city's North End is noted for its fine early-twentieth-century homes. For walking tours or other information, stop by the Blackstone River Valley National Heritage Corridor Commission's office, located in the old train station at Depot Square.

River Island Park is a tiny oasis of green in the industrial heart of Woonsocket. From its riverside walk you get a splendid view of the river, the powerful Woonsocket Falls, and the many mills that draw life from the waterway, a neat definition of the city as a whole. Located on Bernon Street, the park is just a stone's throw from Woonsocket's *Market Square,* home of City Hall and Harris Hall, where Abraham Lincoln spoke in 1860.

Also on Market Square is the *Museum of Work and Culture,* equal parts an examination of nineteenth-century mill life and a celebration of the French-Canadian immigrants who helped launch America's Industrial Revolution. The Acadian workers who came down from Quebec to work Rhode Island's mills developed a rich culture and vibrant family life that stood in stark contrast to the grim conditions in which they worked. Housed in a former textile mill, the museum includes rotating exhibits, a re-created church and mill worker's home, a lecture series, and an annual New Year's Day celebration that re-creates the French-Canadian tradition of visiting family and friends to mark the new year. Open weekday, 9:00 A.M. to 4:00 P.M., Saturday 10:00 A.M. to 5:00 P.M., and Sunday 1:00 to 5:00 P.M. Admission is $5.00 for adults,

Ride Those Rapids

*T*he Blackstone River drops an average 10 feet per mile, and although dams and waterfalls control a significant portion of the river's strength, there are still many parts of the river that canoeists will find fun and exciting. The Blackstone has rapids ranging from Class I to Class III (the latter capable of swamping an open canoe if you're not careful), and the occasional stretches of flatwater give you the opportunity to enjoy the beautiful scenery.

If you put your canoe or kayak in at River Island Park in downtown Woonsocket you'll pass a series of historic mills, then enter a 1,000-foot section of Class I and Class II rapids. City then gives way to forested riverbanks that continue almost to the Manville Dam. Once you portage around the dam there's another stretch of easy canoeing along forests and past the ruins of the 1872 Manville Mill.

The next portage is at Albion Falls, best viewed from the iron-truss bridges spanning the river. After another portage at the Ashton Viaduct, you'll have a choice of paddling down the river or the parallel Blackstone Canal, which dates from the 1820s. The canal is recommended, since it allows you to avoid the dangerous Pratt Dam area. From Lonsdale the river meanders through a large freshwater marsh and past Valley Falls Pond. At this point you can decide whether to call it a day or take on a series of portages separated by short paddles to reach downtown Pawtucket and Slater Mill—the birthplace of the American Industrial Revolution.

For more information and a copy of an excellent canoe guide for the Blackstone River, contact the Blackstone River Valley National Heritage Corridor Commission, One Depot Square, Woonsocket, 02895; 762–0250.

$2.00 for seniors and students, and free for children under ten (when accompanied by an adult). Market Square, South Main Street (exit 9B off I–295), Woonsocket; 769–WORK.

If talk of all this New Year's reverie stokes your hunger, the nearby **River Cafe** is your best bet in Woonsocket for French-Canadian cuisine like pork and beef pies. Located at 446 River Street, just a few blocks from the Museum of Work and Culture, the River Cafe is open Tuesday to Saturday for breakfast, lunch, and dinner (762–1457). Or, take a stroll across Market Square to **Ye Olde English Fish and Chips Restaurant** (25 South Main Street at Market Square, 762–3637), a Woonsocket tradition for more than 75 years. Believe me, if you are a fan of classic English-style fish and chips, it's worth the drive here no matter where in Rhode Island you are coming from. Goodness knows it's not health food, but the deep-fried delights at Ye Olde England remain delicious despite the switch from cooking in animal fat to low-cholesterol oil a few years back. Opened in 1922 by English immigrants, Harry and Ethel Snowden, and currently in its fifth generation of family ownership, the fish and chips shop expanded to include a dining room back in the '70s but still retains its local atmosphere.

For another on-the-go option for lunch, seek out the **Castle Luncheonette** at 420 Social Street (762–5424), where they serve up burgers in a setting straight out of the '50s.

In the annals of quirky restaurant ideas, **Chan's Fine Oriental Dining**, Depot Square at the junction of Main and Railroad Streets (267 Main Street, 765–1900), deserves a mention. After all, at how many places can you get top-quality live jazz, blues, and country music with your fried rice and egg foo young? Every Saturday and Sunday night, owner John Chan brings in performers from around the country, as well as local comedy acts, to entertain diners. The performances are held in Chan's Four Seasons Room, and you can watch the show between trips to the hot buffet and the bar.

If you come just for dinner, you can usually walk right into Chan's dining room, but reservations are required for musical and comedy performances. Ticket prices vary, but generally range from $5.00 to $15.00, depending upon the performer. Showtime is 8:00 P.M., with an occasional second show scheduled at 10:30 P.M. Chan's is open Monday

High School Hockey Heroes

*R*hode Island is a hotbed of hockey, producing such National Hockey League stars as goaltender Chris Terreri, defenseman Mathieu Schneider, and 1996–97 Rookie of the Year Brian Berard. And nowhere does the passion for hockey burn more brightly than in Woonsocket, home of Mount Saint Charles Academy (800 Logee Street, 769–0310).

The Mount, as the school is known, is an incubator for hockey talent, and the school is the perennial winner of the state hockey championships. Watching these high school athletes perform is a treat, especially during one of the annual tournaments when top teams from around the region come in to challenge the Mounties. Plus, there's a good chance you'll see a future star in the making; Schneider, Berard, fellow NHL defenseman Keith Carney, and many other professional hockey players got their start at Adelard Arena.

Even beating the Mounties can be the ticket to success: Current U.S. women's Olympic hockey team goalie Sara DeCosta shocked the state when she led her Toll Gate High School (Warwick) team to a 3-0 shutout over the Mounties during the state championships a few years back. Berard, Schneider, and Carney all played on the men's U.S. Olympic team in Nagano, as well.

and Tuesday 11:30 A.M. to 9:30 P.M.; Wednesday, Thursday, and Sunday 11:30 A.M. to 10:30 P.M.; Friday and Saturday 11:30 A.M. to midnight.

North Smithfield

*H*ow out of the way is **Blackstone Gorge Bi-State Park**? Well, you can't even get to it from North Smithfield, although most of the park is located within the town's borders. The only access point is in Blackstone, Massachusetts, and once you get there, there's not even a sign to guide you to the park. But don't despair, because you can find the 197-acre park, and doing so is well worth the effort.

To get to the park entrance from Rhode Island, take Route 146A north to St. Paul Street in Woonsocket, making a right at Kennedy's Lunch and crossing the state line into Blackstone, Massachusetts. Make the left at Route 122, then another left on County Road, which you will take to the end. At the edge of Rolling Mill Dam is a footpath leading down into the gorge.

Known as the hardest working river in America, 400 feet of the Blackstone's 438-foot vertical drop were controlled for water power to run the dozens of mills along its path. The stretch of the river within the park, then, is a rare exception; here, the power of the flowing water has cut a rocky gorge and flows unfettered downstream. Blazed trails lead from the parking area through undeveloped woodland and to the edge of the gorge, crossing the state line into Rhode Island along the way.

Also located off Route 146A near Woonsocket is **Wright's Dairy Farm** (200 Woonsocket Hill Road, 767–3014). Wright's is a working dairy with 115 cows, super-fresh milk, and blueberry muffins that have been voted the best in Rhode Island. Since 1905 the Wrights have been getting up every morning before sunrise to milk their cows, so the milk in the dairy shop is never more than forty-eight hours old. They also sell fresh cream, which is used in the bakery to create delicious pastries.

Adjacent to the bakery is the dairy barn, where visitors are welcome to stand at an observation window and watch the cows being milked. If you can't make the 4:30 A.M. milking (and who could blame you?) there is another that starts around 3:30 P.M. and continues until dinnertime. Wright's Dairy Farm is open Monday through Saturday 8:00 A.M. to 7:00 P.M. and Sunday 8:00 A.M. to 4:00 P.M. To get there take Route 146A to Woonsocket Hill Road, then head west for $^1/_4$ mile until you see the sign for the farm/dairy on your left. A long driveway leads to the dairy.

Samuel Slater's mill in Pawtucket is known as the birthplace of the American Industrial Revolution, but it was not Slater's only accomplishment. In 1805 Slater and his partners founded the town of **Slatersville,** which today stands largely intact as the first planned mill community in America. Slatersville is not geared toward tourists; it's just a nice place to spend an hour or so walking around and admiring the old homes on Main, School, and Greene Streets.

In 1807 Samuel Slater sent his younger brother John to buy an old mill and create a planned community in northern Rhode Island. After the plans for Slatersville were laid out, John and his wife, Ruth, moved into the town so that he could oversee the operation of the mill, which he did for the next thirty-five years. The Slaters' modest house, not much different from those of his mill workers, is located on School Street. At the top of a curved drive off School Street is the William Slater Mansion, built in 1854 and belonging to the man who eventually became the sole owner of the Slater Mill.

The village centers on a small, triangular common at the corner of Greene and School Streets. Facing the common is the 1838 Congregational Church with its historic cemetery. If you walk west from the common, you will come to Railroad Street; make a left here and walk to the stone Arch Bridge (built in 1855), and you will have a downriver view of the Slater Mill, also known as the Center Mill. Originally built in 1806, the water-powered cotton mill burned and was rebuilt in 1826.

Slatersville is located at the junction of the Providence Pike (Route 5) and Victory Highway (Route 102); you can also get there by taking the Route 146A exit off of Route 146 in North Smithfield. Also on Victory Highway in Slatersville is *Gator's Pub and Restaurant* (1306 Victory Highway, 769–2220), a casual place where you get a sandwich or a simple, family-style meal on the outdoor deck, or work off a beer or two on the beach volleyball court out back.

If you tell a Rhode Islander that you are going to catch a movie at the *Rustic Drive-In* (Route 146, 769–7601), you may get some funny looks. That's because up until a few years ago, the Rustic showed X-rated movies. For the past couple of years, though, the Rustic has been packing in young families and couples on a budget with prices that are an incredible bargain in these days of $7.50 to $8.00 movie tickets. For just $15.00 per carload, you can enjoy a double feature on any of the drive-in's three screens. Second-run movies just out of the expensive theaters are the rule, and the Rustic pulls in more than its share of family films.

The window speakers are long gone, but patrons can tune in the soundtrack on their car radios. The playgrounds and miniature railroads typical of the drive-ins of yore are also missing, but the Rustic's snack bar still offers a wider variety of food and snacks than your standard movie theater, including burgers and clam cakes.

The last drive-in theater in Rhode Island, the Rustic is a landmark on Route 146, with its giant neon marquee pointing the way to the box office. The Rustic gets very busy on warm summer nights, so come early and bring a portable radio and a blanket or lawn chairs so that you can sit outside. (You can bring your own snacks and drinks, too.) The Rustic Drive-In is open nightly during the summer and on weekends and holidays during the spring and fall.

Burrillville

The Rhode Island Red may have a monument in Adamsville (see Newport County chapter), but the state's real shrine to chicken is *Wright's Farm Restaurant* at 84 Inman Road off Route 102 in Nasonville, (769–2856).

Family-style chicken dinners are a Rhode Island tradition, and nobody does it bigger or better than Wright's Farm. Diners have just two choices: all-you-can-eat roasted chicken ($7.95 for adults, $4.50 for children; kids under two are free) or the steak dinner ($17.50). Skip the steak: It's the tender, moist, falling-off-the-bone chicken that makes Wright's Farm famous, along with heaping side dishes of fresh-cut French fries, pasta with homemade tomato sauce, and crisp salads topped with an excellent house Italian dressing (it's all-you-can-eat on the side dishes, too).

The restaurant is tremendous, with six dining rooms that can accommodate 500 people, but the decor is bright and inviting, the service fast and friendly, and the place is immaculate. This impressive operation is the result of more than forty years in business—plenty of time to work out any kinks.

Wright's Farm is extremely popular with Ocean State natives, so expect a wait even with all those tables. A large bar, festooned with carved and painted chickens of all shapes and sizes, is a nice place to pass the time, or you can check out the gift shop (which, surprisingly, is somewhat light on chicken souvenirs) or try your luck at the keno games that run constantly in the lounge. Wright's Farm is open Thursday and Friday 4:00 to 9:00 P.M., Saturday noon to 9:30 P.M., and Sunday noon to 8:00 P.M.; no credit cards accepted.

Burrillville is about as rural and quiet a getaway as you'll find in Rhode Island, so why not take full advantage and spend a night at the **Willingham Manor** bed-and-breakfast (570 Central Street, 568–2468)? Choose from the Elephant Room, with its ledges brimming with decorative pachyderms, or the Shell Room, which features seashells collected from around the world by innkeepers Will and Jan Pinckard. Located in a private wing of an 1840s home, the B&B rooms also afford access to a lovely summer patio for reading and relaxing. Rates are $62 single and $74 double, including a full country breakfast.

The northwest corner of Rhode Island is occupied by one of the state's most out-of-the-way places, the **Buck Hill Management Area.** One of the many undeveloped tracts managed by the state, Buck Hill is teeming with wildlife and is a great place to get acquainted with Rhode Island's still-abundant natural heritage.

Marked trails surround a marsh and follow old roads across both the Massachusetts and Connecticut state lines. Along the way you are bound to see some of the abundant ducks and waterfowl that reside in the marshes and ponds. A sharper eye is required to spot the owls, pheasants, deer, foxes, and wild turkeys that also make Buck Hill their home. Plan on spending a couple of hours here, especially if you come in the early spring or early fall, when the days are cooler and the insect population less oppressive. (Beware: Late fall and early winter is hunting season.)

The entrance to the Buck Hill Management Area is an unmarked gravel road on the right side of Buck Hill Road, approximately $2^3/_{10}$ miles from the intersection with Route 100/Wallum Lake Road. Also in Burrillville are two other state-owned nature preserves worth exploring: the **Black Hut Management Area** (enter off Spring Lake Road, which intersects with Route 102 in Glendale, just south of Wright's Farm) and the **George Washington Management Area** and the adjacent **Casimir Pulaski State Park,** with access from Route 44/Putnam Pike near the Bowdish Reservoir in Gloucester, 5 miles west of the junction of Route 44 and Route 102. Both the Washington and Pulaski parks have beaches for freshwater swimming.

Southeast of Buck Hill on Route 100 near Pascoag is **White Mill Park** (568–4300), a pleasant stop for a picnic lunch or a brief ramble in the woods. A picnic pavilion overlooks the Wilson Resevoir, while a pretty arched bridge crosses a waterfall to a series of hiking paths, one of which will take you to the crumbling remains of the worsted mill that operated here from 1895 through the 1960s.

Gourmet cooks will tell you that preparing a meal can be more fun than eating it. You can put that theory to the test at the **Old Aaron Smith Farm** in Mapleville. Hosts Richard and Claudette Brodeur welcome groups of eight or more persons to enjoy an evening of eighteenth-century cooking and fine dining at their circa 1730 farmhouse. The Brodeurs will teach you how to cook such traditional seasonal dishes as braised duck and Cornish game hens with chestnut stuffing, roasted in an old cast-iron stove and served in the house's formal dining room. You can snack on the appetizers you have prepared and quench your thirst on homemade lavender punch or calendula nectar, or bring your own wine.

All the food you prepare and eat is organically grown and raised on the farm (in season), and all dinners include appetizers, entree, dessert, and beverages. The Brodeurs also are happy to give you the recipes so that you can try these dishes at home.

The Old Aaron Smith Farm is located at 264 Victory Highway, which intersects with Route 102 just south of Lapham Farm Road (568– 6702). Workshops/dinners are available evenings, weekends, and upon request; reservations required. Dinner prices range between $32 and $40.

Just thinking about a doughboy can raise your cholesterol count. Consisting of a slab of dough deep-fried in oil and coated with powdered sugar, doughboys are a flagrant violation of any sensible dietary plan—but worth the indulgence. These Rhode Island favorites occupy a place of honor at *Mr. Doughboy* (1950 Bronco Highway, 568–4897), a classic roadside attraction that lures travelers on Route 102 through Glendale with a restaurant, a miniature railroad, go-karts, batting cages, and miniature golf. You will be amused, and the kids will love it.

Gloucester

The village of *Chepachet* is the heart of Gloucester, the crossroads of three major state roads (Routes 102, 44, and 100) in a town that remains largely undeveloped. Despite its busy main street, however, Chepachet retains much of its charm.

A variety of antiques stores, many in historic homes and buildings, are clustered in the center of Chepachet. An 1814 mill standing beside the Chepachet River is home to the *Stone Mill Antiques & Craft Center* (1169 Main Street, 568–6662). Inside, European furnishings predominate; outside, a collection of old buggies and sleighs catches your eye, including one being "pulled" by a large, white wooden horse. Open Saturday and Sunday 11:00 A.M. to 5:00 P.M.

Across the street, at 1178 Main Street, is *The Old Post Office,* where owner Jere Henault has done such a convincing restoration job that at least once a week somebody comes in looking to mail a letter. (Jere sends them to the new post office down the road.) The collection, which includes merchandise from about a dozen dealers, includes lots of toys and '50s Americana, estate jewelry, books, a kitchen room in the back that will remind you of Grandma's, and an attic full of old radios. The Old Post Office is open Thursday through Saturday 11:00 A.M. to 5:00 P.M. and Sunday noon to 5:00 P.M. (568–1795).

The *Brown & Hopkins Country Store* (1179 Putnam Pike, 568–4830) also has two floors of antiques, but there's much more to the story than that. First opened in 1809, Brown & Hopkins is the oldest continuously operated country store in America. Many authentic touches remain, including a creaky, wide-beamed wooden floor, an old potbellied stove, and an open-beamed ceiling.

As in any good country store, display cases in the front of the building are crammed with penny candies. Staples like flour and rice no longer occupy the shelves, having been replaced by crafts and collectibles; gourmet coffee and fresh breads are sold from behind the counter.

Brown & Hopkins Country Store

Tables and chairs in the rear of the store welcome you to relax to the sounds of the banjo music playing in the background.

Upstairs, the rooms on the second and third floor have been arranged to give the feel of an old country home, with a twist: Everything is for sale. In one room, a long antique table is set with Early American stoneware; another is set up like a bedroom with an old rope bed, while miniature Christmas trees adorned with hand-made decorations fill another. Brown & Hopkins is open Thursday to Saturday 11:00 A.M. to 4:00 P.M. and Sunday noon to 5:00 P.M.

If you need to take a breather, cross the bridge over the Chepachet River to the town fire station. An unmarked path leads along the river to a pretty pond covered with lily pads. There's a good spot to sit right where the pond swells over an old dam and the waterfall gurgles into the stream below.

Another old Main Street business, the *Job Armstrong Store* (1181 Main Street) has been restored as a headquarters and small museum by the Gloucester Heritage Society. The society uses the store as a living museum, featuring workshops by local craftspeople on weaving, quilting, and rug-hooking, and an old loom is a highlight of the small, traditional exhibits that occupy the upper floor. On display are medical artifacts from the Civil War, a drum and uniform from the Chepachet Cornet Band, and displays on the history of the Dorr Rebellion, an 1842 suffrage revolt led by Chepachet resident Thomas Dorr.

The museum is open Saturday noon to 4:00 P.M. and by appointment; call 568–2846.

For such a small town, Chepachet is blessed with two restaurants consistently rated among the best in northern Rhode Island. *The Purple Cat,* on the corner of Route 44 and Route 102 (568–7161), was founded in 1929 as a diner housed in two old trolley cars. It has since shed its lunch-counter image but not its reputation for great Black Angus steaks and fresh swordfish. For lunch The Purple Cat offers a variety of hot sandwiches, and they make a mean cheeseburger. The decor is simple, with old pictures of Chepachet and hand-carved wooden signs on the walls of the dark dining room. One highlight: a lobby photo of former Detroit Tigers pitcher Mark "The Bird" Fidrych, post-stardom and leaning on the cab of his tractor-trailer rig. Open Tuesday to Friday 11:30 A.M. to 2:00 P.M. for lunch and 4:30 to 9:00 P.M. for dinner; open Saturday noon to 9:00 P.M. and Sunday noon to 8:00 P.M.

The *Stage Coach Tavern* (1157 Putnam Pike/Route 44, 568–2275) is another Chepachet building with a storied past. Originally built in the early 1700s as a private home, the building was in use as a tavern in July 1842 when *Thomas Dorr*—the duly elected governor of Rhode Island—began his rebellion against incumbent governor Samuel King, who refused to step down. In quelling Dorr's revolt, King's troops shot through the door of the tavern, set up headquarters in the building, and didn't leave until the end of the summer.

Dorr's Rebellion

*C*ritics who bemoan the sorry state of Rhode Island politics need to put their complaints in perspective: At least the state's present-day political battles don't include actual gunfire. Such was not the case during the brief but all-too-real Dorr's Rebellion of 1842.

Unlike most states, Rhode Island never replaced its Colonial charter—dating back to 1663—after the Revolutionary War. The upshot was that through the 1840s, only property owners could vote. Leading a group of disenfranchised citizens, Thomas Wilson Dorr launched a reform campaign to give the vote to all male citizens. Both Dorr's group and the state legislature drafted versions of a new constitution, but it was Dorr's that emerged victorious in a referendum.

Governor Samuel King's sitting government declared the Dorr constitution illegal. Undaunted, Dorr's party held elections and named Dorr governor in 1842. King refused to step down and called out the militia to crush Dorr's government. There were a handful of armed clashes between Dorr's supporters and the state militia, but Dorr was unable to raise enough popular support to defeat King. Dorr was captured and sentenced to life in prison in 1844.

While Dorr lost the rebellion, his ideals soon triumphed. In 1843 the state adopted a new constitution expanding the vote to non-property owners, and Dorr himself was released from prison after serving just one year. The Dorr Rebellion also led to an important Supreme Court decision that gave Congress and the president the power to determine each state's lawful government.

Once a stop on the stagecoach run between Providence and Connecticut, the Stage Coach Tavern is still luring travelers with a fine selection of seafood, steaks, pasta, and poultry. The house specialty is prime rib, which you can order Governor Dorr–style—smothered with sautéed mushrooms and onions the way old Thomas liked it. The bar in the same building has a local atmosphere. Open Wednesday, Thursday, and Sunday noon to 9:00 P.M.; open till 10:00 P.M. Friday and Saturday. The bar is open until 1:00 A.M. daily, with lighter tavern food available when the dining area is closed; full menu is available in the bar when the dining room is open.

Finally, Chepachet is home to one of the state's most unique public celebrations—the annual **Ancients & Horribles Parade.** Held on the Fourth of July, the parade is described by one local resident as the "anti-Bristol" parade. (For a description of the far more traditional Bristol Fourth of July parade, see the East Bay chapter.) Rather than marching bands playing patriotic themes, local iconoclasts build floats and dress up in costumes parodying the news of the day and skewering local politicians. Anyone who takes the time to make a costume can join the procession, which in past years has included everything from impersonators dressed as Rhode Island's portly governor to a float depicting Mike Tyson's infamous ear-chewing bout with Evander Holyfield. It's a wicked good time.

Given Gloucester's reputation for snowy winters, it seems only fitting that Santa should live here. Stuart Freeman has been playing Santa Claus at the Lincoln Mall for the past fifteen years, but when he's not deciding who's been naughty or nice, he (along with wife, Mimi) runs the **Freeman's Farm Bed & Breakfast** at 65 Jackson Schoolhouse Road (off Route 44 west of Chepachet village).

Freeman's Farm has two spacious, neatly furnished guest rooms. Upstairs, a room with a double bed and shared bath goes for $50 per night. A new three-room apartment downstairs has a private bath, kitchen, and queen-size bed and is a very reasonable $70 per night. The 200-year-old farmhouse is filled with pictures of Freeman in his Santa suit, generally with a beaming child on his lap. The owners' obvious love of children extends to the lodging arrangements—youngsters are welcome and stay free. (The Freemans charge a few dollars for older children to cover the cost of feeding them a full, unlimited breakfast each morning.)

Of course, if you are going to stay at Santa's house, the best time to come is during the winter. Besides his mall duties, Freeman also spends his December weekends hearing Christmas wishes in the special Santa's Workshop he has built behind the farmhouse. Parents are welcome to bring their children and cameras for a free picture in front of the fireplace.

Santa's Workshop generally is open from noon until dark on Saturday and Sunday in December. Call 568–6561 first to be sure.

Spice up your trip through rural Rhode Island with a stop at the *Cherry Valley Herb Farm,* located at 969 Snake Hill Road, 4 1/2 miles from the intersection with Route 116 (568–8585; www.cherryvalleyherbfarm. com). There are eight aromatic herb gardens you can wander through on this fifty-acre farm, and a quaint shop is located in a big red barn that has everything you need to prepare your own herbal teas, potpourri, herb wreaths, and arrangements. Cherry Valley even holds classes if you want to learn more about cooking or designing with herbs.

There also is an abundant selection of herbs to choose from, with fresh plants available from April to September and dried herbs sold year-round. If the children are getting bored, they can go outside for a peek at the farm's cows or play with Buddy the dog—a friendly Samoyed— while you browse among the cookbooks, candles, bath oils, teapots, and dried flowers.

The shop is open Thursday through Saturday 10:00 A.M. to 4:00 P.M. and Sunday 1:00 to 4:00 P.M.

Cumberland

The town of Cumberland occupies the rural northeastern corner of Rhode Island. Flanked by the Blackstone River and the city of Woonsocket, most of Cumberland's attractions are found along Route 114, also known as Diamond Hill Road, named after the town's most prominent feature.

Route 114 is a pleasant, two-lane paved country road running through mixed farms, woodland, and small clusters of homes. From Route 295, travel north from exit 11 (the last exit in Rhode Island) until you see the jolly flags fronting the store at *Phantom Farms* (2920 Diamond Hill Road, 333–2240), a farm stand featuring local produce and pies and pastries stuffed with fruit from the orchard behind the store. There's a sunny porch outside where you can indulge your sweet tooth and admire the farmhouse amid the apple trees. Open every day 6:30 A.M. to 6:00 P.M. year-round; extended hours for Christmas.

About a quarter mile north of Phantom Farms is the unassuming entrance to one of Rhode Island's best-kept secrets, **Diamond Hill Vineyards** (3145 Diamond Hill Road, 333–2751 or 800–752–2505). Keep a sharp eye or you'll miss the small sign on the right (east) side of the road, which leads to a narrow gravel track through the woods, ending at the winery.

Located in a charming circa 1780 farmhouse surrounded by flowers and grapevines, the tasting room/gift shop is a cozy space where, like as not, the person pouring the wine will be one of the owners. Pete and Claire Berntson, with an able helping hand from daughter Chantelle, have been growing pinot noir grapes on their small farm since 1976, producing an eclectic variety of wines including vintages made from apples, peaches, raspberries, and plums. The wines are reasonably priced, and the Berntsons will make up an attractive gift basket for you to take home.

The gazebo outside the vineyard house is the perfect spot to uncork a bottle and relax in this peaceful, bucolic setting. Diamond Hill Vineyards is open daily (except Tuesday) noon to 5:00 P.M.; tours on Sunday or by appointment.

Proceeding north on Route 114 soon brings you to Nate Whipple Highway/Route 120. If you make a right turn here and proceed about ¹/₂ mile, you will see Sneetch Pond Road on your left, just past an old church. Turn here to find **Pentimento** (322 Sneetch Pond Road, 334–1838), a combination eatery and antiques consignment shop in the historic village of Arnold Mills. Located in a beautifully restored former granary building, Pentimento serves coffee, bagels, muffins, and the like. The shop's outside deck alone makes it worth a stop. Shaded by an elm tree that grows through cuts in the wooden floor, the deck hangs over a small waterfall on the Abbott Run River, inviting you to linger with your repast. Open Wednesday to Sunday; hours change seasonally, so call first.

You might want to spend a few minutes longer in **Arnold Mills,** an interesting village that has largely been overlooked by the passage of time. This is an old farming village that got its name from a gristmill built in 1745 by Amos Arnold. (The foundation of the old mill can be seen behind the Pentimento restaurant.) Later, Arnold Mills got involved in a number of industries, including boatbuilding, an odd (although successful) choice for a landlocked town.

After that glory period, Arnold Mills slipped back into its previous role as a sleepy backwater, but visitors can still appreciate the community's old homes, churches, and millpond. Across the street from Pentimento are the remains of an 1825 water-powered machine shop. On your way back out of town, look for the circa 1750 Amos Arnold House on Sneech Pond Road. Better yet, stop in at 202 Nate Whipple Highway, home of the **Llama Farma.** Although northern Rhode Island is the hilly part of the state, you won't mistake it for Tibet—unless you count the wooly denizens at this unique farm. The Llama Farma (334–1873) breeds llamas and also offers day hikes and sunset hikes where guests, riding two to a llama, make a slow circuit of up to 10 miles with a stop for a picnic or wine and cheese. There's also a gift shop selling assorted llama-related products. If you're interested in taking a trail ride, call first for reservations and information.

If Diamond Hill actually were made of diamonds, it would have disappeared under an army of pickaxes long ago. In fact, the area gets its name from a mile-long exposed vein of quartz, formed eons ago by mineral-rich water running through a fracture in the earth's crust. Once a ski area, **Diamond Hill State Park** (Route 114) today provides a wealth of hiking trails over steep terrain, with excellent views of the surrounding countryside from the top of the hill. During your hike look for the massive stone anchors that once held the ski lifts in place. The park explodes with color as the leaves turn in autumn and is a year-round attraction for rock climbers.

At the base of the hill is a band shell set by a small stream, the site of occasional concerts and other town activities. The section of the park on the east side of Route 114 is by far the most popular with visitors, but the bulk of the parkland actually is accessed by a narrow corridor on the west side of the road.

Directly across the street from the park entrance is the **Ice Cream Machine** (4288 Diamond Hill Road/Route 114, 333–5053), home of some of the best homemade ice cream in the state. Nicely landscaped, with painted wooden cows grazing in a small enclosure on a hillside overlooking the parking lot, the Ice Cream Machine promises a wide variety of flavors fresh out of the churn. The cookie dough and maple walnut are wildly popular, and the mint chocolate chip is so minty that it's like biting into a frozen peppermint patty. For a real indulgence try the Diamond Hill Sundae, a mountainous four scoops of ice cream topped with whipped cream and nuts.

The **Valley Falls Heritage Park** also is located on Route 114, but it is on the southern end of the road (3$\frac{1}{2}$ miles south of Route 295, where Route 114 is called Broad Street) in the community of Valley Falls, right across the Central Falls city line.

To their everlasting credit, local preservationists and civic officials a few years back took a decrepit, debris-strewn former mill site and creatively turned it into an interpretive park on the Industrial Revolution. Today the park on the east side of Mill Street (turn at Cumberland Town Hall) is laced with curved walkways and sturdy bridges and has plaques explaining the significance of the river and the surrounding ruins.

In this unique park, all the forces that drove nineteenth-century industry are gathered in one place. Before you is the Blackstone River and the waterfall, flanked by still-standing mill buildings and spanned by an old bridge. Crossing the river downstream is a railroad trestle, still used by the Providence and Worcester Railroad. Finally, below you are the remains of an old mill complex, including remnants of the raceways and turbines that powered the looms. The park is open dawn to dusk.

In the name of progress, the site of William Blackstone's riverside homestead in present-day Valley Falls was flattened in 1886 to make way for the giant Ann & Hope Mill. However, progress also dictated the demise of most of Rhode Island's large textile mills, and in time employment in the service and retail industries replaced mill jobs as the backbone of the economy. So it seemed only fitting when, in 1953, the old mill in Cumberland was converted to the first **Ann & Hope** department store.

Today, Ann & Hope is a Rhode Island institution, sort of what Filene's is to Boston. The selection of clothing, sporting goods, electronics, and other dry goods is impressive, especially at the cavernous Cumberland location, and there's always a sale going on. (Shoppers pushing carts full of a particular sale item, like rolls of toilet paper, are a common sight.)

A catalog store is located in the original 1886 mill building, while a 1901 addition—painted white and red—is home to the main retail outlet. Even if you don't come to shop, it's worth a stop to look around. On the way out, notice the brick homes across Ann and Hope Way, where mill workers once lived.

Ann & Hope is open Monday through Saturday 9:30 A.M. to 9:30 P.M. and Sunday 11:30 A.M. to 6:00 P.M. The mill is located on Ann and Hope Way, off Broad Street in the north end of Valley Falls (722–1000).

Smithfield

Powder Mill Ledges Wildlife Refuge is a small nature preserve with three trails meandering through reclaimed farmland and hardwood forests and leading to a pond where muskrats and great blue herons have been spotted. You can walk the circuit at a comfortable pace in about an hour and a half, then stop at the headquarters of the Audubon Society of Rhode Island, which is located here. The society maintains an extensive library on natural history and operates a gift shop, as well as conducting tours of its half dozen or so refuges around the state.

The **Audubon Society headquarters and library** are located adjacent to the parking lot for the Powder Mill Ledges Wildlife Refuge at 12 Sanderson Road/Route 5, just south of the intersection with the Putnam Pike/Route 44 (949–5454). It's open Monday through Friday 9:00 A.M. to 5:00 P.M.; gift shop open Saturday only noon to 4:00 P.M.

Despite the cars whizzing by on nearby Route 295, an air of serenity pervades the grounds of the **Smith-Appleby House,** a twelve-room farmhouse near Georgiaville Pond. Originally built as a one-room "stone-ender" in 1696, the house later was grafted onto a larger structure moved here from Johnston in the early 1700s to form the present building. The deed for the property was given by Rhode Island founding father Roger Williams to John Smith.

Unlike many of the other historical homes in the area, the Smith-Appleby House has been completely furnished, so visitors can get a good idea of what the everyday lives of the Smiths and Applebys— who lived in the house from 1696 to 1958—must have been like. An old settee and piano dominate the sitting room, while antique teapots and crockery line shelves in the keeping room. A "smoke room" on the second floor of the house was used to cure meat.

Rhode Island's Apple Capital

*S*mithfield *is known locally as Rhode Island's apple-picking capital, with a bunch of orchards located in the vicinity of Greenville.*

Whether you're looking for the perfect pie filling or something to crunch on the spot, you'll find a wide variety of apples at the orchards of Appleland Orchard (135 Smith Avenue/Route 116, 949–3690) and Jaswell Farm (50 Swan Road, 231–9043). Farther afield but worth the drive is Hazard Brothers Orchard on Burnt Hill Road in Hope, which also has a small shop where you can order homemade apple pie topped with ice cream. Spend an hour or so straining for that perfectly symmetrical fruit at the top of the tree and carting around baskets overflowing with green and red orbs, and your family is sure to leave with sore arms and big smiles.

Also located on the seven-acre site is a caretaker's cottage and the tiny shack that once was the Smithfield train depot. Across a small stream lies an old cemetery. The Smith-Appleby House is the headquarters of the Historical Society of Smithfield, which occasionally runs special events such as socials and May breakfasts that feature members dressed in period costumes. Tours are available from May to December by appointment and cost $2.00. Call 231–7363 for more information.

The Smith-Appleby House is located at 220 Stillwater Road, off Route 116 just south of the intersection with Route 7. The house is on your right after the Route 295 underpass.

If you've worked up an appetite, check out the nearby **Kountry Kitchen** (10 Smith Avenue, 949–0840), where the big portions, reasonable prices, and friendly service are excelled only by the views of Hopkins Pond. Open Sunday to Wednesday 6:30 A.M. to 2:00 P.M. and Thursday to Saturday 6:30 A.M. to 8:00 P.M. For family dining with a touch of class, open the door to the **Greenville Inn,** an Italian restaurant that makes a tender, juicy chicken française and a tasty chicken Lorenzo with artichoke hearts, mushrooms, black olives, and diced tomatoes. Every entree is priced less than $15 (36 Smith Avenue, 949–4020). Dinner hours are 4:00 to 10:00 P.M. Monday to Thursday, 4:00 to 11:00 P.M. Friday and Saturday, and noon to 10:00 P.M. on Sunday.

Lincoln

*Y*ou can set out from the Smith-Appleby House on a nice country drive that also has some intriguing historic sites along the way. Making a right turn from the Smith-Appleby House onto Stillwater Avenue, head south until you come to Lime Rock Road, where you will make a left. Enjoy the rural landscape as you head east; after you cross Route 123/Albion Road, the name changes to Wilbur Road. At this point start keeping an eye out for the **Jedediah Smith Homestead** on your left, just before the intersection with Route 246. At the stop sign at the intersection with Route 246, look to your right and you will notice the white facade of the **North Tollgate House,** currently the home of the **Blackstone Valley Historical Society** (725–2847). Built in 1807, the tollhouse was the fee collection point on the north end of the old Louisquisset Pike (Route 246).

Crossing Route 246, you will be dazzled by the limestone quarries and white buildings of the historic **Conklin Limestone Quarry,** established in 1640 and the oldest continuously operated industry in the

United States. Chunks of gleaming limestone taken from this still-active quarry are piled up right to the roadside. Farther along, on your right side, you will see a sign for **Mowry's Tavern.** The old inn, built in 1686 and now a private home, sits close to the road and is shaded by a row of ancient trees.

Turn left onto Simon Sayles Road; the next intersection is Route 126; cross straight over and proceed down Cullen Hill Road until you see a sign pointing left down Lower River Road to the entrance to **Blackstone River State Park.**

As you emerge from your car in the small lot under the Route 116 bridge, you might be tempted to ask, "What park?" And indeed, the charms of the Blackstone River State Park are not readily apparent, and no signs guide your way. But as you walk north on a well-worn footpath, details start to emerge. On your right you can hear the sound of rushing water, and through the trees you catch glimpses of the Blackstone River making its way south to Pawtucket.

Soon enough you see a side path and a small wooden bridge to your left and make a startling discovery: another body of water flowing in quiet obscurity through the woods. You have found a remarkably well-preserved section of the Blackstone Canal, built in the early nineteenth century to move goods down the river from Worcester, Massachusetts, and Woonsocket to Pawtucket and Providence.

Farther along there is an overlook where the remains of an old canal lock are plainly visible. Another viewing platform offers a great look at the waterfall, whose rumbling was audible through the woods long before it came into view.

Waterfall in Blackstone River State Park

From the parking lot the trails following the old canal towpath south actually extend much farther—6 miles in total— and a $3^3/_{10}$-mile section beginning on Front Street in Lincoln has been resurfaced as a premier biking and recreational trail. When completed in 2001, the Blackstone River Bikeway will stretch for $17^1/_{10}$ miles, linking the East Bay Bike Path (see the East Bay chapter) to the Massachusetts border north of Woonsocket. Also on the south side of the parking lot, facing the canal,

Albion Falls

One of the prettiest spots along the entire Blackstone River is at Albion Falls, best reached by taking Old River Road in northern Lincoln to School Street, just north of the Kirkbrae Country Club.

The Albion Bridge crosses the river just downstream from the powerful Albion Dam, built in 1916 to power the Albion Mill, which today survives as a condominium complex. From the center of the bridge you can enjoy the sight and sound of the falls as well as the peaceful wooded surroundings. Or, you can walk along a dirt path between the river and the still-active tracks of the Providence and Worcester Railroad to the west side of the dam, where you can see the old headrace that allowed the river waters to rush through a narrow passage and turn the gears at the mill. Eventually, the Blackstone River bike and jogging path now under construction farther south will come through this spot, as well.

While you're in the area, take a quick stroll through Albion village, another of the Blackstone Valley's well-preserved mill towns.

is the Kelly House, built in 1820 by Wilbur Kelly, a Providence ship captain who backed the construction of the canal. The **Kelly House** is slated to become the park's visitors center.

If you're tempted to linger awhile in Lincoln, you can truly immerse yourself in local history at the **Whipple-Cullen Farmstead** bed-and-breakfast, located on nearby Old River Road (99 Old River Road, 333–1899). Ten generations of Whipples and Cullens (hosts John and Barbara Cullen are the latest) have lived in this post-and-beam farmhouse since 1736. A continental breakfast before a crackling fireplace—one of eight in the house, including some in guest bedrooms—is included with your stay, and guests will find the architectural heritage of the house revealed at every turn, from beehive ovens to pine-plank floors and colonial mantles and moldings. Four guest rooms, with shared baths, are available for $65 to $75 mightly.

There was a time when the Great Road was the only land link between Lincoln and Providence and when the house and farm belonging to Eleazer Arnold were the only sign of civilization for miles around. Much has changed since then, but the **Eleazer Arnold House** remains as a reminder of those quieter times.

Perhaps the best remaining example of Rhode Island stone-ender construction in existence, the circa 1687 Eleazer Arnold House, located at 449 Great Road, is open to visitors on the second Sunday of each month. The house is a veritable museum of historic architecture, from the massive stone wall and fireplace whose stones were taken from nearby quarries, to the original and reconstructed paneling in the downstairs rooms, to the peaked attic, where the original beams that framed the house are still visible. Even the flaws of the old building are fascinating: The attic is adorned by graffiti left by former work crews, including a painter who labored here in 1911. For information call the Society for the Preservation of New England Antiquities (617–227–3986).

Continuing west on the Great Road from the Eleazer Arnold House will bring you to **Chace Farm,** another bit of the Blackstone Valley National Heritage Corridor and an important piece of preserved open space in Lincoln. Walking and hiking trails meander over the sparsely wooded landscape at this old farm, and locals say the best thing going on at the Chace Farm in winter is sledding on the rolling hills that dot the property. Facing the Great Road near the Chace Farm entrance is the historic **Hannaway Blacksmith Shop** (671 Great Road, 333–1100), where smithys demonstrate their art and conduct tours one Sunday a month.

Apart from a few pilots and daredevils, very few people are even aware of the existence of **North Central State Airport,** and therein lies its charm. A terminal building and hangars dating from the fifties and sixties line the airfield, and the airport is surrounded by woodlands. The quiet is only broken occasionally by the sound of a Cessna or Piper taking off or landing. It's a reminder of a time when flying was a simpler, more seat-of-the-pants affair.

There's more to this airport than just watching private planes take off, however. The **Lincoln Flight Center,** located upstairs in the main terminal building, offers a variety of affordable airborne sight-seeing rides and pilot training, including first-time instruction. A flight in one of these trainers provides a good way to get acquainted with the thrill of flying in a small plane while learning the lay of the land from a few thousand feet up; cost is about $60 for a half-hour tour. Call 334–1359 for more information.

Also at North Central is the **Boston-Providence Skydiving Center** (www.skydivetoday.com), which offers beginner skydiving lessons, including ground school and a tandem jump on your very first day for $195 ($185 on weekdays; group discounts available). After a half-hour lesson on such basics as exiting the aircraft and pulling the rip cord, you will be taken aloft in a Cessna 182 or Cessna 206 and jump over the airport runway. At 120 miles per hour, it will take you about eight minutes to free fall and, after the chute opens, slowly glide to earth from 10,000 feet, with a certified skydiving instructor literally strapped to your back the whole way down.

The center also can videotape and photograph your first skydiving experience, and advanced instruction is available if you want to learn how to jump solo. Skydivers must be over age eighteen and weigh less than 230 pounds. Reservations are required, as is a $50 deposit. The center is open for skydiving daily (weather permitting) from 9:00 A.M. to sunset, April 1 through the end of October. Call the Boston-Providence Skydiving

Center at (800) 656–3663 or (800) SKYDIVE (in Massachusetts, Rhode Island, or Connecticut), or e-mail info@skydivetoday.com.

North Central State Airport is located at 6 Albion Road (Route 123), 1 mile from the intersection with the George Washington Highway/Route 116 (from Route 146, take the exit for 116 south).

PLACES TO STAY IN NORTHERN RHODE ISLAND

(ALL AREA CODES 401)

WOONSOCKET
Woonsocket Motor Inn, 333 Clinton Street, 762–1224

NORTH SMITHFIELD
Susse Chalet Inn, 355 George Washington Highway, 232–2400

Hillltop Inn 797 Eddie Dowling Highway, 762–9631

BURRILLVILLE
Willingham Manor B&B, 570 Central Street, 568–2468

GLOUCESTER
Lakeside Motel, 66 Putnam Pike, Route 44, Harmony, 949–3358

White Rock Motel, 750 Putnam Pike, Route 44, Chepachet, 568–4219

Freeman Farm B&B, 65 Jackson School House Road, 568–6561

LINCOLN
Whipple-Cullen Farmstead B&B, 2492 Kingstown Road, 333–1899

PLACES TO EAT IN NORTHERN RHODE ISLAND

(ALL AREA CODES 401)

WOONSOCKET
Chan's Fine Oriental Dining, Depot Square, 765–1900

Ye Olde English Fish and Chips Restaurant, Market Square, 762–3637

The Castle Luncheonette, Social Street, 762–5424

GREENVILLE
The Kountry Kitchen, 10 Smith Avenue, (Route 116), 949–0840

The Greenville Inn, 36 Smith Avenue, (Route 116), 949–4020

BURRILLVILLE
Wright's Farm Restaurant, 84 Inman Road, 769–2856

Mr. Doughboy, Route 102, Glendale, 568–4897

GLOUCESTER
Purple Cat Restaurant, Main Street, Chepachet, 568–7161

Stagecoach Tavern Restaurant, 1157 Putnam Pike, Chepachet, 568–2275

Chester's Restaurant, 102 Putnam Pike, 949–1846

Gautreau's Restaurant, 1006 Putnam Pike, Chepachet, 568–7133

Villa Roma, 2400 Putnam Pike, 968–9007.

FORESTDALE
The Village Haven, 90 School Street, 762–4242

LINCOLN
The Lodge, 40 Breakneck Hill Road, 725–8510

Selected Chamber of Commerce

Northern Rhode Island Chamber of Commerce, *6 Blackstone Valley Place, Lincoln, 334–1000*

CUMBERLAND
Pentimento,
Sneech Pond Road,
334–1838

The Ice Cream Machine,
4288 Diamond Hill Road,
333–5053

OTHER ATTRACTIONS
WORTH SEEING IN
NORTHERN RHODE ISLAND

William Blackstone
Memorial, *Cumberland*

Lincoln Greyhound Park,
Lincoln

Lincoln Woods State Park,
Lincoln

HELPFUL WEB SITES ABOUT
NORTHERN RHODE ISLAND

CITY OF WOONSOCKET,
www.ci.woonsocket.ri.us/

BLACKSTONE VALLEY
TOURISM COUNCIL,
www.tourblackstone.com

The East Bay

The three Bristol County towns known collectively as the East Bay—Barrington, Warren, and Bristol—each has a unique character that, despite their proximity, makes them easily distinguishable.

Of the three, Bristol is the largest and best known, thanks to the town's famous Fourth of July parade and its involvement in America's Cup yachting. Warren is a quiet New England seaside town, while Barrington serves primarily as an upscale bedroom community for the city of Providence.

Adding vitality to all three towns is the **East Bay Bike Path**. Built on the right-of-way of an old railroad line, the path winds its way 14½ miles from India Point Park in Providence to downtown Bristol. Along the way, bikers, strollers, and in-line skaters pass through East Providence, Barrington, and Warren.

About half of the path's length is in Providence and East Providence, but we give it prominence in this chapter because the path is a great alternative to driving if you want to see the best that Bristol County has to offer. The Barrington stretch passes through the cool, wooded confines of **Haines Memorial State Park** (253–7482; a good place to park your car), offering occasional glimpses of the town's beautiful homes as it proceeds south to skirt **Brickyard Pond.** One of the most beautiful spots on the route is where the path crosses the Barrington River just north of Route 114, bringing riders onto the small peninsula that comprises the towns of Warren and Bristol.

In Warren the setting for the bike path changes from woods to suburbia, then passes right through the heart of downtown, gently curving behind Town Hall and past an inviting Del's lemonade stand. Lock up your bike here and all the attractions of Warren are just a few steps away.

Fittingly, the path hugs the shoreline after passing over the Bristol town line, affording an excellent (though occasionally breezy) view of Narragansett Bay. The route then briefly moves back inland, where you can choose to make a detour into **Colt State Park** or continue on to the

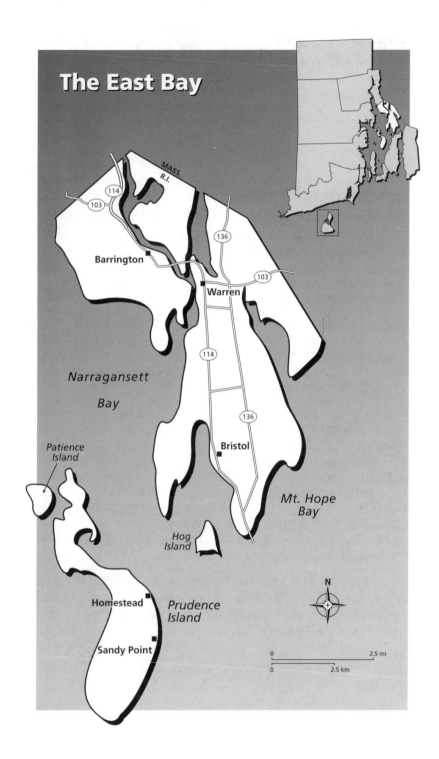

The East Bay

MASS.
R.I.

114

103

Barrington

136

103

Warren

114

Narragansett
Bay

136

Bristol

Patience
Island

Mt. Hope
Bay

Hog
Island

Homestead

Prudence
Island

Sandy Point

N

| 0 | 2.5 mi |
| 0 | 2.5 km |

terminus at *Independence Park* on Bristol Harbor. Once again, your location puts you within easy walking distance of downtown sites, shops, and restaurants.

By car, the best approach to Bristol County is to take Interstate 195 east to Route 114 south, which takes you along and then across the Barrington River before narrowing to become Main Street in Warren. The name changes again (to Hope Street) once you enter Bristol, but Route 114 remains the main drag in both Warren and Bristol. Most of the attractions in this chapter are in close proximity to Route 114, although a few in Bristol are located off Route 136 (Metacom Avenue), which runs parallel to Route 114 before the two roads merge near the southern tip of the peninsula, just before the Mount Hope Bridge.

Barrington

As you drive south on Route 114, you're likely to be distracted by the beautiful views of the Barrington River to your left. A little-known nature preserve on the northbound shoulder of the road offers even better vistas. *Osamequin Park* is a forty-two-acre bird sanctuary wedged between the road, a pond to the south, and the Hundred Acre Cove section of the Barrington River to the east. There is a small network of trails and elevated walkways over the marshes that allow you to stroll from the small parking area directly down to the beach or around the property to the pond and a dam. Waterfowl abound.

Brickyard Pond in Barrington looks for all the world like a sliver of natural beauty, carefully preserved so that even the town's founding fathers might recognize it if they were to return. In fact, they would not: Brickyard Pond did not even exist until the 1940s.

If the first settlers remembered the area at all, it would be for the large clay deposits found here. From the seventeenth century on, the Brickyard Pond site was the source of clay for brickmaking. For almost one hundred years, a succession of brick manufacturing firms dug deeper and deeper into the earth, until all the clay was gone.

In 1943 the Barrington Steam Brick Co. shut down for good, and the former clay pits filled with water to form Brickyard Pond, creating the pretty views enjoyed today by thousands of people passing by on the East Bay Bike Path.

Part of the reason the park is relatively unknown is that drivers heading south on Route 114 tend to whiz by without ever seeing it. (Even heading north it's easy to miss.) To get there from the southbound lanes, take the first left after the sign for the Zion Bible College exit, making a U-turn, which will take you a short distance north on Route 114 to the park, which is on your right. Better yet, wait until you're headed back north at the end of the day to stop, when you can catch the sunset reflecting off the water. Osamequin Park is owned by the town of Barrington; call the town recreation department (247–1925) for information.

As you proceed south on 114, you'll pass Barrington's medieval–style **Town Hall** (283 County Road, 247–1900) on your left, built in 1888 on a foundation of natural boulders. Past the town hall, Route 114 intersects with the East Bay Bike Path (watch out for runners, bikers, and strollers!) and takes a sharp jog east to cross the Barrington River. If you make your first right after the bridge onto Barton Avenue, you'll find the **New Tyler Point Grille** (32 Barton Avenue, 247–0017), an acclaimed seafood restaurant adjacent to the Barrington Yacht Club. The restaurant is open nightly for dinner 4:30 to 10:00 P.M., Friday and Saturday 4:30 to 11:00 P.M., and Sunday 4:30 to 9:00 P.M.

Warren

Continue following Route 114 south, and two small bridges will bring you to **downtown Warren.** Although southern neighbor Bristol gets more attention, Warren is a gem of a New England seaside community that should not be overlooked.

Ravaged by the British during the Revolutionary War, Warren rebounded to prosper as a shipbuilding center and as home to Rhode Island's largest whaling fleet during the nineteenth century. The Industrial Revolution took hold when the whaling business dried up after the Civil War, but Warren remains essentially the small town that it was at the turn of the century.

Dominating Main Street (Route 114) is the **1890 Town Hall** (514 Main Street, 245–7340), with a facade featuring an intricate, unusual carving of the Wampanoag sachem Massasoit, an early friend to the white settlers of this area. The "Sowams" referred to in the carving is the name of the large native settlement that existed here by the banks of the Warren River. After being exiled from Massachusetts, Roger Williams lived at Sowams before moving north to found Rhode Island. There's a plaque at the foot of Baker Street marking the spot of **Massasoit Spring,** the supposed site of Sowams (Barrington also claims to be the location of the village).

Also hard to miss on Main Street is the imposing **George Hail Library** (530 Main Street, 245–7686), named for an early Warren industrialist. From the outside, the massive stone construction and stained-glass windows give the building the appearance of a medieval fortress

AUTHOR'S FAVORITE ATTRACTIONS/EVENTS IN THE EAST BAY

East Bay Bike Path

Prudence Island

Downtown Warren

Blithewold Mansion and Gardens

Haffenreffer Museum of Anthropology

Bristol Fourth of July Parade

Old-Fashioned Family Clambake, Warren, July

Coggeshall Farm Harvest Fair, Bristol, September

church. The interior, restored to its original 1889 beauty and watched over by a portrait of Hail, remains a cozy haven for local bibliophiles. Upstairs there is a small museum focusing on Warren history; the collection includes melted window glass from the Baptist Meetinghouse, burned by the Redcoats in 1778, and scrimshaw and ships logs that recall the town's whaling heyday of the 1840s. The museum is open Wednesday from 2:00 P.M. to 4:00 P.M.

The **Delekta Pharmacy** (496 Main Street, 245–6767) is known for its cabinets. Not the dark-stained wood cabinets cluttered with old apothecary bottles that line the walls (although they were here when the pharmacy opened in 1858). No, it's the coffee cabinets—also known as a milkshake or a frappé, depending upon your state of origin—that are the Delekta's claim to fame. Owner Eric Delekta, whose family has run the pharmacy since the 1940s, brews the coffee syrup every morning, and Warren residents and savvy bike path veterans alike make the pilgrimage here.

A true throwback, the Delekta is the kind of pharmacy that you usually only read about nowadays, with an old-fashioned soda fountain dominating the front of the store and medicine and sundries lining the shelves in back. The tin ceilings are original, as are the gaslight globes hanging in the windows. Open 8:00 A.M. to 8:00 P.M. Monday to Friday, 8:00 A.M. to 5:00 P.M. on Saturday, and 8:00 A.M. to 1:00 P.M. on Sunday.

If the coffee cabinet's close cousin—coffee milk—is the state drink (and the state's General Assembly says it is), then Rhode Island's unofficial state junk food undoubtedly is the hot wiener. At **Rod's Grill** (6 Washington Street, 245–9405), they serve armfuls of these little fire-red hot dogs (known affectionately as "gaggers") right off the grill to a jam-packed lunchtime crowd. Open 6:30 A.M. to 4:00 P.M. Monday, Wednesday, and Saturday; 6:30 A.M. to 7:30 P.M. Tuesday and Thursday; 6:30 A.M. to 6:30 P.M. on Friday; closed Sunday.

Farther north on Main Street is the circa 1840 **Baptist Church in Warren** (407 Main Street, 245–3669), actually the third Baptist house of worship to stand on this spot. (The first was burned by—you guessed it—the British.) The congregation's first minister was James Manning, who also started a Latin school that later became Brown University.

Between Main and Water Streets are a series of *quiet historic streets* that could have been lifted straight out of a Victorian-era stereograph. The short walk to the river anywhere between Wheaton Street and Liberty Street yields a fascinating mix of architectural styles from the eighteenth and nineteenth centuries. Particularly lovely is the area around Church and Baker Streets. Look for the towering white columns fronting the **First Methodist Church** (25 Church Street), built in 1845 and based on a design of Sir Christopher Wren. Across the street, and between Church and State Streets, is a small commons centered on a veteran's memorial and a Civil War–era cannon.

At 59 Church Street is **Maxwell House,** a circa 1755 Colonial-style home with a large central chimney and twin beehive baking ovens. The home is operated by the Massasoit Historical Association and is open by appointment and for occasional cooking demonstrations and Colonial craft displays. Call 245–7652 for more information.

The oldest **Masonic Temple** in New England can be found on nearby Baker Street. Built in 1798 and still used for meetings by the local Masonic Lodge, the Federal-style building (Baker Street, 245–3293) was constructed using beams from British frigates sunk in Newport Harbor. You can call for a tour to get a closer look at the twin Ionic doors and the hall's elaborate, hand-painted Egyptian murals. The **Warren Fire Museum** (38 Baker Street), located at the Narragansett Steam Fire Engine Company station, features historical artifacts from the 250-year-old department and exhibits of old fire-fighting equipment, including "The Little Hero," a hand-operated water pump purchased in 1809. Call the fire chief's office at 245–7600 to view the collection.

The Greek Revival **St. Mark's Episcopal Church** (25 Lincoln Street), designed by famed local architect Russell Warren, broods alongside Lyndon Avenue with its Ionic portico and canted double doors. The 1829 church is guarded by two stone lions, and an old bell sits on the lawn.

Wharves, many dating from the Revolutionary period, line **Water Street,** along with historic homes and small shops and restaurants, including the flag-bedecked **Nathaniel Porter Inn** (125 Water Street, 245–6622). Built in 1795 as a sea captain's home and named after a thirteen-year-old participant in the Battle of Lexington, this National Register property has been carefully restored and continues life as a top-notch restaurant and small bed-and-breakfast.

In a region that abounds with faux Colonial trappings, the Nathaniel Porter Inn with its compact rooms, creaky wooden floors, and low, open-beamed ceilings is the real thing. Guests have a choice of five dining areas, including two formal parlor rooms, a tavern room, and a courtyard.

Signature dishes include beef Wellington and Grand Marnier chicken stuffed with apricots and basil. The inn really comes to life in December with an annual Colonial yule log celebration that features a fife-and-drum corps and Christmas carols, and the restaurant's Twelfth Night in January is highlighted by a traditionally prepared goose dinner. More casual fare is served in the tavern.

Less well known than the restaurant is the small **bed-and-breakfast** maintained on the second floor. Three rooms, all dressed in simple Colonial style with fireplaces and private bathrooms, are offered at a reasonable $80 per night, including a continental breakfast served in a private dining room. Open for dinner Tuesday to Saturday 5:00 to 9:00 P.M. and on Sunday from 4:00 to 8:00 P.M. Lunch is served Saturday from 11:30 to 2:00 P.M. and Sunday brunch from 10:30 A.M. to 2:00 P.M.

Another excellent choice for a fine meal is the **Wharf Tavern** (215 Water Street, 245–5043), for forty years a landmark situated on the Warren River. At least six varieties of lobster dishes are served here, as well as a wide range of other seafood, steaks, pasta, and poultry. The moorings that surround the restaurant attract diners from sea as well as land. Even if you don't come to eat, take a few minutes to walk out on the restaurant's dock, open to the public, for a great view of the river. Open 11:30 A.M. to 9:00 P.M. Sunday to Thursday and until 10:00 P.M. Friday and Saturday; the lounge, which features live music on the weekend, stays open later.

The *Vista Jubilee* is proof that the sea remains intrinsic to Warren's character. Built here, the 350–passenger ship is operated by **Bay Queen Cruises** (461 Water Street, Gate 4, 245–1350 or 800–439–1350 in Rhode Island; www.bayqueen.com). It leaves the docks at the foot of Miller Street for four- and six-hour tours of Narragansett Bay. Passengers can enjoy a variety of themed lunch and dinner cruises, from Caribbean to murder mysteries; there's also a lighthouse cruise, comedic staged weddings, and, occasionally, a hypnotist on board for entertainment.

The cruise is a great way to see the state from the inside looking out, as the *Vista Jubilee* offers spectacular views of Prudence Island, Jamestown, and the Newport Bridge. For special events, such as the annual Oktoberfest and the Great Chowder Cookoff, the ship makes a two-hour layover in Newport.

Lunch cruises are $23.50, high-season (June to September) dinner cruises are $33.50 on weekdays, $34.50 on Friday and $36.50 on Saturday. Off-season (October to May) dinner cruises are $31.00.

No walking tour of Warren would be complete without a stop in at least one of the town's dozens of **antiques shops,** located mostly on Main Street, Child Street (Route 103), and Water Street. The largest, and the first one you're likely to spy, thanks to its gaily painted hunter green and eggplant exterior, is the **Warren Antique Center** (corner of Main and Miller Streets, 245–5461). The former Lyric Theater has been completely renovated and converted to use as a multilevel repository for thousands of items of kitsch and collectibles, representing the wares of 150 dealers. Permeating the barnlike structure are delicious emanations from **Ocean Coffee Roasters,** located just inside the front door.

Right across Main Street is **Horsefeathers Antiques**, featuring high-quality furniture, silver, china, and linens in the 1802 Cromwell Child House (382 Main Street, 245–5530). Upstairs, Marie King proffers an eclectic collection of '50s Americana, with some international oddities thrown into the mix, like a Russian Pepsi bottle. **Alanjays Music and Gift Shop** is an entertaining mix of antiques, collectibles (mostly music related), used CDs and LPs, and used musical instruments. Owners Alan Botelho and Jay Santos have collected more than 20,000 45s, 10,000 LPs, and thousands of CDs and tapes, guaranteed to keep audiophiles browsing for hours (438 Main Street, 247–1336). Open 9:00 A.M. to 7:00 P.M. Monday through Saturday.

The granddaddy of Warren antiquers, Gilbert Warren, offers a wide range of collectibles and old hardware at **The Square Peg** (51 Miller Street; no phone). Just up Child Street from Main Street you'll find **Yankee Consignment** (18 Child Street; also a door on Market Street, 245–6569), specializing in antique and used furniture. For a slightly different take on antiquing, shoot up to the **Black Marble** (76 Child Street, 245–0112), where owners Robin and Bob Grace restore and decorate nonprecious furniture and sell hand-painted mirrors, glassware, and other items.

At the address where for years Casala's Market sold groceries to local residents, John Devine has opened **Water Street Antiques** (147 Water Street, 245–6440), which features a large selection of Art Deco furniture and lighting. Sandy Nathanson is **The Lady Next Door** (196 Water Street, 831–7338), and she has a nice selection of vintage clothing, jewelry, pottery, and antique toys.

For our last stop in Warren, you need to leave downtown. From Main Street/Route 114, proceed north of Town Hall to Child Street/Route 103, and make a right. Follow Child Street until you cross a small bridge over the Kickemuit River, proceeding approximately ¹/₂ mile to Long Lane. Make the right here and continue until Long Lane ends at Barton Avenue; proceed east (left) on Barton Avenue to Touisset Avenue; make a right, and follow this road until you come to the Touisset Fire Station, on your right. Pull into the fire station parking lot, and you'll find the trailhead of the **Touisset Wildlife Refuge** (949–5454).

A seventy-acre nature preserve, the Touisset Wildlife Refuge features open fields still farmed for hay, as well as paths that cut through forest and open up onto salt marshes, a small inlet (Chase Cove), and the banks of the Kickemuit River. Along the well-marked trail you can see an abundance of wildlife, especially in the marsh area that is home to herons and egrets. The trail also crosses a small brook, and at high tide some of the trails can get muddy, so pack some water-resistant footgear if you come. One main trail circles the periphery of the property, while several smaller paths allow access to the interior. Open dawn to dusk year-round.

Bristol

Despite its somewhat isolated location, Bristol has never been a backwater. Founded in 1680, the town briefly served as headquarters for Lafayette during the Revolutionary War, when town fathers paid a ransom in cattle and sheep to keep a British naval squadron from leveling the place. In the eighteenth and early nineteenth centuries, a number of seafaring Bristol residents made their fortunes in the infamous triangle trade, running molasses, rum, and slaves between America, Africa, and the West Indies. The great homes lining Hope Street, including Linden Place, an impressive Federal-style mansion, are the lasting legacy of this prosperous (if morally questionable) period for the town.

The collapse of the triangle trade nearly ruined Bristol, but the town bounced back to become a shipbuilding center of world renown from the late 1800s on.

Shipbuilding still is a vital part of the local economy, but today Bristol's main claim to fame has more to do with the Stars and Stripes than with semaphore flags. The town's annual **Fourth of July parade** has made Bristol nearly synonymous with patriotic celebration in southern New England. Held since 1785, the parade today is an extravaganza of bands, floats, Clydesdales, mummers, and fireworks that attracts thousands of spectators. The red, white, and blue stripe painted down Hope

Street attests to the fact that the parade is serious business hereabouts, and many folks stay in town from the time the church bells ring at 6:00 A.M. to signal the start of festivities, until long after the last of the fireworks have boomed across the bay.

Nearly as legendary as the parade are the traffic tie-ups associated with it; even the bike path gets clogged, although it remains one of the better ways of getting into town for the big show. Fortunately, the town begins celebrating weeks in advance, with festivals and free concerts to get you into the patriotic spirit without having to brave the big holiday weekend crowds. If you plan to stay at one of the handful of inns located downtown during the holiday, make your reservations well in advance—as in years, not months.

As you head south from downtown Warren on Route 114, passing over the town line into Bristol, keep a sharp eye out for one such inn, the **Joseph Reynolds House** (956 Hope Street, 254–0230). The oldest three-story home in New England, the Joseph Reynolds House was built between 1693 and 1695 and was the Marquis de Lafayette's headquarters

Bristol's "Patriotic Exercises"

*B*eginning with the first observance in 1785 (conducted by Revolutionary War veteran Dr. Henry Wright), many of Bristol's early Independence Day celebrations contained elements at once strange and familiar to those of us who associate the Fourth of July with fireworks and backyard barbecues. While the day was marked by cannon fire, music, and dancing, the centerpiece of Bristol's patriotic celebrations during the seventeenth and eighteenth centuries was more solemn: a prayer service held at one of the town's many houses of worship.

While most people from outside Bristol know only about the Fourth of July parade—officially the "Grand Military, Civic, and Fireman's Parade"—the town has proudly clung to the traditional "Patriotic Exercises" that

have marked Independence Day since Colonial times. Each year, prior to the parade, residents gather at Colt Memorial School in downtown Bristol for a ceremony that includes prayers, the singing of the national anthem, and the award of a U.S. flag to the Bristol native who has traveled the greatest distance to be home for the parade.

The parade itself has been held almost every year since 1834, except for a few years in the nineteenth century when the town was hit by hard times and could not afford to pay for the official procession (also, the 1881 parade was canceled because of the assassination of President James Garfield). Today, as many as 10,000 marchers take part in the parade as it proceeds along its 3-mile route through downtown Bristol.

during his 1778 stay in Rhode Island. Thanks to its military importance, the house was shelled by the British during the war, and a cannonball that was shot into the parlor currently rests on a windowsill.

The house abounds with interesting architectural touches, reflecting not only the prosperity of the original owners but also three centuries' worth of modifications (including a second house that was grafted onto the back of the original structure to create the present L-shaped building). The age of the Joseph Reynolds House is evident in the crazy angles around door frames and the sloping hardwood floors in the upstairs bedrooms.

The Andersons, the current owners, offer visitors a self-guided tour of the house, but the best way to get a feel for this National Register country mansion is to spend the night. Innkeeper Wendy Anderson offers rooms and suites, along with a generous breakfast spread, at reasonable prices. Double rooms are $79 to $95 and one suite with an efficiency kitchen goes for $165 nightly; weekly rates also are available.

Rearing up over the east side of Route 114 are a pair of copper bulls, which mark the entrance to **Colt State Park** (253–7482). The park, a sprawling recreation area carved out of the former Colt estate, features bike paths, beaches, and a 3-mile shoreline drive with magnificent sunsets. Just south of the park but before you enter downtown Bristol, look for Poppasquash Road on your right. Turn here and follow the road around Bristol Harbor (slowing to enjoy the view across the water to downtown Bristol) to **Coggeshall Farm Museum** (253–9062).

Coggeshall's raison d'être is to re-create the life of a typical Rhode Island coastal farm family of the 1790s, and it involves a lot more than dressing the staff in period costumes. All the vegetables and herbs grown here, as well as the livestock, are what would have been raised by a family of the eighteenth century, and the products of the farm are used in demonstrations for visitors. Depending on what time of year you come, you'll find workers shearing sheep, tapping maple trees for their sugar, pressing cider, or working the smithy's forge. It's best to call ahead to schedule your visit to coincide with one of the farm's many special events, topped by the annual Harvest Fair (held the third week of September). The fair features traditional music and games like tug-of-war and—a big hit with the kids—pumpkin-seed spitting contests. More sedate is the blessing of the livestock, held each August. Open 10:00 A.M. to 5:00 P.M. October through February and 10:00 A.M. to 6:00 P.M. March through September. Admission is $1.00 for adults and 50 cents for seniors and children under age twelve; additional fees charged for special events.

Downtown Bristol is a stroller's paradise. Hope Street (Route 114) is unusual in that one side of the street is lined with shops, while grand old homes line the other. Best known of the latter is *Linden Place* (500 Hope Street, 253-0390), the Federal-style-with-a-flair mansion of the DeWolf family. Linden Place is open Thursday through Saturday 10:00 A.M. to 4:00 P.M. and Sunday noon to 4:00 P.M., May 1 to Columbus Day. It is also open from noon to 6:00 P.M. every day from the second Monday in December to December 31, except December 24 and December 25. Admission is $5.00 for adults and $2.50 for children under age twelve.

Linden Place is nice to visit, but if you wonder what it would be like to be a guest in such a grand old home, you have a couple of choices: the *Bradford-Dimond-Norris House* (474 Hope Street, 253–6338) and the *Rockwell House Inn* (610 Hope Street, 253–0040), each architecturally similar to the DeWolf mansion, though in more modest proportions.

Known as the "Wedding Cake House," the Bradford-Dimond-Norris House is named for a former deputy governor, governor, and sugar magnate, respectively. Originally a two-story building, a third floor was added after the Civil War, giving the house its confectionery appearance. Recently opened as a bed-and-breakfast by owners Lloyd and Suzanne Adams, the house is steeped in history and Colonial trappings, and the quiet garden veranda is a favorite spot for breakfast or just to relax and read a book. The Bradford-Dimond-Norris House has four guest rooms with rates ranging from $90 to $125 per night.

Most inns boast about being romantic, but the Rockwell House has the history to back up the claim. The "Courting Corner" at the back of the house—a cozy alcove warmed by a stone fireplace—was built by Captain Rockwell for his daughter after she was jilted by a ne'er-do-well suitor. Happily, the concept was a success: The daughter's eventual husband proposed to her before the fire, and six more couples have gotten engaged in the Courting Corner over the years.

Innkeepers Debra and Steve Krohn also put out a nice breakfast, and the location means you can walk to almost everything the town of Bristol has to offer. The four guest rooms all have private baths and range in price from $95 to $125.

Another benefit of staying at either of these two Hope Street B&Bs is that they're right around the corner from the *Bristol Cinema* (91 Bradford Street, 253–4312), a movie theater noted not for its architecture or ambience but for the fact that all shows are still just $2.50.

Built in 1798, the Federal-style *Parker Borden House* (736 Hope Street,

253–2084) was situated so that Captain Parker Borden could keep an eye on his ships. Borden's gift to modern-day guests at the Parker Borden House bed-and-breakfast is the excellent views of Bristol Harbor from two of the bedrooms. A third room overlooks the garden. Innkeepers Jean and Bob Tischer treat guests to a full breakfast that sometimes includes Irish porridge. Rates range from $75 to $95 per night.

Other prominent Hope Street buildings include the *1880 Town Hall* and the *Burnside Memorial,* honoring native son and Civil War general Ambrose Burnside.

Bristol in some ways is Rhode Island in microcosm; everybody knows everyone else, many residents have lived here their whole lives, and most would never dream of leaving. A walk around the *town commons,* located just a block east of Hope Street (either State Street or Church Street will get you there), provides some insight into the sense of community that local residents share. In the center of the grassy commons is the town band shell, right next to an extensive children's playground. There is a ball field where, for generations, young sluggers

Antiquing Along Hope Street

*N**earby** Warren's antiques stores may get the lion's share of the attention, but Hope Street in Bristol also has a nice selection of shops for collectors and treasure-hunters.*

Alfred's (331 Hope Street, 253–3465) has a fine collection of mahogany furniture, china, crystal, and silver; while the neighboring Alfred's Annex (297 Hope Street, 253–2339) consignment shop has an ever-changing inventory, from tables and beds to pottery. Robin Jenkins Antiques (278 Hope Street, 254–8958) specializes in "chippy-paint" items—indoor and outdoor furniture from the eighteenth, nineteenth, and twentieth centuries.

Just east of Hope Street, toward the harbor on State Street, is another pair of antiques shops with distinct reputations. You won't find western wear at Jesse-James Antiques (44 State Street, 253–2240), but owners Jesse Miranda and James Dumas say their low consignment fees mean low prices and a quick turnover in their stock of furniture, glassware, collectibles, and textiles. Across the street, the Center Chimney (39 State Street, 253–8010) is the only shop in town selling estate jewelry, from rings to brooches to necklaces.

Farther north on Hope Street is Dantiques (676 Hope Street, 253–1122), where owners Dan and Chris Manchester collect all the merchandise they acquire from estate sales around the region. They have a wide variety of antique furniture as well as collectibles like inkwells, perfume bottles, and paperweights.

have been hitting foul balls into the fieldstone back wall of the *First Baptist Church,* built in 1814 and topped with a chubby, open-sided bell tower that still rings residents to services on Sunday mornings. Next to the church, in a neat line fronting on High Street, are two other community cornerstones, the old *Byfield School* and the *1817 Bristol County Courthouse,* which housed meetings of the Rhode Island General Assembly from 1819 to 1852.

Another historic building on High Street is the *William's Grant Inn* (154 High Street, 253–4222), located in the 1808 Colonial/Federal home of Deputy Governor William Bradford. Located in a quiet neighborhood in Bristol's historic district, the inn has five rooms decorated with period furniture and antiques. There's a quiet patio and garden out back, complete with goldfish pond. Breakfast, included with the price of a room, includes Portugese French toast and blueberry pancakes whipped up by innkeepers Diane and Janet Poehler. Rooms with a private bath are $105; two rooms that share a bath are $85 each. (Rates drop as low as $75 during the off-season, October through March.)

East of Hope Street is Thames Street and the Bristol waterfront, where shipbuilders still ply their trade and a pair of eateries wait to tempt your palate and quench your thirst. Directly across from Independence Park and the end of the East Bay Bike Path is a restaurant that's a

Burnside's Sideburns

*C*ivil War General Ambrose Everett Burnside's battlefield prowess was less than legendary: Burnside is remembered more for his facial hair than for his skill in facing the enemy.

A veteran of the Mexican War, Burnside moved to Rhode Island in 1853 and opened a factory to manufacture a breech-loading carbine that he designed, but he was forced to sell the business when the government failed to give him a military contract.

When the Civil War broke out, Burnside rose quickly from command of the First Rhode Island regiment to a succession of more significant posts, cul-

minating in his being named commander of the Army of the Potomac— the standard-bearer for the Union Army— in 1862. But Burnside's career as a commander was uneven; earlier successes leading smaller groups of men were followed by blunders as head of larger units. He resigned from the army in 1865.

Burnside's limited military successes were enough to help get him elected governor of Rhode Island three times, but his most lasting legacy sprung from his copious facial hair, trimmed into bushy muttonchops. Pundits switched the syllables of Burnside's last name and dubbed the style "sideburns."

favorite with Bristol residents, **S.S. Dion** (520 Thames Street, 253–2884). With tongue-and-groove walls adorned with nautical knick-knacks and photos, S.S. Dion is an unpretentious setting in which to enjoy generous portions of well-presented seafood, especially the swordfish dishes for which owner Steven Dion and his staff are best known. Open Monday to Saturday, 5:00 to 9:00 P.M.

A 1932 Narragansett Brewery truck garage on Thames Street has been thoroughly renovated to become the new home of **Redlefsen's Rotisserie and Grill** (444 Thames Street, 254–1188), formerly located on Hope Street. A two-sided gas fireplace, a variety of warmly finished wood and stained-glass windows, and a large skylight make the interior of this eclectic, European-style restaurant cheerful and inviting. The roomy bar side is awash in yachting memorabilia and decor, and Redlefsen's pours a unique selection of tap beers you aren't likely to find at your local tavern, including Worsteiner, Spaten Munchen, Pilsner Urquell, and Franzickaner Weisbar.

The German beers salute the heritage of owner Walter Guertler, who also hosts a lively Oktoberfest each fall, complete with lederhosen-clad dancers and singers, sauerbraten, and festival beers. Although chef Michael Kocsis features weiner schnitzel as the specialty of the house, the menu draws inspiration from around the world. That includes Africa, home of the ostrich, a dinner entree described by Guertler as having the flavor of beef without the fat and cholesterol. Open for lunch Monday to Saturday 11:30 A.M. to 2:30 P.M., for Sunday brunch from 10:00 A.M. to 2:30 P.M., and for dinner Monday to Friday 5:00 to 9:00 P.M. and Saturday and Sunday until 10:00 P.M.

For a cold pint of ale or lager after a brisk workout on the bike path, there's no better place than **Aidan's Pub,** located a couple of blocks south of S.S. Dion on the corner at 5 John Street (254–1940). A neighborhood bar and restaurant that does not feel the need to hit you over the head with shamrocks to prove its Irishness, Aidan's pours a number of hearty brews from its taps, the perfect companion to the pub's excellent fish and chips. Open daily 11:30 A.M. to 1:00 A.M.

Nearby, at the end of Constitution Street, is the gateway to one of Rhode Island's most out-of-the-way locales, **Prudence Island.** The Prudence Island ferry (253–9808) leaves from the docks here.

Located in the heart of Narragansett Bay, Prudence Island is big enough ($6\frac{1}{2}$ miles long, $1\frac{5}{8}$ miles wide) to make you wonder why it never was developed like its sisters to the south: Aquidneck Island (Newport, Middletown, and Portsmouth) and Conanicut Island (Jamestown). The bulldozer's loss is our gain, though, as Prudence remains an isolated oasis just minutes by boat from the state's most densely populated areas.

Home to about 150 year-round residents and a large deer population, Prudence begs to be explored on foot, especially since large chunks of the island are accessible only by gravel roads (hardier souls could try a mountain bike). Most points of interest are along the island's main drag, Narragansett Avenue, which runs parallel to the eastern shoreline. About a mile south of the ferry landing at Homestead is the *Sandy Point Lighthouse,* built in 1851 and overlooking a small adjacent beach. Another half-mile brings you to the beginning of a *nature trail,* which accesses the *Heritage Foundation of Rhode Island parkland* in the center of the island. Continue south to reach *South End State Park,* established on the site of an abandoned naval base.

The more adventurous can head north from the ferry to explore the undeveloped Pine Hill area, which includes a *beach at Pine Hill Point.* A grassy cart path extends from here to the northern tip of the island, at *Providence Point.*

Prudence Island is a nice place for a little outdoor activity, but be fore-warned: There are no restaurants and only two small stores (*Marcie's General Store* on Narragansett Avenue at the ferry landing and *Dino's General Store* on Daniels Avenue in Homestead). *The Lighthouse Bed and Breakfast,* however, does give visitors a chance to spend the night on the island. A waterfront cedar chalet, the B&B is run by resident innkeeper Brad Holman, who provides guests with both breakfast and dinner in recognition of the island's limited (actually nonexistent) dining choices.

As the name implies, visitors can enjoy great views of the Sandy Point Lighthouse as well as much of Narragansett Bay. Guest quarters include a bedroom with queen-size bed, a living room with fireplace and wood stove (the B&B welcomes visitors year-round), sitting room, and private bath. Rates range from $85 to $150 per night. Call 683–4642 for information, or e-mail Brad at fyrtorn@aol.com.

Thanks to the large deer population, Lyme disease–bearing ticks also are an unfortunate hazard for hikers on Prudence Island, so wear long pants.

As you travel south from downtown Bristol on Hope Street/Route 114, you'll be tempted to look right to catch occasional glimpses of Bristol Harbor. Instead, keep an eye out to your left. At the corner of Burnside Avenue, you'll see the juxtaposed hulls of the 1913 yacht *Spartan* and the modern *Defiant,* which illustrate the evolution in design of America's Cup contenders. Turn here and you'll be at the doorstep of the *Herreshoff Marine Museum.*

As Bristol is to sailing, the name Herreshoff is to yachts. It was here that five generations of the Herreshoff family built some of the world's fastest and most beautiful wooden vessels, from the eight consecutive America's Cup–winning yachts of the late nineteenth and early twentieth centuries, to the patrol torpedo boats of the Second World War. The museum, housed in the company's former manufacturing plant, tells the story in scores of photos and with the gleaming hulls of the dozen or so boats on exhibit.

Inside, you can run your hand along the elegant and graceful lines that mark the designs of "the Wizard of Bristol," Captain Nat Herreshoff, and his progeny. Amid the great sailing vessels, don't miss the *Thania,* used in the filming of the movie *The Great Gatsby.*

Across Burnside Street from the Herreshoff exhibits is another tribute to racing yachts, the *America's Cup Hall of Fame* (One Burnside Street, 253–5000). Included in the hall are America's Cup memorabilia, photos of all of the winning captains, and models of the hull of every Cup winner.

The Herreshoff Marine Museum and the America's Cup Hall of Fame are open daily May through October from 10:00 A.M. to 4:00 P.M. Admission is $5.00 for adults, $4.00 for seniors, and $1.00 for students; children under twelve are free.

The *Lobster Pot Restaurant and Gallery*'s name betrays its humbler origins as a family-oriented seafood joint. They've been serving fresh seafood here for sixty years, but about a decade ago the Lobster Pot underwent extensive renovations and emerged as an upscale eatery. It's been a successful transition; many Ocean State residents call the Lobster Pot the best seafood restaurant in the state. Lobster, swordfish, and a raw bar are prominent features, and most entrees are under $20. (Surf and turf, featuring a 1-pound lobster and filet mignon, was priced under $25 when we visited.) Expansive windows offer a panoramic view of upper Narragansett Bay and two small isles, Hog Island and Prudence Island; a new outdoor patio offers similar vistas.

If the Lobster Pot's high ceilings and bright atmosphere remind you of an art gallery, that's because it is: Seascapes and other works from Rhode Island, national, and international artists adorn the walls and are for sale; along with a selection of fine jewelry. The Lobster Pot is located at 119 Hope Street/Route 114 (253–9100). Open Tuesday to

Sunday for lunch and dinner 11:30 A.M. to 9:30 P.M. on weekdays and 11:30 A.M. to 10:00 P.M. on weekends.

There's a touch of California at Bristol's **Blithewold Mansion and Gardens**, 101 Ferry Road/Route 114, just north of the Mount Hope Bridge (253–2707; www.blithewold.org). Towering over the other trees in the mansion's "enclosed" garden is a **90-foot giant sequoia,** the largest redwood tree east of the Rockies. Planted in 1911, the tree grows about a foot each year and is the highlight of just one of the many beautiful gardens at Blithewold. The former estate of a Pennsylvania coal magnate, Blithewold has **thirty-three acres of gardens** centered on a **forty-five-room mansion** resembling an English manor house. The mansion, built in 1908, sits before a sloping lawn that affords a terrific view of Narragansett Bay.

Many of the plants, shrubs, and trees at Blithewold convey the spirit of the Orient as well, reflecting a turn-of-the-century passion for Asian horticulture. In one garden stands a **Chinese toon tree,** the first ever planted in America; another corner of the estate has been turned into a **Japanese water garden,** with an earthen bridge that crosses a pond to a tiny island, a maple tree, and a decorative Japanese lantern. The grove of yellow bamboo on the property actually was something of a mistake of fortune: The bamboo originally was planted simply to provide garden stakes, but it began growing beyond all expectations. Today the bamboo stalks grow 20 feet tall, and visitors can follow a trail through the grove.

Tours of the grounds and the mansion are available mid-April to mid-October, Wednesday to Sunday from 10:00 A.M. to 5:00 P.M., but the grounds are open for self-guided tours year-round. Admission to the grounds alone is $5.00 for adults and seniors and $3.00 for children ages six to seventeen (maximum fee per family is $13.00). The guided tour of the grounds and mansion is $8.00 for adults, $6.00 for seniors, and $4.00 for children (maximum fee per family is $20). The mansion also is open most of the month of December for an annual Christmas exhibit.

Proceeding south of Blithewold, you reach an intersection where you can either go straight across the bridge or turn left and head back north on Route 136. Make the left.

As you bounce down the seemingly endless wooded road leading east to the **Haffenreffer Museum of Anthropology** (Tower Street off Metacom Avenue/Route 136, approximately 2 miles north of the Mount Hope

Bridge), it's easy to forget that you're on a peninsula measuring about 3 miles across at its widest point. Your jaunt through the woods is rewarded, however, as the trees part and the road ends at the museum grounds overlooking Mount Hope Bay, with a lovely view of downtown Fall River and the Braga Bridge. A grassy hillside slopes down toward the bay—a nice place for a picnic lunch on a sunny day.

The museum itself is located in part of an old dairy farm, converted in

King Philip's War

If you've ever wondered why Native Americans never tried to push the early European settlers back into the sea once they realized that the newcomers intended to take away their lands, the answer is: They did. Unfortunately for the native population, however, the effort was too little, too late.

By the time the Pilgrims landed in Plymouth, Massachusetts, in 1620, native tribes like the Wampanoag, Patuxet, and Narragansett had already been ravaged by a series of epidemics, unwittingly introduced by the earliest European explorers. These plagues, which continued on and off throughout the seventeenth century, killed 75 percent of the Wampanoags; other tribes were completely decimated.

While early relations between the white settlers and the Native Americans were harmonious, by the 1660s the English craving for land brought the settlers into conflict with the weakened but still formidable native tribes. After the English poisoned his brother Wamsutta (Alexander) in 1661, the surviving son of the great Wampanoag sachem Massasoit, Metacomet (Philip), began preparing for a war to drive the white settlers out of New England.

Lasting from 1675 to 1676, King Philip's War was the Native Americans' last, best chance to reclaim their homelands. At a war council at Mount Hope (Montaup), Philip united tribes that for generations had fought each other, including the Nipmuc, Pocumtuc, and Narragansett, and fighting broke out across Massachusetts, Rhode Island, New York, and Connecticut. Early raids and battles favored Philip's forces. But the English trapped the Narragansetts in their swamp fortress near Kingston, Rhode Island, in December 1675 and nearly wiped out the tribe. In early 1676, Philip led a series of raids on English settlements, burning Providence and Warwick, among other towns. But he lost a valuable ally in April when Canonchet, the leader of the Narragansetts, was captured and executed. After a losing battle at Turner's Falls in Connecticut, Philip's tribal alliance fell apart, and the English eventually trapped Philip at Mount Hope in August 1676.

Betrayed by an informer, Philip was shot on August 12, and his severed head was put on display at Plymouth. With him died the last hope of the native New England tribes, which by the beginning of the eighteenth century had almost ceased to exist on their former lands.

The Price of Pragmatism

People in Rhode Island complain as much about their politicians as anyone anywhere else, if not more so. But every so often, local pols' inbred Yankee pragmatism temporarily outweighs the bureaucratic impulse.

Case in point: Not too long ago, state officials were in a quandary over the tolls collected at the Mount Hope Bridge. Seems the 30 cents per car being collected wasn't enough to maintain the tollbooths, let alone make a profit for the state.

Predictably, some lawmakers proposed raising the tolls to a level that would cover the cost of collecting them. In some places, that would have been the end of the matter.

But after not too much discussion, the state came up with a surprising, commonsense alternative: Eliminate the cost by eliminating the tollbooths. Even more shockingly, that's exactly what the state did. So as you drive across the Mount Hope Bridge totally free of charge, perhaps you should toss a token of gratitude to that most unusual of beasts: the pragmatic politician.

1928 to house brewing magnate Rudolf Frederick Haffenreffer's personal collection of Native American artifacts. Today the museum is operated by Brown University and contains ceremonial clothing, pottery, weapons, and jewelry representing not only the Wampanoag tribe native to this area but also other tribes from throughout the United States, South and Central America, and around the world. The Plains Indians collection is especially extensive. The museum also has an African display, and a new exhibit slated to open in April 2000 will detail the science of anthropology.

Extending south of the museum buildings to Mount Hope Point is the crowning jewel of the Haffenreffer property: 435 acres of history-filled forest, swamp, and shoreline highlighted by **King Philip's Chair** and nearby Cold Spring, the spiritual center of Wampanoag life and the seat of government of King Philip. Philip led his tribe into a disastrous final conflict with the white settlers of Rhode Island and Massachusetts, and was killed in Mirey Swamp in 1675 in the final act of a war that saw the near-annihilation of the Wampanoags.

The museum and grounds are open Saturday and Sunday 11:00 A.M. to 5:00 P.M. from September through May and Tuesday to Sunday 11:00 A.M. to 5:00 P.M. from June through August. Museum admission is $3.00 for adults, $2.00 for seniors, and $1.00 for children. Call 253–8388 for information.

Contiguous with the museum property is the 127-acre **Mount Hope Farm,** recently saved from development and now open to the public for hiking and biking. This 319-year-old farm includes a 1745 Colonial home where George Washington stayed with Deputy Governor William Bradford in 1789. More recently, this was the home of the Haffenreffer family, whose legacy includes the Cove Cabin, a log building with great views of the Mount Hope Bridge and Seal Island, a refuge for harbor seals.

Back on Route 136 and heading south, keep an eye out for Mount Hope Avenue on your left and a small sign for *Tweet Balzano's Family Restaurant* (180 Mount Hope Avenue, 253–9811). Ever since Tweet and Millie Balzano opened the place in the 1950s, this has been the Bristol mecca for generous seafood and Italian dinners served family style and at a reasonable price (entrees are under $10 except for an occasional twin-lobster special).

A short drive farther and you'll reach the end of the Bristol peninsula; fortunately, the *Mount Hope Bridge* awaits to carry you over Mount Hope Bay to Portsmouth. As you pass over this narrow, two-lane span, drive slowly to admire the architecture that won the designers international acclaim when the bridge was built in 1929. The bridge is especially pretty on a warm summer night, when all the old lampposts are lit in silent accord with the lights dancing on the waters below.

**PLACES TO STAY
IN THE EAST BAY**

(ALL AREA CODES 401)

WARREN
Nathaniel Porter Inn,
125 Water Street, 245–6622

BRISTOL
Bradford-Dimond-
Norris House,
474 Hope Street, 253–6338

Joseph Reynolds House,
956 Hope Street,
254–0230 or
(800) 754–0230

King Philip Inn,
400 Metacom Avenue,
253–7600

Parker Borden House,
736 Hope Street, 253–2084

Rockwell House Inn,
610 Hope Street,
253–0040 or
(800) 815–0040

William's Grant Inn,
154 High Street,
253–4222 or
(800) 596–4222

**PLACES TO EAT
IN THE EAST BAY**

(ALL AREA CODES 401)

BARRINGTON
New Tyler Point Grille,
32 Barton Avenue,
247–0017

WARREN
Bullock's,
50 Miller Street,
245–6502

Delekta Pharmacy,
496 Main Street, 245–6767

Nathaniel Porter Inn,
125 Water Street, 245–6622

Rod's Grill,
6 Eashington Street,
245–9405

Wharf Tavern,
215 Water Street, 245–5043

BRISTOL
Aidan's Pub,
5 John Street, 254–1940

S.S. Dion,
520 Thames Street,
253–2884

The Lobster Pot Restaurant
and Gallery,
119 Hope Street, 253–9100

Redlefsen's Rotisserie
and Grill,
444 Thames Street,
254–1188

Tweet Balzano's Family
Restaurant,
180 Mount Hope Avenue,
253–9811

Bristol Art Museum,
Bristol

Bristol Train of Artillery,
Bristol

Charles W. Greene
Museum, *Warren*

Colt State Park, *Bristol*

Historical and Preservation
Society Museum, *Bristol*

OTHER ATTRACTIONS WORTH SEEING IN THE EAST BAY

Barrington Town Hall,
Barrington

HELPFUL WEB SITES ABOUT THE EAST BAY

Bristol Online,
www.bristolri.com/

Town of Barrington,
www.ci.barrington.ri.us/

Town of Bristol,
www.town.bristol.ri.us

Town of Warren,
www.intap.ne/~warren

Welcome to Barrington,
www.ltdaxis.com/
barrington.html

Newport

The mansions of the Gilded Age are the siren song for Newport visitors. But while the elegant "cottages" of the Vanderbilts and Astors are well worth a visit, don't let them lure you away from Newport's many other treasures.

By the time the mansions off Bellevue Avenue were built, Newport already had been a thriving seaport and intellectual center for more than 200 years. Until a prolonged British occupation stunted the city's progress during the Revolutionary War, Newport rivaled New York and Boston in importance. To this day Newport deserves much more than its reputation as a playground for the rich and famous.

Even those who come to town seeking the history of this old seaport tend to gravitate toward Thames Street, which means that neighborhoods like *Easton's Point* can be overlooked. Yet the Point section of Newport has as much history packed into a few small streets as just about any other place in America.

Founded by Quakers, most of the Point's quiet streets are either numbered or named after plants, trees, or geographic features, since Quaker theology frowned upon such "man-worship" as naming things after people or artificial objects. One exception is Washington Street—the Quakers' Water Street was rechristened after the Revolution in honor of the war's greatest hero.

Washington Street runs along the water roughly from the Newport Bridge to the parking lot of the Newport Visitor and Information Center, and many of the Point's finest homes, spanning centuries of history and changing architectural styles, line this beautiful avenue. Most famous of these is *Hunter House* (54 Washington Street, 847–1000; www.newportmansions.org), built in 1748 and considered the finest example of Georgian architecture in North America. Unlike many of its Newport neighbors, the Hunter House was spared destruction by the British during the occupation, probably because the owner was a staunch supporter of the Crown. When the British left town, so did the house's Tory owner, and Hunter House became the headquarters for

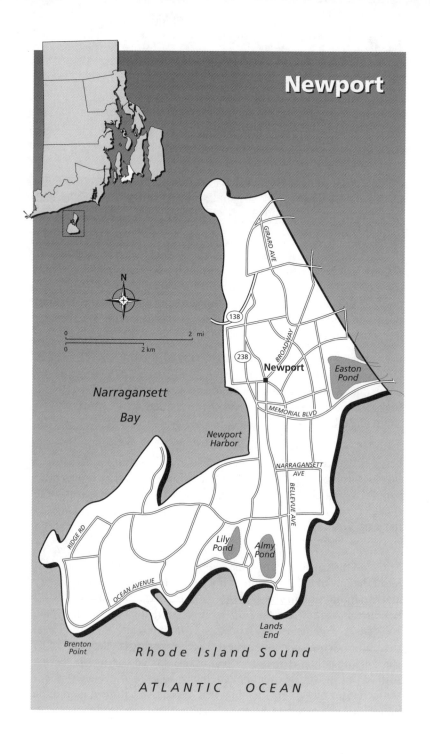

NEWPORT

Admiral de Ternay, commander of the French fleet dispatched to help the colonists in their fight against the British. Later, Senator William Hunter bought the house and lived there for forty-four years, and it's his name that stuck.

Hunter House was the first property restored by the Preservation Society of Newport County and features a fine collection of period furniture made by the Townsends and Goddards, the Newport cabinet-making families (and in-laws) whose work has sold for as much as $13 million at auction. Stepping through the ornate front door is a step back into a world of eighteenth-century luxury. Open 10:00 A.M. to 5:00 P.M. on weekends in April and October, daily from May through September. Admission is $6.50 for adults and $3.00 for children.

In sharp architectural contrast to Hunter House is the **Sanford-Covell Villa Marina** (72 Washington Street, 847–0206), a circa 1869 Victorian summer home with a magnificent, 35-foot entrance hall. Whether arriving by land or sea, guests at the Sanford-Covell Villa Marina are welcome to stay in rooms in the stately house, which has its own dock and a bayfront saltwater swimming pool off the porch in back. Rates in season are $125 to $295, including continental breakfast and complimentary afternoon port and sherry in the parlor.

Across the street from the Sanford-Covell property, at the corner of Washington and Willow Streets, is the **Church of Saint John the Evangelist,** a fine Gothic parish church built of stone in 1894.

Newport bills itself as America's First Resort, but municipal boasting doesn't stop there. According to the Newport County Convention and Visitors Bureau, Newport also can claim America's first

- *ferry service, begun in 1657*

- *gas streetlights, installed in 1803*

- *circus, hosted in 1774*

- *female newspaper editor, lighthouse keeper, and telephone operator*

- *passenger airline service, with regular flights to and from New York*

- *public roller-skating rink*

- *auto race, in 1895*

- *arrest for speeding, in 1904 (the driver was barreling through town at 15 mph)*

- *open golf tournament, international polo match, and National Lawn Tennis Championship*

- *synagogue*

- *church steeple*

The **Stella Maris Inn** (91 Washington Street, 849–2862) represents yet another architectural style. Originally called Blue Rocks, this French Renaissance–style mansion was built in 1853 as a private home and later sold to the Sisters of Cluny, who used it as a convent and renamed the house Stella Maris, or "Star of the Sea." Now a bed-and-breakfast, the inn has eight guest rooms with views of either the bay or the lovely garden out back. The wide, white porch that fronts the house invites you to linger over breakfast and enjoy the cool salt air.

Rose Island Lighthouse

Weekend room rates are $175 to $195 in the high (summer) season and $110 to $125 off-season; rooms are $125 to $150 on summer weekdays and $95 to $110 off-season.

Directly across Washington Street from Stella Maris is *Battery Park,* a local secret that offers one of Newport's best bay views. Take a break from your stroll through the historic Point and watch the traffic passing over (cars and trucks) and under (boats and windsurfers) the *Newport Bridge* looming to the north. To the south is *Goat Island,* which currently is cluttered with hotels and condos, but during World War II it was used to manufacture and store thousands of highly explosive torpedoes.

Battery Park also affords an excellent view of Rose Island and the historic *Rose Island Lighthouse* (www.roseislandlighthouse.org). The Rose Island Lighthouse Foundation invites guests to stay overnight at the lighthouse, located on a tiny island in the middle of Narragansett Bay. Actually, it's more of a challenge than an invitation: The lighthouse, built in 1869 and restored in 1993, has no running water, no maid service, and no electric appliances. You bring your own food and make your own bed. Everything in the guest quarters is manually operated, from the ice cream maker to the washing machine to the alarm clock, with the goal being "to see if modern man can manage a few days having to pump his own water," explains Foundation Executive Director Charlotte Johnson. When guests are done with their chores, they are free to explore the one-and-one-half-acre lighthouse property and walk the shoreline of Rose Island, which is cluttered with old Navy buildings and populated mainly by seabirds. Nightly rates range from $130 to $155 and vary seasonally. For $650 to $1,200 (depending upon the time of year), you can even become the keeper of the week, tending to the lighthouse while staying in a modern apartment on the building's second floor.

For the less intrepid, the foundation also operates a museum at the lighthouse, which reproduces the life and lodgings of a turn-of-the-century lighthouse keeper. The museum is open 10:00 A.M. to 4:00 P.M., and the foundation runs a launch service to Rose Island on demand during the summer and by appointment during the winter. Private boats also can dock at Rose Island's pier, and the Jamestown-Newport Ferry also will make a stop at the island upon request. Visit the Rose Island Lighthouse Foundation's offices at 365 Thames Street, second floor, call 847–4242 for more information, or visit www.roseislandlighthouse.org on the Web.

Leaving Washington Street via any of the "tree" streets (Elm, Poplar, Willow, Walnut, Chestnut, Cherry, and Pine) allows you to sally past a virtually unbroken line of Colonial homes, the feature for which the Point probably is best known. At 29 Elm Street is the aptly named **Third and Elm Press** (846–0228), whose wares doubtless would have been familiar to eighteenth-century Point residents: woodblock carvings, prints, Christmas cards, and notepaper. Open Tuesday to Saturday, 11:00 A.M. to 5:00 P.M., and by appointment.

Following a "rhumb line" in nautical terms means keeping a steady course between destinations, but you'll want to make a detour to **The Rhumb Line** (62 Bridge Street, 849–6950), a restaurant and tavern serving lunch and dinner in an old Colonial home on Bridge Street. In contrast to the weathered exterior, The Rhumb Line's light-wood interior is refreshingly bright and welcoming and the menu varied and interesting, with entrees ranging from grilled stuffed pork chop, chicken and broccoli Alfredo, and sea scallops casino. For lunch, sandwiches and burgers are reasonably priced. Tucked away on a side street, The Rhumb Line boasts of being "The Place You Wish You Found First." Open daily for dinner 5:00 to 9:30 P.M. and for lunch in the summer.

The Newport Historical Society leads walking tours of the Point from April through October. Tours leave from the Museum of Newport History and cost $7.00; call 846–0813 for more information. Newport on Foot also has a walking tour of the Point; call 846–5391.

Right on the edge of the Point district, across the street from the **Newport Visitor and Information Center,** is one of the town's real treasures, **Cardines Field.** One of the oldest baseball parks in the country, Cardines

Cardines Field

Field is a wonderful place to spend a warm summer evening appreciating the labors of ballplayers who still do it for the love of the game. Built between 1937 and 1939, Cardines is home to the amateur Newport Sunset League, founded in 1919, which has games on weekday nights at 7:00 P.M.and Saturday at 1:00 and 3:00 P.M.

Like Fenway Park in Boston and Wrigley Field in Chicago, the stadium itself is as much an attraction as the game. The bleachers are set on a fieldstone foundation, while a green, wooden pavilion wraps around the corner of Marlborough Street. Beyond the high outfield fence stands a line of fine Colonial homes, doubtlessly dented over the years by home runs off the bats of local heroes as well as baseball legends Jimmie Foxx and Satchel Paige, both of whom played here in their younger days.

Admission to Sunset League games is just $1.00 for adults and 50 cents for children. For the price of a beer, however, you can see the game for free from the back patio of adjacent **Mudville's Pub** (8 West Marlbor-

Not a Road, and Not an Island: What's With That Name?

When it comes to place names, Rhode Island is a state of confusion. Properly noting that most of the state is not an island at all, visitors are often stumped by the Ocean State's curious moniker (which in fact is an abbreviation of the state's full name—the State of Rhode Island and Providence Plantations).

Here's the story: When Italian explorer Giovanni Verrazano sailed up the East Coast in 1524, he came upon a triangular island, which he noted was about the size of the Greek island of

Rhodes. He was actually referring to Block Island, but the early settlers of modern-day Rhode Island thought Verrazano was talking about Aquidneck Island, where Newport is located. So they renamed Aquidneck Island "Rhode Island."

Later, the islands in Narragansett Bay were united politically with the plantation settlements that stretched south from Providence along the east and west sides of the bay— thus giving Rhode Island its extra-long appellation.

ough Street, 849–1408), an excellent sports bar crammed with memorabilia from the Celtics, Bruins, and Red Sox. Open 11:30 A.M. to 1:00 A.M. daily; excellent food, including a thick, meaty clam chowder, is served until 11:00 P.M.

From Mudville's it's just a short walk to the heart of downtown Newport, with its historic Brick Market, wharves, and Colonial homes as well as fine restaurants, shops, and pubs. Many of these attractions are geared to Newport's phenomenal summer tourist trade, but there are still a few odd and overlooked gems waiting to be discovered.

Unlike almost everything else on Bowen's Wharf, **Aquidneck Lobster,** located at the end of the dock, past the Chart House Restaurant (846–0106), is no tourist trap. Its "facade" is a loading platform, and your "guides" are brawny, bearded men with greasy smocks who usually are too busy to acknowledge your presence. But you didn't come to see *them*: You came for the lobsters.

Inside huge green holding tanks are as many as 10,000 lobsters, pulled from local waters and unloaded at the docks here for distribution to the restaurants of Newport and the rest of Rhode Island. There are blue lobsters, orange lobsters, and albino lobsters. There are little chicken lobsters, and there are giant, twenty-five-pound monsters that are hundreds of years old.

Evan Smith, marketing director of the Newport Visitors and Convention Bureau, likes to bring guests to Aquidneck Lobster to give them a taste of the "real" Newport. Although this is a working fishing center, visitors are always welcome. There always is a selection of super-fresh seafood on ice, and, of course, the lobsters are for sale. For an authentic souvenir of your visit to Newport, an Aquidneck Lobster hat or T-shirt beats all of those nautical-themed paperweights from local gift shops, claws down. Open 6:00 A.M. to 6:00 P.M. daily, year-round.

From yachts to schooners to powerboats to catamarans, there are many options for tourists who want to charter a boat or book an excursion to explore Newport Harbor and Narragansett Bay. One of the more unusual, however, is the **Rumrunner II,** which in summer departs four times daily from Bannister's Wharf in downtown Newport (dockside, 847–0299; office, 849–3033 or 800–395–1343).

With its numerous unpopulated islands and hidden coves, Narragansett Bay was an active center for bootlegging liquor during Prohibition. Under cover of darkness, small, fast boats like the *Rumrunner II* would venture out past the 12-mile limit to meet ships from Canada and the West Indies and load up their decks with cases of alcohol. To avoid the Coast Guard on the way back to shore, rumrunners would use camouflage, superior speed, and knowledge of local waters. But sometimes their luck ran out: In one famous 1929 incident, the Coast Guard fired on an escaping rum-runner, the *Black Duck,* killing three men and wounding another.

With Roaring Twenties music in the background (and complimentary Black Duck Rum cocktails on evening cruises), the *Rumrunner II* crew mixes Prohibition lore with the standard descriptions of bay sites, including the Newport mansions, Rose Island, and Jamestown. Once powered by triple 500-horsepower engines capable of 60 miles per hour, the 1929 motor yacht *Rumrunner II*—originally built to the specifications of two New Jersey bootleggers—was refurbished a few years ago but still manages a breezy 30 knots, permitting the tour to cover a lot of water in an hour and a half. The East Passage Express Tour, departing Memorial Day through Labor Day at 11:30 A.M.; 1:30 P.M., and 3:30 P.M., is $15 per person and includes complimentary juice and soda; children are $10, and a 10 percent senior citizen's discount applies. The Smuggler's Cocktail Cruise departs at 5:30 P.M. and 7:00 P.M. and costs $20 per person.

Looming over lower Thames Street is the imposing brick facade of the **Samuel Whitehorne House** (416 Thames Street), a circa 1811 Federal-

Nordic Newport

*C*ould Rhode Island have been discovered almost 500 years before Columbus "sailed the ocean blue"? Some Norwegian scholars think that the Vikings, led by Leif Ericsson, actually sailed up Narragansett Bay, and that Vinland in fact was coastal Rhode Island. Some of the geographic details of the area match the descriptions of Ericsson and his brother, Thorwald, who also spent time in Vin-land. Believers point to evidence such as Bristol's "singing rocks" (see the East Bay chapter) and the discovery of an ancient battle ax in North Kingstown in 1889; skeptics say that Ericsson's Vinland probably was farther north.

Legend also has it that Newport's Old Stone Mill, located in Touro Park at the corner of Bellevue Avenue and Mill Street, was built by the Vikings. The purpose and ori-gin of this odd circular structure, with its arched stone walls, is a mystery. Some say it is a mill dating to the seventeenth century, while some scholars and local residents insist that Ericsson built it during his stay in "Vinland" about the year A.D. 1000.

What do you think? You can weigh the evidence as you walk around the small park, open daily until sunset—then perhaps retreat to the bar at the Hotel Viking (where else?) to ponder it some more.

style mansion preserved by the Newport Restoration Foundation. Once the home of a shipping merchant, the house has been grandly restored and filled with elegant furnishings from the period, including many pieces by Newport craftsmen. Highlights include the Pilgrim period furniture in the brick-floored summer kitchen, the large fireplace and side-bake oven in the winter kitchen, and an herb and fruit garden typical of fine homes of the Federal period.

The Newport Restoration Foundation (847–2448) previously offered tours of the house only by appointment but recently began regular museum hours. The house is now open Saturday and Sunday 10:00 A.M. to 4:00 P.M. and Monday, Thursday, and Friday 11:00 A.M. to 4:00 P.M.

Newport's Gilded Age "cottages"—the mansions lining Bellevue Avenue and surrounding streets—are smack in the middle of the beaten path. Most of the well-known mansions, including the Breakers and Chateau-sur-Mer, are maintained and operated by the Preservation Society of Newport County (849–9900), whose tours and activities tend to reflect the genteel surroundings.

On the other hand, the independently operated and less-well-known **Belcourt Castle** (657 Bellevue Avenue, 846–0669) has a deserved reputation for user-friendliness. Guided tours of the mansion are the rule, but if you ask, they'll let you explore the public rooms on your own. Belcourt Castle hosts an array of unusual special events, including a ghost tour, murder mystery nights, and medieval banquets.

Belcourt, a reproduction of King Louis XIII's hunting lodge at Versailles, claims to have more ghosts per square foot than anywhere else in Newport, if not the country. Among the spirits you may encounter during the two-hour Ghost Tour are the Monk, who always appears in close proximity to a wooden seventeenth-century German statue, and a screaming ghoul who haunts a fifteenth-century suit of armor in the ballroom.

Regular tours of Belcourt Castle are from 9:00 A.M. to 5:00 P.M. during the summer, 10:00 A.M. to 5:00 P.M. in the spring and fall, and 10:00 A.M. to 4:00 P.M. during the winter months. Admission is $8.50 for adults, $6.50 for seniors and college students, $5.50 for other students, and $3.50 for children ages six to twelve.

Speaking of ghosts, Newport has plenty of 'em, as detailed in Eleyne Austen Sharp's book, *Haunted Newport*. This old town is a hotbed for bloodsuckers, too, if you take vampire scholar Christopher Rodina's word for it; he calls New England "The Transylvania of the Western

World." Austen Sharp and Rodina help headline a quirky newcomer on the city's cultural calendar: **Haunted Newport Week.**

First held the week before Halloween in 1999, the celebration of things spooky in Newport features lectures, ghost tours to sites such as Belcourt Castle and the Cliffside Inn (home to the ghost of artist Beatrice Turner), psychic readings, a horror film festival and, of course, a blood drive. For information, visit the Haunted Newport Web site (www.hauntednewport.com) or write to Haunted Newport Week, P.O. Box 12, Newport, RI 02840-0001.

For a bargain, you can't beat nearby **Ochre Court** (100 Ochre Point Avenue, 847–6650, extension 2347), the first of the opulent Gilded Age mansions built by Richard Morris Hunt in Newport. Set on the center of the campus of Salve Regina University, Ochre Court now houses the school's administrative offices; admission is free (although donations are encouraged). There are no tours unless you are with a student who's

The Ghostly Images of Beatrice Turner

*A*rt was Beatrice Turner's life, even if her subject matter was oddly limited. The only child of Adele and Andrew Turner, Beatrice spent her summers in Newport dreaming of becoming a painter. But her father, who wrote love poems to his beautiful daughter and turned away potential suitors, made Beatrice quit art school and stay home to paint self-portraits for his enjoyment.

When Andrew died in 1913, Beatrice refused to let officials take his body away until she painted his portrait. Her next work was an exterior one: she had her entire house painted black in tribute to her late father.

For years after Beatrice and her mother were instantly recognizable denizens of Newport, decked out in full Victorian costume even as the nineteenth century became a distant memory. When Beatrice died a spinster in

1959, workers found more than 1,000 self-portraits in her house.

Today the ghost of Beatrice Turner is said to inhabit her old home, now Newport's elegant Cliffside Inn bed and breakfast. Even if you don't find Beatrice's luminescent visage hanging over your bed some night, however, you can find many reminders of this sad, eccentric lady. Most of Beatrice's artwork was destroyed after she died, but the owners of Cliffside have managed to acquire about one hundred of her self-portraits and other works, which now adorn the walls of the inn.

The Cliffside Inn (2 Seaview Avenue, 847–1811; www.cliffsideinn.com) has thirteen rooms in the main house—an 1880 Victorian mansion—plus three luxury suites in the nearby Seaview Cottage. For information or reservations, call 800–845–1811 or e-mail cliff@wsii.com.

thinking of attending the school, but visitors can admire the exterior details of this replica of a French medieval chateau, as well as the grand hall, with its carved stone walls and massive marble table. Ochre Court is open Monday through Friday 10:00 A.M. to 4:00 P.M.

If your idea of high society resonates with images of white-gloved butlers serving dinner from a silver platter, then make a beeline to **Vanderbilt Hall** (41 Mary Street, 846–6200). This redbrick Georgian Revival mansion, built by the son of Cornelius Vanderbilt, is both a fine restaurant and an elegant hostelry, with touches of class that recall Newport's glory days.

The owners of Vanderbilt Hall want guests to feel like they're staying at the home of a very rich friend, so there's no check-in counter at the lobby. Instead, a formally attired butler greets you at the door and escorts you to your room. A stroll around the house reveals that all the classic hallmarks of a fine gentleman's home remain in place: Guests can relax in grand comfort in the music room, card room, morning room, billiard room, or conservatory.

Lights, Camera, *Amistad!*

*V*isiting downtown Newport not only is a step back into history, it's also a visit to a movie set—specifically, the set of the Steven Spielberg 1997 epic, Amistad.

Spielberg, his cast, and crew, spent nearly the entire month of March 1997 in Newport, filming key scenes for Amistad, the true story of an 1839 slave rebellion and the trial that followed. Courtroom scenes, featuring actors Matthew McConaughey, Anthony Hopkins, and Morgan Freeman, were filmed inside Newport's 1739 Colony House (846–2980), which is open for free tours daily 9:30 A.M. to 4:00 P.M. from July through Labor Day, and by appointment the rest of the year.

During filming, all of adjacent Washington Square was transformed to resemble a street scene from the early nineteenth century. Street signs were removed, new facades were placed over the two movie theaters on the square, and dirt and sand were thrown down to cover the pavement. Making the work easier was the fact that many of the buildings on the square date from the 1840s or earlier. When actors in costume and horse-drawn carriages and wagons were added, the cameras began rolling.

Spielberg also constructed the Colonial jail seen in the movie right in the middle of historic Queen Anne Square, but a week after filming wrapped, there was no hint that the seemingly formidable stone building was ever there. Other Newport locations included Clarke Street and St. John's Church.

Service that begins with twenty-four-hour in-room dining and full valet and laundry service carries over to dinner in Vanderbilt Hall's four private dining rooms, which are open to overnight guests and nonguests alike. Meals ($55 per person) include such specialties as quail soup, warm duck salad, hollyberry sorbet, and hearty Anglo-American entrees like venison and wild mushroom stroganoff for the main course. There's an extensive dessert menu and wine list to round out the evening, too.

The **Newport Casino** (194 Bellevue Avenue, 849–3990) is known as the host of an annual pro tour tennis tournament and as the home of the International Tennis Hall of Fame, where Chris Evert (1995), Jimmy Conners (1998), and John McEnroe (1999) joined the ranks of the illustrious. The Hall of Fame exhibits—greatly expanded in the past few years—are well worth a visit for any tennis buff, and the sprawling 1880 casino itself is a treat for the eyes, an excellent example of the shingle style pioneered by the famed architectural firm of McKim, Mead & White.

One of the ways the Hall of Fame preserves the history of the game of tennis is by maintaining the casino's original **court tennis** court. Court tennis, also known as royal tennis, is the ancestor of modern tennis, dating back to the sixteenth century. Players use a curved racquet, and the ball can be played off the walls of the court as well as the surface, a la racquetball.

The court tennis court in Newport is one of only thirty-four left in the world. To get a real feel for the history of tennis, catch a match by members of the National Tennis Club, who occasionally don old-fashioned tennis whites and play the ancient game. In 1998 the U.S. Court Tennis Professional Singles Championships were held at the casino.

Although it is known today as a tennis mecca, the casino actually was built with a whole range of sport in mind. One of these was **croquet,** that favorite pastime of backyard cookouts. Croquet is taken seriously here, though, with regular tournaments and regional championships on the schedule. Real diehards can check out the **Croquet Hall of Fame,** housed in the nearby Newport Art Museum (76 Bellevue Avenue, 848–8200).

Four dollars will get you onto the grounds of the casino and thus into the stands for any court tennis or croquet matches that are going on. Call ahead for schedule information. The casino's historic grass tennis courts also are available for rental if you want to play where the stars have played.

For $8.00 per adult ($6.00 for seniors, members of the military, and students; $4.00 for children), you get access to the grounds plus admission to the Hall of Fame's museum, where you can test your stroke on a simulated tennis court and learn about the sport and its stars through a series of brand-new, interactive exhibits. Open 9:30 A.M. to 5:00 P.M. daily.

Another Bellevue Avenue landmark is the **Redwood Library and Athenaeum** (50 Bellevue Avenue, 847–0292). The oldest library building in America, the Redwood Library was built in 1750 and features a handsome, classic portico which—like the rest of the building, and outward appearance to the contrary—is constructed entirely of wood. Inside, the library's book collection includes almost all of the original volumes it opened with 250 years ago (members of the occupying British army are thought to have swiped the rest while they used the library as an officers' club during the Revolution). Many of these ancient tomes, purchased in England in 1749, can be seen in barred cases in the library's quiet Roderick Terry Reading Room.

Only museum members may take out books, but visitors can check out the library's history on a short tour offered by the staff on weekdays at 1:30 P.M. or by reservation; ask at the main desk for information. Highlights include a copy of Gilbert Stuart's famous painting of George Washington and fine furniture by Newport's own Goddard and Townsend families. Open Monday 9:30 A.M. to 5:30 P.M., Tuesday to Thursday 9:30 A.M. to 8:00 P.M., Friday and Saturday 9:30 A.M. to 5:30 P.M., and Sunday 1:00 to 8:00 P.M.

Touro Synagogue (85 Touro Street, 847–4794; www.tourosynagogue.org) is the oldest Jewish house of worship in America, built in 1763. But the Jewish population in Newport predates the structure by a century, attracted by the gospel of religious tolerance preached by state founder Roger Williams.

The magnificent but unrevealing Georgian exterior of the synagogue gives way to a rich interior, featuring a dozen Ionic columns representing the twelve tribes of Israel. The synagogue features separate galleries for men and women, and a painting of the Ten Commandments by Newport artist Benjamin Howland provides a backdrop to the Holy Ark, where the congregation's Torahs are kept. Contrary to legend, there's no evidence that a trapdoor in the synagogue ever led to an underground passage out of the building—supposedly so that congregants could escape anti-semitic oppressors. But the room below was used as a stop on the Underground Railroad to hide escaped slaves.

Tours of Touro Synagogue are conducted every half-hour, Sunday through Friday 10:00 A.M. to 3:30 P.M. in July and August; 1:00 to 1:30 P.M. Monday through Friday and 11:00 A.M. to 2:30 P.M. Sunday in September and early October; Sunday 1:00 to 2:30 P.M. from mid-October to late May; and Monday through Friday 1:00 to 2:30 P.M. and Sunday 11:00 A.M. to 2:30 P.M. from late May through June. Tours are also offered by appointment but never on the Sabbath (Saturday) or on Jewish holidays. For an interesting sidelight, you can also peer into the nearby Jewish cemetery, which dates from the seventeenth century.

The massive stone walls of **Fort Adams** (841–0707) never were needed to repel the enemy, but for years they presented an effective barrier to visitors. Although it is the centerpiece of well-traveled **Fort Adams State Park** (perhaps best known as the home of the Newport Jazz Festival), the 1825 fort itself was closed from 1983 to 1995 because of deteriorating and dangerous conditions. However, a subsequent restoration effort led the state to reopen the fort.

Some areas still are undergoing reconstruction, but visitors can explore the walls, gun emplacements, and parade grounds of the fort, one of a series of fortifications built after the War of 1812 to protect East Coast harbors. Guides explain not only the fort's architectural nuances but

A Fortress Never Tested

*T*here's an old saying that generals are always fighting the previous war, and it holds true for Fort Adams. Built over the course of thirty-three years at the then-astronomical cost of $3 million, when completed in 1857 Fort Adams provided a formidable defense against wooden sailing ships armed with cannons. The problem was that by the time it was completed, advances in artillery made the fort's granite walls vulnerable.

Happily, Fort Adams was never put to the test. Without a significant navy, the Confederacy had no way of attacking Newport or Narragansett Bay. In fact, the Union considered Fort Adams so safe that it relocated the U.S. Naval Academy here during the Civil War. The fort also served for a time as home base for the aging U.S.S. Constitution—the fabled "Old Ironsides" of the Revolutionary War.

Defenses at Fort Adams were upgraded during the Spanish-American War around the turn of the century, but the fort's military usefulness continued to fade until, finally, it was decommissioned in the 1950s. Today, however, the imposing fortress has reclaimed a place of prominence, not only as a fascinating site to explore, but also as an excellent example of military architecture and evolution.

also the military tactics and weaponry that made it an effective deterrent to sea attacks on Narragansett Bay.

Admission to Fort Adams is $5.00 for adults and $2.00 for children (children under age six are free). Proceeds benefit the Fort Adams Trust, which conducts the tours from May to Columbus Day and is restoring the fort. Open Wednesday through Sunday; tours are conducted regularly 10:00 A.M. to 4:00 P.M. (Note: There's also a per-car admission fee to enter Fort Adams State Park.)

If Fort Adams sparks an interest in learning more about Newport's military history, shoot on over to the *Artillery Company of Newport Museum,* located at 23 Clarke Street (846–8488 or 849–6968) just off Washington Square in the heart of downtown. Chartered in 1741 by King George II, the unit served in the French and Indian War, the American Revolution, the War of 1812, the Civil War, and the Spanish American War. The company's circa 1836 armory houses a collection of military uniforms from around the world, artifacts representing the unit's colorful history, and a number of historic artillery pieces, including four brass cannons cast by Paul Revere in 1797. Admission is free, but donations are encouraged; open May to October on Saturday from 10:00 A.M. to 4:00 P.M. and by appointment year-round.

The popular *Ben and Jerry's Folk Festival* and *JVC Jazz Festival* (847–3700), held each August and featuring a who's-who lineup of artists, are just two of many special events held in Newport each year. Perhaps the most interesting is the annual *Black Ships Festival,* held each July in commemoration of the opening of Japan by favorite Rhode Island son Commodore Matthew Perry in 1854.

Each year hefty sumo wrestlers descend on Newport, while delicate kites fill the air at Brenton Point State Park and the pounding of taiko drums shakes the walls of the Newport Casino. Local restaurants host sushi demonstrations, Japanese beer tastings, and elaborate tea ceremonies, while the Newport Art Museum presents origami (paper folding), bonsai (tiny tree pruning), and ikebana (flower arranging) exhibitions. You can even learn some conversational Japanese and get your face painted like a Kabuki dancer.

Most events are free, although admission fees are required for some of the more popular events, including the drum exhibition and the craft workshops. For tickets or information contact the Black Ships Festival Office (28 Pelham Street, 846–2720).

More than 600 dolls of all shapes and sizes inhabit Newport's **Doll Museum** (520 Thames Street, 849–0405). The cheerful pink building, looking somewhat like a doll's house itself, is split between a doll store and the museum, which contains antiques from the eighteenth and nineteenth centuries as well as more modern playthings. Museum exhibits include a fine "Tynietoy" dollhouse, manufactured in Providence in the 1920s, as well as a Queen Anne doll from the 1740s and figures from forgotten television shows such as *Mork and Mindy* and the '70s revival of *The Wizard of Oz, The Wiz.*

Artists' dolls—hand-painted, one-of-a-kind originals crafted by doll artisans like Ashot Gregorian and Sonja Hartmann—are sold in the shop adjoining the museum and fetch prices as high as $2,000. A selection of popular Madame Alexander dolls also is on display.

The museum is the passion and business of owner Linda Edward, who frequently is behind the counter to answer visitors' questions. The museum and shop are open on Monday and Wednesday to Friday 11:00 A.M. to 5:00 P.M. and Saturday 10:00 A.M. to 5:00 P.M. Museum admission is $2.00 for adults, $1.50 for seniors, and $1.00 for children over age five. Children under five are free.

Overexuberant sailors and seamen in Newport's bygone days sometimes found themselves guests at the Newport County Jail, located at 13 Marlborough Street. Since 1987, the former jail has been operating as the **Jailhouse Inn** (847–4638), with twenty-three "cells" adorned with striped bedsheets and a lobby that retains the feel of an old police station—a function the circa 1772 building had until a few years ago. Huge iron gates frame the entry to the inn's common room, which is adorned with photos of intimidating-looking officers of years past.

The inn doesn't go overboard with the jail theme, however. Rooms are air-conditioned and pleasantly furnished and have refrigerators, private baths, and televisions; a complimentary continental breakfast is served. Room rates range from $45 off-season to $275 in high season.

Some may be born to be sailors, but admirals are made. Many of America's greatest naval leaders were shaped at Newport's Naval War College, located on Coasters Harbor Island. Founded in 1884, the college is the Navy's top school on the art of naval warfare, and it is the oldest school of its type in the world.

Housed in the college's Founder's Hall, the former Newport Asylum for the Poor (1820), is the **Naval War College Museum,** which provides a fascinating look at the history of the U.S. Navy in Narragansett Bay, as well as exhibits on the history of naval warfare. Torpedoes on display are a reminder that thousands of these explosives were manufactured and stored on tiny Goat Island, just offshore downtown Newport, during World War II. Models and pictures depict the clash between the sloop *Katy* of the Rhode Island Navy and the sloop *Diana* of the Royal Navy in 1775, the first naval battle of the Revolutionary War. (The *Katy* was later rechristened the *Providence* and joined the Continental Navy; you can visit a replica of the *Providence* at Fort Adams State Park.) The exploits of Naval War College graduates like World War II Admiral Chester W. Nimitz are detailed in a special gallery.

On your way in or out of the museum, take a moment to appreciate the beauty of Founder's Hall, a white-painted fieldstone masterpiece that sits on a grassy hillside with a commanding view of the bay. Set on a small stone on the lawn is a plaque noting that Coasters Island was the site where European settlers first landed on Aquidneck Island in 1639.

Admission to the museum is free, and the exhibits are open year-round Monday through Friday 10:00 A.M. to 4:00 P.M. and June to September on Saturday and Sunday noon to 4:00 P.M. Follow the signs from the Newport Bridge to the Admiral Kalbfus exit; enter the Naval Education and Training Center through Gate 1 to get to the museum. Call 841–4052 or 841–1317 for information.

The problem with most aquariums is that the fish are in there, but you're out here. Not so at the **Newport Aquarium,** located at Easton's (First) Beach in Newport (849–8430). This hands-on aquarium aims to be as user-friendly and as kid-friendly as possible, a place where you can pick up a fiddler crab and sea urchin or pet a dogfish shark. The aquarium's educational mission is to teach visitors about the creatures that inhabit the waters of Narragansett Bay, and staff troll the local seashore and pick through fishing boat nets searching for interesting specimens. There's no need for any "Free Willy" concerns here: At the end of the season, the public is invited to a "setting free" party where children can grab fish and crustaceans, run them down to the beach, and toss them back into the sea.

Besides eels, horseshoe crabs, and other more familiar creatures, each summer the waters of the bay also are home to an interesting variety of tropical fish carried north from the West Indies by the Gulf Stream. As a result, the aquarium tanks also hold such colorful species as damsel fish and butterfly fish.

The Newport Aquarium is located downstairs from the **carousel,** which is another attraction worth a visit. The aquarium is open daily April to

September 10:00 A.M. to 5:00 P.M. and until 8:00 P.M. on summer Thursdays when the town of Newport sponsors family nights at the beach. Admission is $3.50 for adults and $2.50 for children. There also is a fee for parking at the beach, but if you tell the lot attendant you're going to the aquarium, you'll get all but $2.00 back when you leave. (If you come after 4:00 P.M., there's no charge to park.)

The **Rhode Island Fishermen and Whale Museum** (849–1340; www. edgenet.net/seachurch/museum) is another hands-on experience geared toward children, only here the emphasis is on the lives of the people who depend on the sea. Kids can try on fishermen's clothing and take the helm at a wheelhouse equipped with a working marine radio. They can also touch real whale blubber and baleen, the fibrous substance used by whales to gather tiny plankton for food. A skeleton of a dolphin stands next to that of a human, a graphic illustration of the surprising similarities between these two distant cousins. Open 10:00 A.M. to 5:00 P.M.; closed Tuesday and Wednesday. Admission is $2.50 for adults and $1.50 for children ages two to twelve; kids under two are free.

The museum is located in the **Seamen's Church Institute** (847–4260; www.edgenet.net/seachurch/) building at 18 Market Square on Bowen's Wharf. The building also houses the Chapel of the Sea, a small room with a tile floor inlaid with seashells, seascape murals on the walls, and a holy water font shaped like a clam shell, as well as a second-floor library

A Haven for Men of the Sea

*T*he Seamen's Church Institute is one of Newport's most interesting—some might even say incongruous—institutions. Located smack-dab in the middle of tourist land, the institute is a throwback to a time when Newport's economy was driven by fishing, not summer rentals. The nonprofit group provides housing and emergency financial help to fishermen who have hit rough waters, giving them money to pay for health care, fishing gear and supplies, and other necessities.

Rooms at the institute building on Bowen's Wharf are $65 per month—a price that might make high-season vis-itors green with envy, until they ponder the true cost of seeking shelter here: Tenants are fishermen beset by declining fish stocks, closed fisheries, and industry downsizing.

Still, it's not all bad news: The Seamen's Church Institute helps fishermen find new jobs and deal with addiction and other problems. If you want to get away from your touristy surroundings for a few minutes and learn a little about Newport's seafaring economy, stop in at the institute's St. Elmo's lunch counter and meet some of the men and women who still go down to the sea in ships.

with a spyglass for peering out over Newport Harbor. If you enjoy the sights, be sure to drop some coins in the donation box in the lobby.

Newport's scenic **Ocean Avenue** starts near the end of the cliff walk in the mansion district and runs along the ocean for 10 miles, passing some breathtaking scenery and eye-popping homes—stately old mansions and angular contemporary designs alike—along the way. After crossing over Goose Neck Cove and passing the Newport Country Club, Ocean Drive enters **Brenton Point State Park,** famous for spectacular views and constant sea breezes that make the park a mecca for kite enthusiasts. Although some drivers simply turn around at this point and head back to town, Ocean Avenue actually continues past the park before ending at Castle Hill.

Near the end of Ocean Avenue you'll see a sign for the **Castle Hill Inn and Resort** (849–3800 or 800–398–7427; www.castlehillinn.com) at 590 Ocean Avenue. Turn off here and follow the long driveway to this popular but out-of-the-way restaurant and inn. Once the home of naturalist Alexander Agassiz, this impeccable 1874 Victorian has a commanding view of Newport Harbor and the ocean, with a broad expanse of grassy lawn that runs to the edge of some impressive cliffs. Some of the guest rooms share similar views, including the magical room in the turret described by Thornton Wilder in *Theophilus North.*

The lobby of the inn is dark and woody, in sharp contrast to the sunny, brightly decorated dining room overlooking the lawn. Dinner here is formal by Newport standards: Jackets are required for men, and jeans

Submarine Graveyard

*O*ne of the last battles between German and American forces in World War II took place in Narragansett Bay in May 1945. The German submarine U-853 was operating off Rhode Island's Point Judith when the head of the U-boat fleet officially ended hostilities with the Allies. But the commander of the U-853 didn't get the message, and on May 5, 1945, the U-boat torpedoed and sunk the U.S.S. Black Point. It proved a fatal decision; the U-boat was quickly detected and sunk by a pair of American sub hunters, the U.S.S. Moberly and the U.S.S. Atherton.

Today the wreck of the U-853, which went down will all hands, sits upright at the sandy bottom, her conning tower still pointed at the surface more than 100 feet above. The only thing missing from the sub are the propellers, which you can see in the driveway of the Inn at Castle Hill. Certified scuba divers can view the U-853 on a guided tour conducted by Newport Dive Center (call 847–9293 or e-mail ndf@ids.net) or Ocean State Scuba (423–1662 or oss@scuyak.com).

Castle Hill Inn and Resort

are forbidden. But you can dress down for the inn's popular Sunday brunch, which you can enjoy in the dining room or outside from 11:30 A.M. to 3:30 P.M.

Also on Sunday the inn has an excellent lawn party, with an open grill serving up hamburgers, hot dogs, chicken, and steak and a jazz band that plays while couples stroll around the grounds or lounge on the grass until evening, cocktails in hand. From the inn you can take a short walk east along the water to the *Castle Hill Light,* a small lighthouse perched precariously on the edge of a cliff.

The Castle Hill Inn and Resort accepts overnight guests year-round, but the restaurant is open only from Labor Day through the end of October.

One of the things that lures hordes of tourists to Newport each year is its scads of shops selling antiques, fine clothing, jewelry, and home furnishings. Everyone, it seems, wants to come away from the City by the Sea with a little piece of the Gilded Age. With so many retail shops, it stands to reason that Newport would have a fair number of unusual specialty shops, as well.

One such shop is the *Animation Art Gallery* at 192A Thames Street (849–2577 or 800–964–2541; www.animart.com), which has a large selection of animation cels on display and for sale. Part art gallery, part retail store, here's a place where you can spend $275 for a machine-printed Disney limited-edition sericel or $3,000 for an original cel from *The Little Mermaid.* Animation art from Warner Brothers, Hanna-Barbera, and other studios also are available. Open daily 10:00 A.M. to 5:00 P.M.

The *Rue de France* catalog is nationally famous for its fine assortment of French country home furnishings, including custom lace curtains, elegant bed coverings, and dainty linens. Almost unknown is the fact that the company's one and only retail store is located in Newport. Decorated with the products that have made the catalog famous, Rue de France (78 Thames Street, 846–3636) has been described as the most beautiful store in town—which should only encourage you to pick out a few things to give your home that special touch of *je ne sais quoi.* Open Monday through Saturday 10:00 A.M. to 5:30 P.M. and Sunday noon to 5:00 P.M.

Down on Lower Thames Street is a veritable jungle of stone creatures, statues, and fountains, all the domain of **Aardvark Antiques** (475 Thames Street, 849–7233 or 800–446–1052). "Urban archaeologist" Arthur Grover scours local estates and backyards looking for unique outdoor statuary, which he sells from his distinctive lot in the heart of Newport. Neat to walk through; even neater to buy. Open daily 10:00 A.M. to 5:00 P.M.

Themes restaurant (Brown & Howard Wharf, off lower Thames Street; 848–5745) bills itself as offering "unique dining," but it's not the menu that's unique—it's the decor. Every few months, designer Richard Carbotti—who has gained international fame for creating unique environments for corporate parties, upscale weddings, and other events—completely reinvents the interior of this waterfront restaurant. Dine here once and you're surrounded by the grandeur of the Italian Renaissance; come two months later, and the place looks like a ski lodge, or reflects the party atmosphere of Mardi Gras.

Staff costumes often change with the themes, as does the menu. Themes is open daily during the summer from 5:30 to 11:00 P.M., and Tuesday to Sunday from 5:30 to 10:00 P.M. during the off-season.

If you're heading back to the visitors center parking lot after spending a day seeing the sights, consider a short detour to the **Newport Dinner Train** (841–8700 or 800–398–7427; write P.O. Box 1081, Newport 02840). You can meet the train at 19 America's Cup Avenue (near the visitors center).

Departing from a small station on America's Cup Avenue, the dinner train takes a leisurely three-hour tour of the Newport, Middletown, and Portsmouth shoreline. As the train slowly moves along, guests are served drinks and appetizers at neatly trimmed tables in the dining cars, while outside the windows there are views of U.S. Navy ships docked at Coddington Cove, the bushy inhabitants of Green Animals Topiary Gardens, and quiet country streets and woods. Within sight of the Mount Hope Bridge, the train comes to a rest, and a gourmet dinner is served as the sun sets over Narragansett Bay and the lights of the bridge come on. You linger in this beautiful spot over award-winning babyback ribs, seafood, or chicken Vanderbilt, followed by dessert and coffee.

As well as the dinner-only excursions, the Dinner Train has murder mystery dinners and a wine excursion featuring vintages from Newport Vineyards. The dinner train operates Friday to Sunday from May through the end of December. Dinner for two and an approximately three-hour excursion (7:00 to 10:00 P.M.) will run you about $85.

If you want the train ride but not the meal, the **Old Colony & Newport Scenic Railway** (624–6951; www.ocnsr.com) offers eighty-minute excursions along the same route, with both coach and parlor seating available. In December there's a special North Pole Express run on weekends to pick up Santa in Middletown and deliver him to Newport. You can meet this train at the same place as the Dinner Train. Regular excursions are $8.00 for first-class seating, $5.75 for adult coach seating, $4.50 for seniors, and $3.25 for children. The North Pole Express is $7.75 for adults and $4.75 for children; reservations required. The train operates on Sunday only from January 16 to March 30, with departures at 11:30 A.M. and 1:30 P.M. Saturday excursions are added between April and November 19; Saturday departures are at 11:00 A.M. and 1:00 P.M.

PLACES TO STAY
IN NEWPORT

(ALL AREA CODES 401)

Castlehill Inn & Resort,
590 Ocean Avenue,
849–3800

The Cliffside Inn,
2 Seaview Avenue,
847–1811 or (800) 845–1811

Elm Tree Cottage,
336 Gibbs Avenue,
849–1610 or (800) 882–3356

Hotel Viking,
One Bellevue Avenue,
847–3300

The Ivy Lodge,
12 Clay Street,
849–6865

The Jailhouse Inn,
13 Marlborough Street,
847–4638

Murray House B&B,
1 Murray Place,
846–3337

Newport Doubletree
Islander Hotel,
Goat Island,
849–2600 or
(800) 322–TREE

Newport Harbor Hotel
and Marina,
49 America's Cup Avenue,
847–9000

Ocean Cliff,
65 Ridge Road, 841–8868

Stella Maris Inn,
91 Washington Street,
849–2862

Vanderbilt Hall,
41 Mary Street,
846–6200

Villa Liberté,
22 Liberty Street,
846–7444 or
(800) 392–3717

PLACES TO EAT
IN NEWPORT

(ALL AREA CODES 401)

Black Pearl,
West Pelham Street,
846–5264

Jake and Ella's,
636 Thames Street,
846–7700

Brick Alley Pub &
Restaurant,
140 Thames Street,
849–6334

The Cheeky Monkey,
Perry Mill Wharf,
845-9494

Christie's Restaurant,
351 Thames Street,
847-5400

Franklin Spa,
229 Spring Street,
847-3540

Handy Lunch,
462 Thames Street,
847-9480

La Petite Auberge,
19 Charles Street,
849-6669

The Mooring,
Sayer's Wharf,
846-2260

Mudville's Pub,
428 West Marlborough
Street,
849-1408

The Rhumb Line,
62 Bridge Street,
849-6950

Sala's Dining Room,
345 Thames Street,
846-8772

Sardella's Italian
Restaurant,
30 Memorial Boulevard
West,
849-6312

Scales & Shells,
527 Thames Street,
846-FISH or 846-3474

White Horse Tavern,
Marlborough Street,
849-3600

**OTHER ATTRACTIONS
WORTH SEEING IN
NEWPORT**

The Astors' Beechwood
Mansion

The Breakers

Chateau Sur Mer

The Elms

Kingscote

Marble House

The Old Colony House

Rosecliff

**HELPFUL WEB SITES
ABOUT NEWPORT**

Best Read Guide to
Newport,
www.newportri.com/

Newport Chamber
of Commerce,
www.newportchamber.
com/

Newport County
Convention and Visitors
Bureau,www.gonewport.
com/

Newport This Week,
www.newportthisweek.
com/

Visit Newport,
www.visitnewport.com

Welcome to Newport,
www.bbsnet.com/
Newport/newport.html

Selected Chambers of Commerce in Newport

Newport County Chamber of Commerce,
45 Valley Road, Middletown 02842, 847-1600

Newport County Convention and Visitors Bureau,
23 America's Cup Avenue, Newport 02840;

Newport County

Jamestown

J ust as Rhode Island sometimes is overlooked by people speeding on the interstate between Boston and New York, Jamestown is perhaps best known to travelers for its bridge leading to and from Newport. That's a shame, because this Conanicut Island town is full of surprises for the informed visitor to discover.

After reaching the island either from the Pell Bridge to the west or the Newport Bridge to the east, take the North Road exit from either direction on Route 138, then head south toward the village of Jamestown. Looking carefully, the first thing you will see on your right (about $1^6/_{10}$ miles) is a small sign for **Watson Farm** (455 North Road, 423–0005).

Beginning in 1798, Watson Farm was continually operated by the same family for 183 years. Today the 285-acre property is owned by the Society for the Preservation of New England Antiquities and still run as a family farm, raising cows, sheep, and lambs and working the earth to yield hay and vegetables. Visitors are free to explore the farm on their own or to hike the nature trails that offer good views of the bay. The farm managers are usually working around the fields and livestock and are happy to answer your questions. There also is a beautiful old farmhouse on the property, although it is not open to the public, as it's where the farmers live. In addition to fresh produce, you can buy beef and lamb raised on the farm, as well as knitted blankets and clothing.

Visitors are welcome on Tuesday, Thursday, and Sunday, June 1 to October 15 from 1:00 to 5:00 P.M. Admission is $3.00 for adults, $2.50 for seniors, and $1.50 for children ages six to twelve. Children under six are admitted free.

The rich Native American heritage of Jamestown is evident in the **Sydney L. Wright Museum** (26 North Road, 423–7280), which is maintained by the Jamestown Philomenian Library. The small museum features artifacts from the West Ferry archaeological dig, which unearthed both pottery and items received in trade with the English in the mid-seventeenth

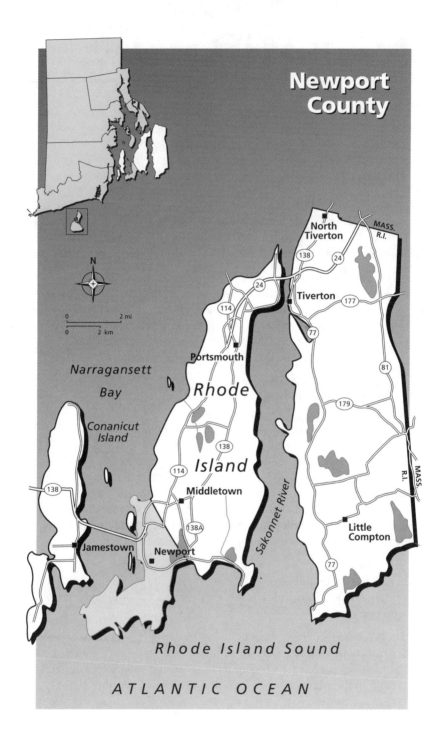

Author's Favorite Annual Events

Fool's Rules Regatta,
Jamestown; August

International Polo Series,
Middletown; June through
September

century. A cemetery cremation site yielded stone bowls thought to be 3,400 years old, and these are on display along with a variety of arrowheads found around the island. Open Monday 10:00 A.M. to 9:00 P.M., Wednesday 10:00 A.M. to 5:00 P.M. and 7:00 to 9:00 P.M., Tuesday and Thursday noon to 5:00 P.M. and 7:00 to 9:00 P.M., and Friday and Saturday 10:00 A.M. to 5:00 P.M. (Saturday 10:00 A.M. to 2:00 P.M., June 15 to September 15), and summer Sundays 10:00 A.M. to 2:00 P.M. Admission is free.

Before construction of the Newport Bridge in 1969, the ferry was the only link Jamestown had to its sister island and the rest of Newport County. The old ferry closed after the bridge was built, and though the glory days are gone forever, the memory lives on in the *Jamestown & Newport Ferry Company* (423–9900), which is based at the East Ferry Wharf in downtown Jamestown.

The tiny ferry *Edgartug* departs eleven times daily from Jamestown and makes stops at Bowen's Wharf, Long Wharf, and Goat Island (if you ask nicely, they'll even drop you off at the New York Yacht Club, Fort Adams, or Rose Island).

For Newport visitors, the ferry is a pleasant way to explore the quiet streets of Jamestown and its growing array of interesting restaurants. For those on the Jamestown side, the ferry presents a good alternative to dealing with the Newport traffic. Either way, you get a scenic ride on the bay. The $12 per person round-trip fare for the short journey is a bargain when you consider that you don't have to worry about the bridge toll or pay for parking in Newport.

Jamestown at night is a pretty place, with streets that grow quieter with each passing hour and lights that twinkle from the restaurants that have set up tables for outside dining. Two notable eateries that offer alfresco dining are the *Schoolhouse Cafe* (22 Narragansett Avenue, 423–3380) and *Trattoria Simpatico* (13 Narragansett Avenue, 423–3731). After dinner you can take the short walk down to the marina, where a small park overlooks the bay, Newport Bridge, and the lights of downtown Newport.

For sophisticated dining in a small-town setting, Trattoria Simpatico can't be beat. Owner Phyllis Bedard and chef Mark Simon have successfully wedded an imaginative menu to a setting that captures Jamestown's quiet charms. Located on Narragansett Avenue in the heart of town, Trattoria Simpatico has a small dining room inside a converted village home, but a screened-in porch and alfresco dining on the lawn are the main draw in the warmer months. There is live jazz in the garden room year-round.

At Trattoria Simpatico, the setting makes for a casual, relaxed atmosphere. The food, on the other hand, is elegant and excellent. Meals start with fresh bread served with rosemary olive oil, then continue with entrees representing both land and sea, including a potato-wrapped, pan-seared salmon, lobster risotto, rack of lamb, and grilled Black Angus tenderloin. The soups and salads are also very good, and Trattoria Simpatico has an extensive wine list. Entrees range from about $16 to $25.

If you want to party in raucous Newport in the summer but still have a quiet place to lay your head when the day is over, then Jamestown's small group of inns are the perfect solution.

What's in a name? For the **Bay Voyage Inn** (150 Conanicus Avenue, 423–2100), quite a lot. The large Victorian house that comprises the inn and restaurant was moved in two pieces across Narragansett Bay in 1889, its owner fleeing Newport for the "more prosperous shores" of Jamestown. The inn was renamed to commemorate the successful transit.

Luckily for latter-day guests, the house did not move too far inland once it reached Jamestown: The Bay Voyage has a great view of the bay, the Newport Bridge, and, across the water, downtown Newport. Many of the rooms and suites have water views, some have private patios, and all inn guests can enjoy the scenery from the pool and patio area.

Overlooking the pool and the bay is one of the inn's two elegant dining rooms, where guests and the general public are welcome to sample the signature lobster thermidor or a selection of entrees served tableside (lighter fare is served in the tavern). The restaurant also is acclaimed for serving Rhode Island's best Sunday brunch, which features breakfast fare like eggs Benedict as well as carving stations and seafood dishes.

Room rates range from $70 to $260, depending on season, view, and day of the week. Open for dinner daily (Sunday nights only during summer) from 6:00 to 9:00 P.M. (last reservation); entrees range from $18 to $23. Sunday brunch, served 10:00 A.M. to 2:00 P.M., is $21.00 for adults and $10.95 for children age 10 and younger.

Lodging is otherwise pretty scarce on Conanicut Island, but there are a couple of bed-and-breakfasts that might catch your eye. **The East Bay B&B** (14 Union Street, 423–2715) is a hundred-year-old Queen

Anne Victorian with three guest rooms. Innkeeper Karen Montoya puts out a generous continental breakfast spread to start your day; then it's just a quick walk to the shops and restaurants downtown. Nearby is the *Jamestown B&B* (59 Walcott Avenue, 423–1338), a simple but comfortable three-room affair highlighted by Mary Murphy's full breakfasts. For just $65 to $75 nightly, you get a great view of the bay; a spacious room with hardwood floors, lace curtains, and Colonial furnishings; and an eye-opening morning spread that may feature Rhode Island jonnycakes, French toast, apple pancakes, or Mary's top-secret "Dutch babies."

Beavertail State Park is simply one of the most beautiful places in Rhode Island. Located at the southern tip of Jamestown, the park is centered on the 1856 *Beavertail Lighthouse,* the third beacon that has shone from this spot since 1749.

Set on a rocky prominence facing the open sea, the park is famous for its pounding surf. From the parking lot you can clamber down a short hillside to a series of huge boulders, a great spot to sunbathe and picnic while the roaring breakers blast spray and foam below. Surf casters love Beavertail for its excellent fishing.

Beavertail also is the place to come to enjoy fantastic sunsets over an expansive ocean horizon. Officially, Beavertail is closed from sunset to sunrise; however, the gates to the park are often left open at night so that you can at least drive the road that loops around the lighthouse and admire the powerful, rotating beacon as it shines its warning out to ships in the East Passage.

The lighthouse itself is closed to the public, but you can get an up-close look at the mechanics of the light at the *Beavertail Lighthouse Museum* (423–9941), which has on display the huge French glass lens used at Beavertail until 1991. Located in the old assistant keeper's quarters, the museum also includes exhibits detailing the lives of the men and women who had the vital, if sometimes perilous, job of maintaining Rhode Island's lighthouses. Eerie before-and-after photos of the *Whale Rock Lighthouse* tell the story of the hurricane of 1938, which ripped the top of the lighthouse off and killed the keeper. From Beavertail Point, the foundation of the Whale Rock light is plainly visible at low tide. (Look west toward the Narragansett shoreline for something that looks like the conning tower of a submarine.)

The museum, which also contains models and descriptions of every lighthouse in Rhode Island, is open daily from June to August, 10:00 A.M. to 4:00 P.M. during the summer and on weekends after Labor Day.

Admission is free. The park and museum are located at the southern end of Beavertail Road; from downtown Jamestown take Southwest Avenue south, then make a right turn onto Beavertail Road.

If you're traveling with a teenager, chances are a favorite part of Jamestown will be exploring the old gun emplacements and watchtowers at **Fort Wetherill State Park** (884–2010).

Perched atop a rocky hillside, the fort was built to guard the entrance to Narragansett Bay during World Wars I and II. The fort's guns, never fired in anger, are long gone, but you can still see the rotating platforms where they once rested and the rails that were used to transport ammunition from the bunkers below.

Save for a handful of picnic tables, the park is undeveloped, and the crumbling fortifications, with their warren of rubble-strewn underground chambers, are no place for unsupervised children or for folks who have trouble getting around. But the public is welcome to walk around the fort, and the view from the top is nothing short of spectacular. Fort Wetherill is located near the end of Highland Drive, south of downtown Jamestown.

Captain Kidd's Booty

*W*hile strolling the shores of Jamestown, it might be wise to bring along a metal detector. Who knows—you could be the one to find the long-lost buried treasure of Captain Kidd.

Captain William Kidd shared a pirate's life with fellow brigand Thomas Paine during the 1690s, but by 1699 Paine had retired to Conanicut Island (Jamestown) and Kidd was on the run from the British. That spring, Kidd anchored a vessel full of loot off Jamestown and went ashore to visit his old friend.

After his stay with Paine, Kidd reportedly sailed to Gardiner's Island and then on to Boston, where he was arrested, taken to England, tried, and later hanged for piracy. During Kidd's trial, Paine told officials that Kidd had asked him to hold his gold for him, but that he had refused.

One theory holds that Kidd buried his treasure somewhere on Gardiner's Island. Yet local lore claims that Kidd really did give Paine his fortune, and that it may have been buried in Paine's yard in Jamestown. While she was in jail, for example, Kidd's wife instructed Paine to bring her a large amount of gold. And when Paine's house was renovated many years later, workers found an ivory tusk and a gold coin.

What really happened to the rest of the treasure? Your guess is as good as anyone's.

More user-friendly is Fort Wetherill's cousin, **Fort Getty** (off Beavertail Road), which has some old fortifications but also a picnic area, trailer hookups, a beach volleyball setup, and a panoramic view of small, undeveloped **Dutch Island** and the old and new **Jamestown Bridges.** There also is a small lighthouse at the tip of the park.

Middletown

I t was a hot summer night in 1777 when a raiding party of American soldiers caught a British general with his pants down, literally. General Richard Prescott, commander of British forces occupying Aquidneck Island, was having an affair with the wife of Henry Overing, whose estate was situated north of Newport in the Middletown countryside. As often happens with such things, word soon got out that Prescott was spending his evenings at Overing's house. Acting on this information, a small band of Colonial militiamen based in Tiverton made a daring nighttime raid across the Sakonnet River and through enemy territory to capture Prescott, who was hauled away in his nightshirt.

Although the daring of Colonel William Barton, leader of the raid, was recognized with the naming of Tiverton's Fort Barton, General Prescott's ignominious foray into Middletown has been memorialized with the naming of **Prescott Farm** (2009 West Main Road/Route 114, 849–7300 or 847–6230). A project of the Newport Restoration Foundation, Prescott Farm is a collection of historic Newport County buildings on the site of the former Overing estate. The property includes **General Prescott's guardhouse,** a fascinating **windmill** (circa 1812), and a **former ferry-master's home** (circa 1715), which was moved here from Portsmouth and restored as an old country store. (The 1730 **Prescott [Nichols-Overing] House** is not open to the public.)

The guardhouse, which once sat next to the Prescott House up the hill, includes old muskets and a remarkably well-preserved drum from a Massachusetts militia corps that fought against the British. In the loft upstairs are two tiny beds, proving that the visitors of Prescott's day were frequently small of stature, if not of rank.

The windmill, moved to this site from Warren, remains in working order and was used to grind flint corn for Rhode Island jonnycakes up until a few years ago. Occasionally, the cotton sails are reattached to their wooden frames, and the gears and stones inside begin to turn as they have for the past 186 years.

Even when the windmill's mechanism is at rest, however, the docent-led tour is captivating. The entire grinding process is explained, and you can marvel at the ingenuity of the eighteenth-century technology that allowed the miller to lift a three-ton millstone with one hand on a lever. In the top level of the mill is the bonnet, a huge central gear powered by the wind-turned sails outside.

The general store features herbs grown in a small, traditional garden behind the building, as well as honey from the beehives located on the Prescott prop-

The Prescott Farm Windmill

erty. Also take a few minutes to look over the eclectic collection of farm implements and children's toys gathered by the Restoration Foundation from the attics and barns of Newport County. Tours are $2.00 for adults and $1.00 for children; tickets can be purchased at the general store. Open Monday to Friday, 10:00 A.M. to 4:00 P.M., April 15 to October 31.

If a tree falls in the forest when nobody's around, would it make a sound? Ponder that and similar thoughts as you follow the signs to

St. George's School

*O*ne *of Middletown's most prominent landmarks is the Gothic Revival steeple of the chapel at St. George's School (847–7565), located on a hilltop off Purgatory Road. Built in 1901, St. George's is one of the best private boarding schools in the country, counting legendary Rhode Island Senator Claiborne Pell among its alumni.*

You can see St. George's steeple from much of Middletown, and a drive up to the school's campus is rewarded by spectacular views of Second Beach and the Atlantic Ocean. Visitors are welcome to visit the chapel when school is in session.

St. George's also plays host to an annual outdoor summer ballet performance; you can picnic on the school's big lawn while you watch the show. For ticket information, contact the Island Moving Company at 847–4470.

Whitehall (311 Berkeley Avenue off Green End Avenue, 846–3116 or 847–7951), the American home of noted philosopher George Berkeley.

Berkeley, an Anglican clergyman who postulated that nothing can exist unless it is or can be seen, heard, or otherwise perceived, came to Newport in 1729 and stayed two years in an effort to build an Anglican school in America. The school never was built, but Berkeley did leave behind his fine country home, which is maintained as a museum by the Colonial Dames of Rhode Island.

By 1897, when three ladies from Newport rediscovered it, Berkeley's home had fallen into such a state of disrepair that it was used as a hay barn. But the home has been fully restored and furnished to represent the fine residence of Berkeley's day. Each summer Berkeley scholars from around the world are invited to stay at Whitehall and act as tour guides, so you can spend your visit discussing *Alciphron*—which Berkeley wrote here—and admiring the rooms and herb garden.

Whitehall is open daily, except Monday, July 1 through Labor Day 10:00 A.M. to 5:00 P.M. and other times by appointment. Admission is $3.00 for adults and $1.00 for children.

A peaceful place to stop for a picnic lunch is the nearby *Paradise Valley Park,* located at the corner of Paradise Avenue and Prospect Avenue. (From Whitehall, proceed south on Berkeley Avenue until it becomes

Far From a Teacher's Paradise

*T**he next time someone bemoans the current state of public education, point him or her to the Paradise School for some perspective. Beautiful and quaint, this one-room schoolhouse nonetheless provides a sharp rap on the knuckles to nostalgia about the "good old days" of reading, writing, and 'rithmetic.*

Typical of nineteenth-century Middletown schools, a single teacher was responsible for presenting all subjects, at all grade levels, to a class of fifty or more. Students ranged in age from seven to sixteen, and school days stretched from 9:00 A.M. to 4:00 P.M., with an hour off for lunch.

Heat was provided by a wood- or coal-burning stove that needed to be stoked frequently. An outhouse served as the bathroom, and water had to be pumped from a well. The school's large windows provided the primary source of illumination: natural light.

For a tour of the Paradise School, call the Middletown Historical Society at 849-1870.

Paradise Avenue south of Green End Avenue.) Located at a quiet country corner, the still-developing park has blue-gravel walking paths that meander through a lush meadow, with the spire of St. George's School ever present in the distance. A pretty gazebo seems the ideal spot for a travel break.

Paradise Park also is home to **Boyd's Windmill,** the only surviving eight-vaned windmill left in the United States. Built in 1810 and moved here from the Boyd family farm in Portsmouth, the windmill has recently been restored to full working order, and public tours are planned. Call the Middletown Historical Society at 849–1870 for information.

A corner of the park is occupied by the *1875 Paradise School,* listed on the National Register and home to the Historical Society, which operates a seasonal museum on the site.

Follow Prospect Avenue to the end and make a right, and on your left at 1038 Aquidneck Avenue is one of the strangest "zoos" you will ever see. The **Newport Butterfly Farm** (849–9519) is home to more than thirty species of butterflies, which are raised by owner Marc Schenck in a large Quonset greenhouse that has had many of its glass panes replaced by screens, allowing a nice breeze to blow through. Visitors are guided on a tour that includes a look at a (dead, but preserved) Goliath Birdwing butterfly. With a wingspan of more than a foot, it is the largest butterfly in the world.

You also get to walk through the screen houses, which are full of fluttering butterflies and the tropical plants and weeds they need for food and reproduction. Thanks to a strict "no touch" rule, the butterflies are so tame that you can get up close and personal with them while they eat, mate, and lay eggs. In addition to the mature butterflies, the plants are home to the caterpillars that one day will turn into a chrysalis and later sprout wings. (Come between 11:00 A.M. and 1:00 P.M. for the best chance to witness this metamorphosis.) Schenck also grows butterfly-attracting plants outside the greenhouse to lure wild butterflies like red admirals, question marks, and tortoise shells to the property.

Any long-term resident of New England can tell you that there are not as many butterflies around as there once were; in fact, Schenck says that some native species are extinct and many others are threatened. On the bright side, he says, by growing the right kinds of flowers and plants you can easily attract butterflies to your own yard; the farm sells kits to help you out. The Newport Butterfly Farm is open May 1 to October 1

11:00 A.M. to 4:00 P.M., weather permitting (sunny days are best; closed rainy days). Admission on weekdays is $6.00 for adults and $4.00 for children ages three to twelve.

Prepare to be awed by **The Inn at Shadow Lawn** (120 Miantomini Avenue, 847– 0902 or 800–352– 3750; http://www. shadowlawn.com). This magnificent mansion of Italianate Stick design, unlike those Newport "cottages" along the cliff walk, welcomes guests to stay for the night.

You approach the grand white building from a curved drive that edges the shady green expanse that gives the inn its name. Once inside, your eyes will feast on the wealth of detail that Richard Upjohn lavished on his home when he built it in 1853. Step into the grand entryway onto mahogany floors laid in a basket-weave pattern, and take a moment to admire the fine staircase in front of you and the French crystal chandelier hanging from the 14-foot ceiling overhead. To your left is the parlor with its stained-glass windows, huge, arched mahogany doors, and elephant-skin wall coverings.

Upstairs, the eight guest rooms—each named for a nineteenth-century female author—are decorated with a Victorian flair and scented with potpourri, and a bottle of wine awaits your arrival. The spacious Elizabeth Barrett Browning room, the honeymoon suite, includes a copy of Browning's famous love poem, "How Do I Love Thee," which guests can take home.

Innkeeper Randy Fabricant left his hectic life as a New York attorney a few years ago to purchase Shadow Lawn, and he welcomes arriving guests by flying the flag of their native country at the front of the house. Room rates range from $85 per night for an off-season weeknight stay to $225 for the honeymoon suite on a summer weekend and include a full breakfast.

The smallness of Rhode Island makes for wonderful contrasts. For example, just minutes from the hustle and bustle of downtown Newport—and just a short walk from the crowds at Third

The Inn at Shadow Lawn

Beach—is the tranquillity of the **Norman Bird Sanctuary** (583 Third Beach Road, 846–2577), a remarkably varied nature preserve covering 450 acres just over the Newport town line in Middletown.

An ornithologist's paradise, the Norman Bird Sanctuary attracts more than 250 species of birds, including waterfowl, nesting songbirds, and pheasants. What attracts winged and two-legged visitors alike is the sanctuary's diverse topography, which runs the gamut from open fields and dense woodland to marshes and beaches.

Seven miles of **hiking trails** make the changing terrain easily accessible to visitors of all ages, and the children will especially enjoy the **trailside museum** at the Paradise Barn, which includes history and science exhibits and a display on the epochal geographic changes that have created the preserve's unique landscape. Be sure to follow the trail to **Hanging Rock,** part of the series of rocky ridges that bracket the isolated wooded valley at the heart of the sanctuary. For centuries artists have sought to capture the beauty of Hanging Rock, and philosopher George Berkeley sought out a shady spot underneath the formation while writing one of his famous tracts. It's a serene place to contemplate the meaning of life—or just to stop for a breather.

The preserve is open daily 9:00 A.M. to 5:00 P.M. from Memorial Day to Labor Day and until dusk on Wednesday evening; winter hours are Tuesday to Sunday 9:00 A.M. to 5:00 P.M. Admission is $4.00 for adults, $3.00 for seniors, and $1.00 for children under twelve. For early risers, there's a free Sunday morning bird walk that starts at 8:00 A.M., spring through fall.

In the same area as the Norman Bird Sanctuary are two other excellent natural sites worth investigating. Just a short jog south at the end of Sachuest Point Road is **Sachuest Point National Wildlife Refuge** (847–5511), 242 acres of grasslands, marsh, and beaches on a peninsula that juts out into Narragansett Bay between Second Beach and Third Beach. Here you can spy a variety of ducks, birds, foxes, and butterflies along the trails, which are open from dawn to dusk.

Closest to Newport is **Purgatory Chasm,** a gaping fissure cut into the cliffs overlooking Second Beach. Legend has it that Purgatory Chasm was made by the Devil, chopping with an ax at the head of an Indian maiden. More likely, the 160-foot-deep crack was the result of centuries of waves battering against the rock.

Some daredevils and lovers (and aren't they the same thing?) have foolishly leaped across the chasm, but you don't have to: A wooden bridge spanning the cleft provides an excellent view of the chasm and the waves crashing into the opening far below. Braver souls can walk out to the edge of the chasm and peer down at the cave that the sea has hollowed out of the base of the cliff and that fills with water at high tide. From this spot you also have a great view of the bay meeting the ocean to the south, while the drifting sounds from Second Beach far below will draw your attention to the north.

A small parking area, located on the east side of Purgatory Road just south of the intersection of Hanging Rock Road and Paradise Avenue at Second Beach, serves visitors to Purgatory Chasm. There is no admission fee.

A shopping center is probably the last place you would expect to find a winery, but then you would miss the tastings and tours offered by the *Newport Vineyards and Winery,* located in the Eastgate Mall at 909 East Main Road/Route 138 (848–5161; www.newportvineyards. com). Founded by a former U.S. Navy captain in 1977, Newport Vineyards Vinland makes up in quality and variety what it lacks in setting. The Sanctuary white, a dry vintage made of local grapes, is a highlight, and red and white ports are new additions to the vineyard's wine list.

Actually, the inside of the winery is quite pleasant, and tours describing the wine-making process are conducted daily at 1:00 and 3:00 P.M. from May through August and on weekends year-round. Hours are 10:00 A.M. and 5:00 P.M. Monday to Saturday; noon to 5:00 P.M. Sunday.

Portsmouth

I f you're playing tourist in Newport, chances are you'll hear or read about *Green Animals Topiary Gardens* (847–1000). Still, this country estate merits a mention, despite being relatively well known. Unlike the other properties maintained by the Preservation Society of Newport County (Kingscote, Chateau-sur-Mer, the Breakers, and other Newport mansions; www.newportmansions.org), Green Animals is located way off in the countryside of northern Portsmouth. And it is so very odd that it demands inclusion in any collection of offbeat attractions.

Those of us whose exposure to topiary animals is limited to a view from the monorail at Walt Disney World may find the idea of carving shrubs into amusing creature-shapes rather, well, silly. But Green Animals was serious business for gardener Joseph Carriero and his successor, George Mendonca, who created and maintained for eighty years the topiary gardens at the former estate of Thomas E. Brayton. Today there are twenty-one green animals throughout the property, including camels, pigs, birds, and giraffes. The kids will love it.

The formal gardens overlook Narragansett Bay, and the estate house includes a Victorian toy exhibit and a gift shop. Admission to Green Animals is $9.00 for adults and $3.50 for children ages six to seventeen; you can also buy a variety of combination tickets that allow you to visit Green Animals and some or all of the other Preservation Society properties.

Open May 1 to October 31 daily from 10:00 A.M. to 5:00 P.M., Green Animals is located on Cory's Lane off West Main Road/Route 114 just south of the intersection with Route 24 and about 3 miles south of the Mount Hope Bridge.

Island Park reminds you of those towns out west that used to sit on Route 66, the main drag before the era of interstate highways. At one time, Point Road led to a stone bridge that crossed the Sakonnet River to downtown Tiverton. But in 1954 Hurricane Carol washed out the center span of the bridge and it was never rebuilt, taking Island Park off the beaten path. (Today, the Sakonnet Bridge to the north makes Route 138/Route 24 Portsmouth's main link to the eastern mainland.)

Still, this is no ghost town, and the chance to view the remains of the old bridge (from the Stonebridge Marina) is worth the detour off Route 138 (if heading north, take a right onto Park Avenue; use Boyd's Lane if traveling south). Also, Island Park has built a solid reputation for its variety of seafood restaurants, including the waterfront *15 Point Road* (15 Point Road, 683–3138).

It might be a stretch to call *Flo's Clam Shack* a restaurant, but Flo's is a must-see if you want a taste of what living in a seaside New England community is all about. They mean it when they say "shack": Flo's is a rough-hewn drive-in adorned with fishing nets and weather-beaten buoys, with a porch supported by old telephone poles and a parking lot of crushed shells. After you order, the person at the window will give you a small beach stone painted with a pick-up number, and a couple of picnic tables make up the dining area. You get the idea.

But the fried clams and fish are fantastic, and Flo's has been here forever. (A sign noting that the place is closed during hurricanes is only half in jest: Flo's has weathered uncounted storms since it opened more than sixty years ago, and a previous shack was washed out to sea in the 1938 storm.) Many folks take their orders across the street and sit on the seawall or go down to the small beach. Flo's is located at Park

Avenue in Island Park. (A second, newer location on Aquidneck Avenue in Middletown offers similar fare but caters to the Easton's Beach crowd and lacks the peculiar ambience of the original.) It is open Friday to Sunday 11:00 A.M. to 8:00 P.M.

Island Park Beach, by the way, is open to the public and parking along the seawall is free, if limited.

For a completely different dining experience, it's well worth the drive down Portsmouth's East Main Road to the *Sea Fare Inn* (3352 East Main Road/Route 138, 683–0577). Those in the know won't hesitate to travel up from Newport or down from Providence to indulge in chef George Karousos's Greek-inspired cookery. An herb garden on the restaurant grounds is the source for many of the fresh ingredients that are the key to the Sea Fare Inn's success. How fresh, you say? Well, consider that the Sea Fare Inn doesn't even have a freezer on the premises.

Dishes like Chicken à la Grecque and steak au poivre complement an array of seafood entrees and have helped Karousos earn high praise both locally and nationally. The grilled swordfish is served in a nice sherry sauce and is topped with lobster, accompanied by julienned carrots and zucchini. The signature Lobster Gourmet is served with a Mornay sauce

Portsmouth Polo

*W*hen polo was introduced to America in nearby Newport in 1876, it was strictly a rich man's game. But while owning a "string of poloponies" (pronounced puh-LOP-puh-nies, to quote the Honeymooners' Ed Norton's famous malapropism) may still be a measure of wealth, those with eight bucks burning a hole in their pockets can attend a polo match at Portsmouth's Glen Farm.

Every summer Saturday at 5:00 P.M., teams from England, India, Spain, and even farther afield saddle up for a few chukkers of world-class polo, part of the annual Newport International Polo Series. Along with the hoi polloi, you may rub shoulders with nobility, actors, and other tony Newport visitors.

Despite polo's country-club image, the sport is fast-paced and occasionally dangerous (to players, not spectators). The version of the game you'll see at Glen Farm is nearly identical to that played more than a century ago.

Glen Farm, a hundred-acre park that features a grand old manor house, is located on Route 138 in Portsmouth. Tickets for polo are sold at the Newport County Convention and Visitors Bureau (23 America's Cup Avenue, Newport; 800–976–5122) and at the Glen Farm gate on match days (call the Glen Farm box office at 846–0200).

A Farm With a Berry Nice View

*T*here's plenty of pick-your-own farms in Cranston, Foster, Johnston, North Smithfield, and throughout the West Bay half of Rhode Island. But my friend's father—who lives in Cranston and seeks out only the best berries for making pancakes, muffins, and jam—insists on making the long drive out to Portsmouth to pick blueberries and strawberries at Quonset View Farm (895 Middle Road, 683–1254).

Not only are the berries here bigger, better, and cheaper, but the beautiful views of Narragansett Bay and Quonset Point are well worth the trip. Plus, the steady breeze off the water keeps amateur pickers cool, even during the height of the summer harvest season.

To get to Quonset View Farm, take Union Street from either Route 114 or Route 138 to Middle Lane. For brochures listing Rhode Island's pick-your-own farms and roadside farm stands, contact the state Department of Environmental Management's Division of Agriculture, 22 Hayes Street, Providence 02908; 277–2781.

and surrounded by shrimp, scallops, and crabmeat. Service is professional, attentive, and unhurried.

Thanks to its reputation and popularity, the restaurant has grown to take over most of the 1887 Colonial-style estate house that once belonged to the Webb family. Speaking of family, that's how you'll be treated by the Karousoses, who also operate the Sea Fare American Cafe in downtown Newport.

Practically next door to the Sea Fare Inn you'll fine the **Sakonnet River Inn** (3338 East Main Road/Route 138, 683–0035), a pretty bed-and-breakfast. A room with a working fireplace at this restored 1850 farmhouse will cost you $125 a night and includes a continental breakfast.

Rhode Island's newest winery, **Greenvale Vineyards** (582 Wapping Road, 847–3777; www.greenvale.com) is also located off East Main Road/Route 138 in Portsmouth. The vineyard, within hailing distance of the Sakonnet River, takes advantage of the moderating effect of the ocean and the rich soil of Aquidneck Island to produce complex vintages from young vines. Greenvale only began producing its chardonnays, cabernet francs, and vidal blancs in 1993, yet its wines are already appearing on the lists of such upscale eateries as the Gatehouse restaurant in Providence. For a simple table wine, try the Skipping Stone White.

The vineyards center on an 1860s Victorian Gothic house and stable, which has been refurbished into a tasting room. Greenvale Vineyards is open Thursday to Sunday noon to 5:00 P.M. To get there, take East Main Road to Sandy Point Avenue, then turn right on Wapping Road. The winery is about $1/2$ mile down on your left.

Tiverton

Although officially part of Newport County, Tiverton and Little Compton share Bristol County's geographic isolation from the rest of Rhode Island. Like their neighbors to the north, the two towns are located on a small peninsula jutting into Narragansett Bay, with far more secure land links to Massachusetts than to the Ocean State.

What's especially engaging about Tiverton is the way the town quickly gives way to country as you head south. One minute, you're passing between the rows of homes that make up the modest seaside village; the next, you're driving through a pastoral landscape where glimpses of the water are an ever-present companion.

Rising above the village of Tiverton is **Fort Barton,** the launching point for one of the most heralded military exploits in American history. Built in 1777 to prevent the British occupiers of Newport from attacking Boston or Providence, the redoubt known as the Tiverton Heights Fort was the base for Colonel William Barton. Just a week after the fort was commissioned, Barton led a party of soldiers on a daring raid to British-held Aquidneck Island and captured General William Prescott, commander of the Newport garrison. The mission was such a morale boost to the beleaguered Continental Army that the fort was renamed in Barton's honor.

Two centuries later, Fort Barton is a tranquil plateau crisscrossed with **nature trails** that lead through a narrow right-of-way to a larger preserve known as the Fort Barton Woods. There's not much left of the fort itself besides some earthen walls, but a modern **observation tower** provides a nice view of Narragansett Bay and the Mount Hope Bridge. Birdsong and children's laughter drifting upward from a nearby school serve as accompaniment to this otherwise quiet spot. The main Red Trail leads you to a pond and four bridges crossing the **Sin and Flesh Brook,** whose grisly name recalls the murder of a white settler by a renegade Indian.

Parking for the fort is located on Highland Road. There's no office on the park grounds, but **Tiverton Town Hall** is across the street and the folks there are very helpful in answering questions.

Continue south on Highland Road and you will intersect with Main Road (Route 77). Make a left turn, and you almost immediately will be greeted by **Evelyn's Drive-In** (2335 Main Road, 624–3100). A stop at Evelyn's is a great topper to a hot summer day spent at the beach or driving around Bristol County. You could take your meal inside the small dining room, but in nice weather the best idea is to order from the outside window and dine alfresco on the canopied picnic tables overlooking Nannaquaket Pond. Nothing fancy about this busy roadside seafood shack, just great fried fish, shrimp, and clams. Open seasonally.

Route 77 continues south, hugging the shore of the pond and affording a nice view of a small peninsula and the Sakonnet River beyond. At this point you are truly in the country, as evidenced by the abundance of nature preserves in the area. The first one you can visit is the **Emile Reuker Wildlife Refuge,** located about $1/8$ mile west on Seapowet Road. (It's a right turn at the next crossroads you will come to on Route 77.) This Audubon Society of Rhode Island (949–5454) property features short, easy-to-walk trails along the salt marshes to **Jack's Island Beach.** Fiddler crabs patrol the beach and herons and ducks ply the waters of the marsh and river, while a feeding station attracts a variety of birds in the winter.

If you exit the parking lot and turn right, Seapowet Road ends almost immediately at Seapowet Avenue. Head south (left turn) and you will soon come to a small bridge that crosses Seapowet Creek, which leads into the undeveloped **Seapowet Marsh Wildlife Refuge.** Slow down for a view of the river (which looks more like a bay) on one side and the creek on the other.

Seapowet Avenue ends at a bend in Puncatest Neck Road; bear left, and a short drive past pretty Nanquit Pond will bring you to **Tiverton Four Corners** (crossroads of Main Road/Route 77 and East Road/Route 179).

Locals boast of Tiverton's rural character by pointing out that this intersection has the only traffic signal in town, but there's more reason than a red light to stop at Four Corners. This crossroads has always been a prominent part of Tiverton: A sawmill and gristmill were erected here in the late 1600s, and Robert Grey—the explorer who discovered the Columbia River and established the United States' claim to modern-day Idaho, Oregon, and Washington—had his home here.

In more modern times, many Providence families have taken a ride in the country as an excuse to stop at **Gray's Ice Cream** (624–4500), at 16 East Road, often called the best in the state. Dozens of ice cream flavors are offered, and there's also a decent selection of sherbet and frozen yogurt varieties. Order from the outside window or go inside the shop, which doubles as a convenience store.

For a picnic lunch, you can't do much better than the deli sandwiches served at **The Provender** (3883 Main Road, 624–8084). Typical is the Mamma Mia, with sliced turkey topped with roasted garlic basil mayo, provolone cheese, and marinated peppers. Provender's fresh soups lean heavily on the veggies, including broths flavored with Brazilian black beans and a carrot-and-tomato soup with fresh dill.

Located in a three-story Victorian, which for years was the local general store (evidenced by the high ceilings and squeaky wooden floors), Provender also serves muffins and coffee for breakfast. Call ahead and they'll pack you a box lunch tied up with a pretty bow, or you can settle into one of the benches on the wraparound porch and watch the world (slowly) go by. Open daily 9:00 A.M. to 5:00 P.M. in summer; winter weekdays 9:00 A.M. to 3:00 P.M. (closed Monday; closed Tuesday after Christmas through March 1); and winter weekends 9:00 A.M. to 5:00 P.M. The Provender also closes for the entire month of February.

"Shopping the way it used to be" is the other reason folks come down to the Four Corners. Located at the crossroads itself is the **Donovan Gallery** (3879 Main Road, 624–4000), which features the original work of New England artists. It's open Tuesday to Saturday 10:00 A.M. to 5:00 P.M. and Sunday noon to 5:00 P.M. in summer. Weekday hours are trimmed to 11:00 A.M. to 4:00 P.M. in spring and fall, and the shop is closed Tuesday January through March. Also at the crossroads is **The Cottage at Four Corners** (3847 Main Road, 625–5814), which sells antiques and home accessories and features the work of local crafts-people and all-maple furniture made in Maine. The Cottage is open Tuesday through Saturday 10:00 A.M. to 5:00 P.M. (plus Monday in the summer) and Sunday noon to 5:00 P.M.

Next door is **Abigail and Magnolia's,** a funky, eclectic shop that mixes clothing handwoven from natural fabrics with an assortment of archi-tectural garden pieces—go figure. Open 10:30 A.M. to 5:00 P.M. week-days and 1:00 to 5:00 P.M. Saturday and Sunday in summer; the same hours from Wednesday to Sunday in the winter.

The **Four Corners Grille** (3841 Main Road, 624–1510), with its pine floors, wooden booths, and small dining room, has a Colonial, almost rustic feel. They've got a great selection of sandwiches here, from chicken cordon bleu served on a French roll ($6.95) to mixed vegeta-bles on grilled rosemary focaccia bread ($5.50), all served with excel-lent, beer-battered fries on the side. Dinner entrees focus on comfort foods, such as shepherd's pie and meat loaf, and seafood. Salads and soups—including a creamy lobster bisque full of bits of lobster meat—are also served. Open daily 8:00 A.M. to 8:00 P.M. during winter and 7:00 A.M. to 9:00 P.M. during summer.

Just down the road—a few hundred feet south on Route 77—are the charming *Mill Pond Shops,* located in a converted mill complex connected by a wooden bridge that spans a stream-fed raceway. The specialty shops include *Little Purls,* a children's clothing store (625–5900; open 10:00 A.M. to 5:00 P.M. Monday to Saturday, 10:00 A.M. to 5:00 P.M. on Sunday; closed on winter Mondays except between Thanksgiving and Christmas); *Pond Lilies,* a women's clothing shop that also features original sea glass jewelry by Newport artist Sue Gray Fitzpatrick (3964 Main Road, 624–2594; open 10:00 A.M. to 5:00 P.M. Monday to Saturday, noon to 5:00 P.M. on Sunday; closed Monday January to March); and *Courtyards,* which specializes in garden statuary, decorative fountains, and "eccentricities" selected by owner Wendy Prazak Dutton (3980 Main Road, 624–8682; open Monday to Saturday 10:00 A.M. to 5:00 P.M., Sunday noon to 5:00 P.M.; closed Monday January through April).

The *Magic Garden of Tiverton* (3988 Main Road, 625–1344), located just a few steps from the Mill Pond Shops, is a showcase for the genius of environmental artist Michael Higgins, who uses a chainsaw to create whimsical and unique wooden figures. Higgins has turned tree stumps into noble eagles, provided schools with painted mascots, carved a nativity scene for the nearby Amicable Church, and even sculpted an entire Wizard of Oz troupe for a homeowner's backyard. Populated by wacky birch "bugs," dragons, and other products of Higgins' imagination, the Magic Garden serves both as a studio for custom jobs and a retail stop. Carvings range in price from $10 to thousands.

Finally, the *Tiverton Historical Society* operates a small museum at the *Chase Cory House,* located a few steps south of Four Corners at 3908 Main Road (624–4013 or 624–8881). A typical Colonial-era home (listed as built in 1730, although local historians think it might actually date from 1690), complete with a tremendous fireplace and tiny doorways, the Chase Cory House is open to visitors on Sunday from 2:00 to 4:30 P.M., June to September.

After this brief stop in civilization, our journey takes us back to nature again. About a half-mile east of Four Corners on East Road (Route 179) is the entrance to secluded *Weetamoo Woods,* a sweetheart of a nature park that boasts some great natural and artificial attractions.

Named after the queen of the Pocasset Indians (the name translates as "sweetheart"), Weetamoo Woods consists of 450 acres of woodland, swamp, and rocky prominences surrounding the remains of an old mill and mill village. When you first enter the property, you will be standing on the remains of **Eight Rod Way,** a seventeenth-century cobbled road lined with stone walls. A large cedar swamp feeds the streams that cross the property, and hikers will cross a number of **ancient slab bridges** as they follow the paths to the old **Borden Mill.** Here you can see the overgrown remains of an eighteenth-century sawmill, including the dam and raceway that once fed water to the wheel that powered the mill. There is also a pretty **arched bridge,** and the remnants of the homes of mill workers also are visible. Weetamoo Woods is open sunrise to sunset. Call the Town of Tiverton, which owns the property, for more information at 624–2105.

Also worth a stop on East Road—especially if you love horses— is **Roseland Acres** (594 East Road, 624–8866), a year-round equestrian center offering guided trail rides on wooded trails and a whole lot more. Roseland Acres has horses ranging in size from 26 inches (no, not to ride) to 18 hands, and offers family hayrides and turn-of-the-century carriages for hire. The children will delight in the petting zoo with its pot-bellied pig, four-horned lamb, and Barbados sheep, and a pony ride for the little ones is simply a must.

Roseland Acres also has an indoor track available for day and evening lessons and hosts major equestrian competitions. Open daily 9:00 A.M. to 9:00 P.M.

If you've seen enough forest and crave the sounds and sights of the sea instead, head south from Four Corners on Route 77 for about $1^1/_2$ miles and look for Pond Bridge Road on your right. Take this road, past the small dam that gives it its name, until you reach Fogland Road. Make a left and look for the sign for **Fogland Beach** on your right.

The rocky beach itself is nice enough, with a small picnic area and playground located along the bay. The lack of any significant waves makes this a great spot to take the little ones. Kids of all ages, however, will enjoy looking for Tiverton's **Speaking Rocks.** Since they were discovered in the mid-1700s, the hieroglyphics carved in a set of boulders along the beach here have mystified local residents and scholars. Various theories have attributed the carvings to Norsemen, Native Americans, or other early explorers, but to this day there is no consensus as to their origin. At one time there were six carved rocks, but some were hauled away and others claimed by the sea, so today there remains only one. The carvings

Sakonnet Vineyards produces some of the East Coast's best wines, and Rhode Island is home to New England's best restaurants and one of the nation's top culinary schools, Johnson and Wales University. At the Sakonnet Cooking School, you can learn how to put fine wine and great food together to create memorable meals.

Held each spring and fall, the daylong cooking classes at Sakonnet Vineyards feature guest chefs from around the region. The hands-on instruction includes basic cooking techniques and meal preparation, with a big banquet to end the day. Visiting chefs also share their favorite recipes with students.

The one-day classes cost between $100 and $150 and include lunch, dinner, and wine. For more information, contact Sakonnet Vineyards at 635–8486.

have faded over time, but to see if you can find the last of the speaking rocks, walk along the shore about ¹/₂ mile south of Fogland Beach.

Little Compton

Nothing much has changed in Little Compton over the past couple of centuries, which suits locals just fine. From the time the area was settled in 1674 until well into the twentieth century, Little Compton's residents primarily were farmers, both working the land and raising livestock, including the famous Rhode Island Red rooster. Gentrification has come in the form of fine homes for some of the state's wealthier residents, but Little Compton still retains most of its rural charm and Yankee character.

If you do happen to find the Speaking Rocks, you may be in the mood to celebrate (especially if you've figured out what they mean). If so, you're in luck, because just over the Tiverton/Little Compton border are the cool cellars of **Sakonnet Vineyards** (left turn off Route 77/West Main Road, 635–8486; www.sakonnetvineyards.com).

Sakonnet's hospitality center lies at the end of a winding, rutted dirt road, and the abstract sculptures on the lawn lend a modern touch to an otherwise rustic setting. Inside the cool, dark center you can sample any of a dozen or so vintages available (the tasting room is open 11:00 A.M. to 5:00 P.M. daily October 1 to Memorial Day, 10:00 A.M. to 6:00 P.M. in summer). Tours of the winery run every hour on the hour; you can also pick up a map and take a self-guided tour of the vineyards themselves.

Sakonnet's chardonnays and *gewürztraminers* have received rave reviews, and the signature wine is a dry vidal blanc that is a great accompaniment to Rhode Island's fresh seafood. Sakonnet also recently released its first sparkling wine, the 1995 vintage Samson Brut, named after the winery owners. The most popular seller, however, is the Eye of the Storm, a fruity blush wine so named because it was created when white and red grapes accidentally were mixed during a hurricane. It's a great wine for a picnic, and Sakonnet is happy to oblige. You can buy the fixings for your lunch at the hospitality center, pick up a bottle of chilled wine, and sit outside to admire the rows of grapes destined to become this year's vintage.

Sakonnet Vineyards also operates a bed-and-breakfast, **The Roost,** which is in the original farmhouse on the property. The three guest rooms all have private baths, and a continental breakfast is served in the common room downstairs. Rooms are $100 nightly, plus tax. The inn is located off West Main Road, the first left south of the road that leads to the winery. Call 635–8486 for information or reservations.

It's no surprise that Sakonnet Vineyards chose a rooster as its logo; the world-famous Rhode Island Red breed was developed here, and there's even a monument to the plucky little bird in the nearby village of **Adamsville.** Perhaps the most out-of-the-way town in Rhode Island, Adamsville is located in the far northeastern corner of Little Compton and has firmer ties to Westport, Massachusetts, than to any community in Rhode Island. To get there, either follow Route 179 east from Tiverton Four Corners or make a left on Peckham Road just south of Sakonnet Vineyards. At the end of Peckham Road, make a left on Long Highway, then a quick right onto Colebrook Road, which will take you right into Adamsville.

For such a small town, Adamsville has a decent number of attractions for back-roads explorers.

The aforementioned **Rhode Island Red Monument,** located on Main Road in downtown Adamsville, is no big deal, just an inscribed plaque, really. Then again, how many towns can claim they have a monument to a chicken? Right across the street from the monument is the **Abraham Manchester Restaurant** (635–2700). Built in 1820, the restaurant building served for generations as Adamsville's general store and post office, stocking "everything from a pin to a locomotive," according to famed proprietor "Uncle Abe" Manchester.

Looking at the yellow-and-black facade fronted by a porch that still bears a sign with Manchester's name, it's not hard to imagine the days when children came to buy penny candy and travelers rode into town for some of Manchester's famous Adamsville cheese. These days, the restaurant serves a straightforward selection of steaks, seafood, chicken, and pasta dishes. Manchester's menu staples include fresh cod prepared how you like it and a weekend sautéed-dinner special. The bouillabaisse is also well regarded. Open Sunday to Thursday 11:30 A.M. to 9:00 P.M. and

Friday and Saturday, 11:30 A.M. to 10:00 P.M.; the adjoining tavern, which also serves food, stays open until 1:00 A.M.

Adjacent is **The Barn** (1 Main Road, 635–2985), which readers of *Rhode Island Monthly* say has the best breakfast in the state. This is no greasy-spoon; gourmet breakfasts served inside or on the patio out back include eggs Benedict topped with a homemade pesto hollandaise sauce, traditional Rhode Island jonnycakes, and fresh-squeezed orange juice. Open 6:00 A.M. to 11:30 A.M. weekdays and 7:00 A.M. to 1:00 P.M. on weekends.

Gray's Store (4 Main Street, 635–4566) is an Adamsville institution. Built in 1788, the store is one of the oldest in America, and it has been in the Gray family since 1879. Gray's still serves a vital function as Adamsville's sundries and grocery store, and its long history is reflected in the old soda fountain (order a malted or a frappé), antique penny-candy cases, and freestanding ice chest. Current owner Grayton Waite (his grandmother was a Gray) keeps up the Adamsville cheese tradition by carefully turning and aging his stock of Cabot cheese, and the store shelves are filled with locally made jonnycake meal and pancake mixes. Antiques, cigars, and Hannah's gifts and collectibles round out the inventory.

For many years Gray's and Manchester's across the street took turns housing the local post office, until a separate post office building finally was built to serve the town. The **old post office**, circa 1935, is still preserved in one corner of Gray's Store, including the original blotters and clerk's station.

Gray's is open 9:00 A.M. to 5:00 P.M. from Monday to Saturday and noon to 4:00 P.M. on Sunday and holidays.

Just down the road, at 26 Main Street, is **Stone Bridge Dishes** (635–4441), which over the past forty years has built an excellent reputation on its wide selection of everyday dinnerware. Located in a 130-year-old former Oddfellows Hall, Stone Bridge Dishes forgoes the fancy china in favor of durable stoneware and pottery. There are about one hundred patterns of dishes in stock, and nothing is ever discontinued by the store, so if you break a cup or lose a butter dish, chances are Stone Bridge will have a replacement. M. A. Hadley, Bennington, Quimper, and Arabia products are featured. Open Monday to Saturday from 9:30 A.M. to 5:00 P.M. and Sunday noon to 5:00 P.M.; closed Monday January through March.

From Adamsville, you need to double back on Colebrook Road to Long Highway (left) and then Peckham Road (right) to reach the next destination. After turning onto Peckham Road, take the second left onto Willow Avenue, which soon delivers you to the **Commons.**

Most people's vision of the classic New England town would fit neatly into the narrow rectangle known as the Commons, although such a setting is a rarity in Rhode Island. In fact, Little Compton owes its village structure to Massachusetts, which at one time laid claim to the town and where setting important public buildings around an open patch of land accessible to all residents was, if you'll pardon the pun, common practice.

At the green center of the Commons is the 1832 Georgian-style **United Congregational Church** and its *old graveyard.* Take a few moments to walk the rows of headstones in a setting that is remarkably tranquil considering that it is in the heart of town. This is where **Benjamin Church,** who defeated King Philip, is laid to rest. Also buried here is **Elizabeth Padobie,** daughter of John and Priscilla Alden and the first white girl born in New England. Look for the grave of **Elizabeth Palmer,** whose headstone notes that she "should have been" the wife of the man she married but refused to live with.

Surrounding the refreshingly untouristy village green are all the municipal buildings that make up the structure of a prosperous New England farming community. Individual buildings house the **Wilbur School, Grange Hall, Legion Hall,** police station, library, post office, and **Town Hall.** At the east end of the square is the **Commons Restaurant,** also known as the Commons Lunch (635–4388), which offers seafood platters at reasonable prices. The clam chowder (New England–style, of course) is excellent, lobster rolls and boiled lobsters are a specialty, and the restaurant is known for serving the East Bay's best jonnycakes.

The restaurant draws a crowd of locals as well as tourists, and you can sit at the dinerlike counter in front, the dining room in back, or out on the patio in warmer weather. Open daily 5:00 A.M. to 8:00 P.M. in summer; in winter the hours are 5:00 A.M. to 6:00 P.M. from Monday to Thursday and 5:00 A.M. to 7:00 P.M. from Friday to Sunday.

Next door to the restaurant is the **C. R. Wilbur General Store** (635– 2356), which remains essentially unchanged since it opened more than one hundred years ago. Staying true to its name, you can find almost anything you need for sale at Wilbur's—it's bigger than it looks. Open daily 7:00 A.M. to 6:00 P.M. from Monday to Saturday and 7:00 A.M. to 1:00 P.M. on Sunday.

A pair of small bed-and-breakfasts keep each other company on Long Highway, about a mile or so from the water in the quietest corner of Little Compton (and that's pretty quiet!). The **Land's End B&B** (410 Long Highway, 635–9557) offers rooms and an efficiency apartment in a bright, open contemporary home with two decks and a cookout area that guests can use. The in-ground pool is a welcome bonus for summer visitors. By contrast, the **Harmony House B&B** (456 Long Highway, 635–2283) is located on an eighteenth-century farm, the house surrounded by stone walls and gardens. Guests can choose from four rooms decorated with antiques or a cottage that's available for weekly rental. Open May through December.

Doubling back to Route 77, our next stop is the 1690 **Wilbor House** (635–4559), currently operated as a museum by the **Little Compton Historical Society.** Visitors may tour the house, with its period furniture, as well as an 1860 barn that houses a collection of horse-drawn carriages and sleighs. There also is an old one-room schoolhouse on the property. The museum is open late June to September, Tuesday to Sunday from 2:00 to 5:00 P.M. Admission is $4.00 for adults and 75 cents for children under twelve.

Not quite as old as the Wilbor House, but with perhaps a more colorful history, is **The Stone House Club,** located at the bend in the road where West Main Road becomes Sakonnet Point Road (122 Sakonnet Point Road, 635-2222; www.stonehouseclub.com). Built in 1836 by David Sisson, an engineer who built Sakonnet Point's first breakwater, the Stone House was a popular speakeasy during Prohibition and currently operates as a membership club, inn, tavern, and restaurant.

Given his experience with seaside construction, it's not surprising that Sisson built a house that has weathered more than a century of hurricanes and nor'easters, despite an exposed hillside location overlooking

Disturbing the Peace

*H*ow did the town of Little Compton come to possess such a prize piece of real estate for its Town Landing—almost five acres of beautiful waterfront property on the Sakonnet River?

Some locals say that two neighbors in the area had a long-running spat about access to the property. No sooner would one of the feuding ladies open the gate on the road, then the other would shut it.

The story goes that the fight carried over into the hereafter: When one of the women died, she left the waterfront property to the town, hoping to annoy the surviving neighbor by allowing other residents to come down and launch boats, fish, play, and picnic—presumably creating a lot of noise and traffic in the process.

If so, the strategy was not especially successful. Like most of Little Compton, the Town Landing is still a pretty sleepy place—by outsiders' standards, anyway.

a freshwater pond and the ocean beyond. The exterior of the aptly named Stone House Club is somewhat forbidding—the house is constructed of 2-foot-thick granite walls—but the inn is bright and inviting inside, with a parlor and common areas on the first floor and eleven guest rooms (including two suites) on the second and third floors.

The basement Tap Room, with a fireplace that's in use during cooler months, serves both as a cozy tavern and restaurant. True to its English pub flavor, the tavern offers a wide selection of brews, while the restaurant pays homage to the sea nightly with fresh seafood specials. Saturday is soup and sandwich night, and several interesting pasta dishes are the feature on Sunday night.

Since the Stone House is a membership club, overnight stays and use of the restaurant are limited to members and their guests. Membership fees are $25 annually per person and $40 per couple; nonmembers who want to eat at the restaurant pay a $5.00 per table fee. Excluding membership fees, the inn's room rates range from $58 to $175 per night in the high season ($48 to $150 November to April). In addition to the rooms in the Stone House Club, there also are two lofts in a converted barn on the property. Room rates include continental breakfast.

From this point, Route 77 continues south for a couple of miles and ends at **Sakonnet Point.** If you take the road to the end, you may see local fishermen pulling in their catch at the **Town Landing,** and you also can get a look at the offshore **Sakonnet Light.**

PLACES TO STAY IN
NEWPORT COUNTY

(ALL AREA CODES 401)

JAMESTOWN
Bay Voyage Inn,
150 Conanicus Avenue,
423–2100 or
(800) 225–3522

The East Bay B&B, 14
Union Street, 423–2715

Jamestown B&B,
59 Walcott Avenue,
423–1338

MIDDLETOWN
Atlantic House B&B,
37 Shore Drive, 847–7259

Bartram's B&B,
94 Kane Avenue, 846–2259

Courtyard by Marriott,
9 Commerce Drive,
849–8000 or
(800) 321–2211

The Inn at Shadow Lawn,
20 Miantonomi Avenue,
847–0902 or
(800) 352–3750

Sea Breeze B&B,
36 Kane Avenue,
847–5626

Wolcott House By the Sea,
467 Wolcott Avenue,
846–9376

PORTSMOUTH
Bestemor's House B&B,
31 West Main Road,
683–1176

Best Western Bay Point
Inn, 144 Anthony Road,
683–3600 or
(800) 289–0404

Founder's Brook Motel &
Suites, 314 Boyds Lane,
683–1244

Holiday's B&B, 20 Silva
Lane, 683–2416

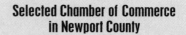

The Sakonnet River Inn,
3338 East Main Road,
683–0035

LITTLE COMPTON
Land's End B&B, 410 Long
Highway, 635–9557

**PLACES TO EAT IN
NEWPORT COUNTY**

(ALL AREA CODES 401)

JAMESTOWN
The Bay Voyage Inn,
150 Conanicus Avenue,
423–2100

Chopmist Charlie's,
40 Narragansett Avenue,
423–1020

Jamestown Oyster Bar,
22 Narragansett Avenue,
423–3380

Schoolhouse Cafe,
14 Narragansett Avenue,
423–1490

Trattoria Simpatico,
13 Narragansett Avenue,
423–3731

MIDDLETOWN
The Atlantic Grille,
91 Aquidneck Avenue,
849–4440

Sea Shai,
747 Aquidneck Avenue,
849–5180

PORTSMOUTH
15 Point Road Restaurant,
15 Point Road, 683–3138

Selected Chamber of Commerce in Newport County

Newport County Chamber of Commerce,
*45 Valley Road, Middletown 02842;
www.newportchamber.com/*

Flo's Clam Shack, Island
Park (no phone number)

Sea Fare Inn,
3352 East Main Road,
683–0577

TIVERTON
Evelyn's Drive-In, 2335
Main Road, 624–3100

Gray's Ice Cream,
16 East Road, 624–4500

Stone Bridge Restaurant,
1848 Main Road, 625–5780

The Provender,
3883 Main Road, 624–8084

LITTLE COMPTON
Abraham Manchester
Restaurant, Main Road,
Adamsville, 635–2700

The Barn, Main Road,
Adamsville, 635–4566

Commons Lunch,
The Commons, 635–4388

Crowther's, 90 Pottersville
Road, 635–8367

The Stone House Club, 122
Sakonnet Point Road,
635–2222

**OTHER ATTRACTIONS WORTH
SEEING IN NEWPORT COUNTY**

Butts Hill Fort, *Portsmouth*

Jamestown Fire Department
Memorial and Museum,
Jamestown

Memorial to Black Soldiers,
Portsmouth

Wilbor House,
Little Compton

**HELPFUL WEB SITES
ABOUT NEWPORT COUNTY**

Jamestown Community
Homepage,
www.jamestownri.com

Tiverton Guide,
http://tiverton.org

Town of Middletown,
www.middletown
ri.com/

Town of Portsmouth,
www.portsmouth
ri.com/

Discover the Coastal
Villages,
www.coastalvillages.com

South County— North Kingstown and Inland

People talk a lot about how small Rhode Island is, yet more diversity is packed into South County than is found in some whole states. Here you run the gamut from the genteel resort ambience of Watch Hill to the honky-tonk of nearby Misquamicut, from dense wilderness to waves crashing onto pristine beaches. There are the subdivisions of North Kingstown and the country lanes of Exeter, surfing in Narragansett and skiing at Yawgoo Valley. And there is the otherworldly atmosphere of secluded Block Island, with its mix of Victorian hotels and natural wonders that led the Nature Conservancy to name the island one of the last great habitats left on earth.

If South County lacks anything, it's a big city, but that's fine with folks around here, who have fought casinos and giant retailers alike to preserve the rural character of their home. By the way, if you look at a map, you'll see that the region is called Washington County. Don't call it that, though, because no one will know what you're talking about. South County is not only a name, it's a state of mind.

North Kingstown

One of the oldest highways in America, **Post Road** follows the course of the old Pequot Trail, a main thoroughfare for native tribes even before Europeans settled the shores of Narragansett Bay in the seventeenth century. Later, Post Road became the major mail and stagecoach route between New York and Boston (in fact, in many stretches it still is known as the Boston Post Road) and remained a major artery until the advent of the national highway system and the construction of Interstate 95 some fifty years ago.

In Rhode Island, much of the northern part of Post Road remains a well-traveled byway, while in the southern part of the state a large stretch of

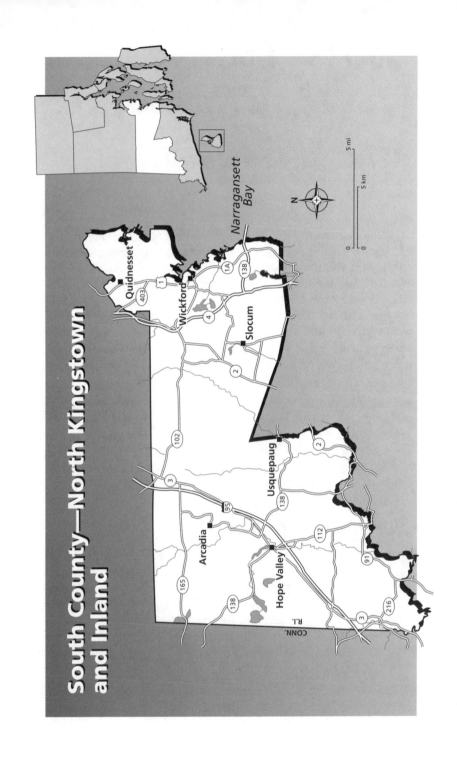

South County—North Kingstown and Inland

Narragansett Bay

CONN.
R.I.

Quidnesset
Wickford
Slocum
Usquepaug
Arcadia
Hope Valley

403
1
1A
138
4
2
102
3
95
165
138
138
112
91
216
3

N

5 mi
5 km
0
0

superhighway was built between North Kingstown and Westerly. This is the express route to South County's beautiful ocean beaches, although on beach mornings and evenings it can sometimes resemble a very long parking lot. This part of Route 1 actually bypasses much of Old Post Road, which still exists in many places as Scenic Route 1A.

A great way to sample many of North Kingstown's hidden treasures is to take a drive on one of the older stretches of Route 1/Post Road, starting at the intersection of Route 1/Post Road and Route 403/Devil's Foot Road. (Route 403 is the second exit off Route 4 south; bear left off the ramp.)

Quonset Point lent its name to the famous domed huts created here by the Seabees during World War II, and the mascot of the Naval Construction Battalion ("CBs," get it?)—a giant, wrench-carrying honeybee—guarded the entrance to the military base (The Seabee was recently restored and returned to public display.) During the war, just about every American naval fighter, dive-bomber, and torpedo bomber pilot was trained at the former Quonset Point Naval Air Station or one of its satellite bases.

This remarkable period of Rhode Island history is preserved at the **Quonset Air Museum** (Hangar 488, Eccleston Avenue; 294–9540), located at Quonset Point State Airport. Route 403/Devil's Foot Road ends at the base, and to get to the museum you make a right turn at the

The Devil's Footprints

*L*ocal legend has it that the Devil, old Satan himself, once stomped his way across North Kingstown, leaving his cloven hoof-prints on a spot known since at least 1671 as Devil's Foot Rock.

There are a number of stories about the strange markings on Devil's Foot Rock, located just off Post Road (Route 1) near the intersection with Devil's Foot Road (Route 403) near Quonset Point. The most interesting tale involves a local Indian woman who supposedly sold her soul to the Devil and would brew up potions and spells on the rock ledge. When the Devil came to claim her soul, the story goes, the woman ran off, and the Devil left his footprints as he chased her.

Although parts of Devil's Foot Rock (also known as Devil's Foot Ledge, the Devil's Footprint, and the Devil's Tracks) have been lost to road construction and quarrying, two of the "footprints" remain visible. There's a spot on the west side of Post Road just south of the railroad bridge near Quonset Point where you can park, and from there it's a quick scramble up the rock formation that overlooks the railroad tracks, to the footprints themselves.

traffic signal onto Quonset Road, then drive approximately 2 miles and make a left on Eccleston Avenue. Look for the Quonset Air Museum hangar on your right.

Described by the late curator, Howard Weekley, Jr., as a "working museum in progress," the Quonset Air Museum will not be mistaken for the Smithsonian. Located in the air base's old, brick Hangar 488, this fledgling museum has grown by leaps and bounds in recent years and now contains an impressive collection of vintage and unusual aircraft. Staff are constantly working to restore their fifty-year-old planes and repair the aging hangar.

It is fascinating to watch the restoration process and realize the amount of work it takes to bring an old aircraft back into presentable shape after decades of neglect, as is the case with the museum's Grumman F6F Hellcat. Salvaged from the bottom of the ocean off Martha's Vineyard, the World War II fighter is undergoing a restoration expected to take another decade to complete.

Awesome Air Show

*M*y family and I recently moved to a beautiful new home, but the one thing we really miss about our modest ranch house in North Kingstown is being within biking distance of the annual Rhode Island National Air Show, held in early June at Quonset State Airport.

The week before the air show was always full of great anticipation, especially with the Blue Angels' FA-18s skating across the sky at treetop height as they rehearsed their incredible precision-flying routine. On the weekend of the big two-day show, we would jump on our bicycles and pedal over to the sprawling, mostly abandoned Quonset Point base. The first time, the longish ride provoked some protests from the children, but all that was cured when a giant C5-A Galaxy transport flew directly over us on the way to the show, barely 200 feet up. The kids weren't scared—they were hooked.

The Quonset air show is one of the nation's best and features some of the most interesting aircraft in the world. In past years we've seen a Russian MIG-29 demonstrate high-performance turns over the airfield and marveled as a Harrier jet showed off its vertical-takeoff capabilities. An F-117 stealth fighter also has made a few visits to the tarmac, guarded by serious-looking soldiers carrying assault weapons (the unspoken but clear message: Look, but don't touch!).

If you can bicycle in, you'll save the parking fee (donated to charity) and a lot of time waiting in traffic at the end of the day. Either way, though, the show is highly recommended.

The Hellcat is just one example of the aircraft Quonset Point; others include the Grumman TBM Avenger torpedo bomber and the Sikorsky SH3 Sea King helicopter, both of which also are part of the museum's collection. In all, the Quonset Air Museum has seventeen aircraft on permanent display, including a Polish Air

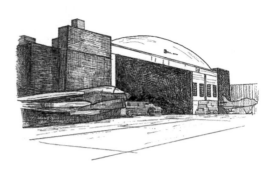

Quonset Air Museum

Force MiG-17F, a couple of Douglas A-4 Skyhawks, and a huge Russian Antonov AN-2 "Colt," the world's largest biplane. New additions include the world's only surviving Curtis X-15C jet and an F4 Phantom. Other assorted military equipment and memorabilia also are on display, including a 1940s-vintage U.S Army half-track.

The Quonset Air Museum is open year-round Friday to Sunday from 10:00 A.M. to 3:30 P.M. Admission is $4.00 for adults and $2.00 for children under age twelve.

Smith's Castle at Cocumscussoc (55 Richard Smith Drive, 294–3521) frequently surprises visitors, who turn onto the access road off Route 1/Post Road looking for some sort of medieval fortress and find only a simple wooden house. When first raised around 1638, the original structure on this site was a fortress, a blockhouse that could be used by early settlers to defend against attack from the native tribes in the area.

Thanks to the efforts of Roger Williams, for more than half a century no such defense was needed against the local inhabitants. Williams lived and preached at Cocumscussoc for many years and established peaceful relations with Conanicus and Miantinomi, the chiefs of the Narragansetts. It was not until 1675 that hostilities broke out between the white settlers and the native tribes, resulting in the 1676 burning of Smith's Castle and ending with the Great Swamp Massacre, where the Narragansetts were nearly annihilated by armies from Massachusetts and Connecticut. Rebuilt in 1678, Smith's Castle later became a prosperous plantation and political center for the former Narragansett territory.

Presently maintained by the Cocumscussoc Association, the house and grounds are open to visitors from May through September. Not only are

Author's Favorite Attractions/ Events in South County— North Kingstown and Inland

Wickford

Step Stone Falls

Yawgoo Valley Ski Area and Water Park

Casey Farm

Allie's Donuts

Wickford Art Festival, North Kingstown; July

Wickford Festival of Lights, North Kingstown; December

International Quahog Festival, North Kingstown; August

Strawberry Festival, Smith's Castle, North Kingstown; June

Rhode Island National Guard Air Show, North Kingstown; June

National Guard Leapfest (skydiving show), Richmond; July

Washington County Fair, Richmond; August

Cajun and Bluegrass Festival, Exeter; September

Colonial Crafts Festival, Hopkinton; September

the historic house and its eighteenth-century garden worth a visit, but the plantation also sits on a lovely cove facing a small island, deeded by the wife of Conanicus to Roger Williams so that he could graze his goats.

House tours are conducted from noon to 4:00 P.M. Thursday through Monday from June through August and Friday through Sunday in May and September. Tours also can be arranged by appointment. You can visit the grounds any time of year. Admission to the house and tour is $3.00 for adults, $1.00 for children under age twelve. The turnoff for Smith's Castle is located on the east side of Route 1/Post Road, approximately 1½ miles south of Quonset Point.

Just south of Smith's Castle, on the right side of the road past the state police barracks, is a small wooded spot called **Richard Smith's Grove.** This is a nice place to stop for a picnic lunch, and it also offers access (but no trail) to undeveloped Cocum-scussoc State Park, a dense, stream-fed woodland.

The next intersection you will come to is the turnoff for Route 1A, which leads south through the village of Wickford and into Narragansett. If you keep going straight on Route 1, you'll soon come to **Duffy's Tavern** (235 Tower Hill Road, 294–3733), the place to stop for good, inexpensive seafood right off the boat. Duffy's is notable for its big patio area (complete with outdoor bar and a small stage for live music), which is used for summer clambakes and lobster cookouts. Open 11:30 A.M. to 9:00 P.M. Monday through Thursday, 11:30 A.M. to 10:00 P.M. Friday and Saturday, and noon to 9:00 P.M. on Sunday. If you make this pit stop, though, be sure to double back and pick up the road to Wickford.

The seaside village of **Wickford** gets a lot of attention for its distinctive, upscale specialty shops and its annual art festival, one of the largest on the East Coast. But this charming little town also has a sometimes overlooked series of quiet residential streets dating from the eighteenth and nineteenth centuries. On Church Lane, accessible via a narrow footpath off Main Street, sits the **Old Narragansett**

The Navy's Fightin' Engineers

*F*ile clerk Frank Iafrate was working at the massive Quonset Point Naval Air Station in January 1942 when a Navy lieutenant approached him with a strange request: Could he design an insignia for a new unit of construction engineers, one that would reflect both their building and fighting prowess?

Iafrate, an amateur artist, agreed. His first choice for a mascot was a beaver, praised for its industriousness. But research showed that beavers usually run away when confronted with danger—not exactly the image the Navy wanted for its fightin' engineers.

Instead, Iafrate settled upon the bee—another hard worker that has a nasty sting when provoked. Asked to draw a Disneyesque character, Iafrate sketched a honey-bee wearing a sailor's cap and holding a machine gun, wrench, and hammer in his white-gloved (à la Mickey Mouse) hands. It was a fitting mascot for men who built airfields on islands across the Pacific, driving payloaders with a gun at their side—which they often were forced to use.

When Iafrate took his bee and stuck a naval reference in front of it, the famous nickname for the Construction Battalions was born: the Seabees.

Church (294–4357), built in 1707 and one of the oldest Episcopal churches in America. The church, moved to its present location in 1800, has a fine collection of Queen Anne communion silver and houses the oldest church organ in North America, manufactured in 1680. Famous portrait artist Gilbert Stuart was baptized here, and there's an old cemetery across the quiet, shady street. Open 11:00 A.M. to 4:00 P.M., Friday to Sunday from mid-June to mid-September.

Perhaps the town's most intriguing (and mouthwatering) shop is *Wickford Gourmet Foods* (21 West Main Street, 295–8190 or 800–286–8190), a two-story building stuffed with exotic pasta, canned fruits and vegetables, spices, cookware, and dishes, not to mention a gourmet deli counter, a coffee bar, and a small cafe upstairs. "Rhode Island elves" are credited with creating the Rhode Island Gift Basket, full of such goodies as Kenyon's jonnycake and pancake mixes, Eclipse coffee syrup, and jam from a Little Compton berry farm. Open Monday through Saturday 8:30 A.M. to 6:00 P.M., Sunday 8:00 A.M. to 5:00 P.M., and an hour later each day during the summer.

Not only is the *Seaport Tavern* (16 West Main Street , 294–5771) the only restaurant with a liquor license in the village of Wickford, it's the only one that's open for dinner. But those are far from the only reasons to check out this charming little eatery. Owner and chef Efendi Atma offers a remarkably large menu of hot and cold appetizers, gourmet pizzas (including one that honors his Turkish heritage, made with feta cheese, roasted garlic, and black olives), soups, salads, sandwiches, and a variety of seafood, steaks, pasta, and other entrees.

The dining room is tiny, so it's best to come when the weather is favorable and you can relax under an umbrella on the restaurant's two-level deck, which looks out over the tidal channel and pond that bisect the village. The Seaport Tavern is open 11:00 A.M. to 10:00 P.M. every day, except Monday, when only lunch is served (11:00 A.M. to 5:00 P.M.).

For an even closer look at Wickford Harbor, you group can charter the yacht **Brandaris,** which you'll find anchored across the street from the Seaport Tavern. This beautiful wooden sailing vessel is available for nature excursions and sight-seeing tours; call 294–1481 for information.

The annual **Wickford Art Festival** is held on the second weekend in July and attracts more than 200 artists, who display their work up and down Brown Street. The festival always is a lot of fun, although the crowds may have you wishing the town fathers had installed wider sidewalks. (For more information call the Wickford Art Association at

Beware the Quahog

*G*lance at the menu in a Rhode Island restaurant, and chances are you'll find an exotic-sounding dish alongside the more familiar scrod, shrimp, and lobsters: the quahog, or quahaug . But don't go asking the waiter why there's some kind of pork dish listed with the seafood: Quahog is the fancy name for a native Rhode Island clam.

Officially Artica islandia, *the ocean quahog is a bivalve mollusk that populates the ocean waters off Rhode Island as well as Narragansett Bay. Locally, it's used to make quahog chowder, quahog cakes, stuffed quahogs—even quahog chili. Local cartoonist and humorist Don Bousquet has even made a tidy living playing off Rhode Islanders' fondness for this funny-sounding clam. (For the record, Webster's says it's pronounced "KWA-hog," but if you want to sound like a local you should say "KO-hog.")*

Quahogs are so popular in Rhode Island that an International Quahog Festival was launched a few years back. Held in August in Wickford, the festival includes a quahog shucking contest, live music, a stuffie cooking contest (a stuffie being a stuffed clam or quahog), and, of course, quahogs cooked in every imaginable way. For more information, visit the festival Web site at www.quahog.com, or call Duffy's Tavern at 294–9606.

294–6840). An equally pleasant time to visit Wickford, but with a much more local flavor, is during the village's annual *Festival of Lights*, held in early December to herald the arrival of the Christmas season. The town Christmas tree is lit, as are festive lights all along the business district, the streets come alive with the sounds of carolers, and horses drawing hay wagons clip-clop around town. The lights stay on throughout the holiday season. For information contact the North Kingstown Chamber of Commerce at 295–5566.

Gilbert Stuart Birthplace and Museum

Other than during the annual art festival—when the town fairly bustles—Wickford is a pretty quiet place year-round, making it a nice setting for a cluster of *bed-and-breakfasts*, most located in historic homes in or near downtown. In the heart of the village is *The Haddie Pierce House* (146 Boston Neck Road, 294–7674), a three-story Victorian topped by a widow's walk—a standard feature for almost every seaport home built in the seventeenth and eighteenth centuries. A bit farther away from "town" you can immerse yourself in Victoriana at *Mount Maple of Wickford* (730 Annaquatucket Road, 295–4373), a B&B in an 1862 home that's surrounded by a huge veranda. Mount Maple has three rooms with private baths, ranging in price from $90 to $110 nightly.

Leaving Wickford, you must make a left at the end of Brown Street and cross a small bridge to continue on Route 1A. Drive south for roughly 4 miles until you reach Snuff Mill Road; make the right and follow Snuff Mill Road until it ends at Gilbert Stuart Road. Make a left here and you will almost immediately come to a small bridge crossing the Mattatuxet Brook. On the right side of the road is the beautifully restored *Gilbert Stuart Birthplace and Museum* (815 Gilbert Stuart Road in Saunderstown, 294–3001).

Whether you know it or not, a little bit of Gilbert Stuart likely passes through your hands each day. Stuart, born in 1755, is the portraitist who painted the most famous likeness of George Washington, which appears on the face of the dollar bill. Fittingly, the museum includes reproductions of Stuart's greatest works, including portraits of the first five presidents of the United States.

Stuart's family home, one of several structures on the museum site, is an interesting combination of dwelling and workplace. The upper floors of the two-and-a-half-story, gambrel-roofed home (circa 1751) is where the family ate and slept, warmed by corner fireplaces in each room. But in the basement, in the same room as the kitchen, stands a water-powered snuff mill, the source of the Stuart family's prosperity. The mill, powered by a waterwheel under the house, has been fully restored, and tour guides show how the mill was used to grind tobacco into snuff.

The museum grounds are especially lovely, located in a remote spot next to a rushing stream fed by an impressive waterfall. Behind the house is tranquil Carr Pond, and nearby bubbles the Eye Spring, which local legend says has curative powers for conditions ocular. The other major structure on the site is a wooden gristmill filled with old grindstones.

The Gilbert Stuart Birthplace and Museum is open April through October, Thursday through Monday 11:00 A.M. to 4:00 P.M. Admission is $3.00 for adults and $1.00 for children ages six to twelve.

Return to Route 1A and proceed south for another half-mile. Watch for a farm surrounded by an old stone wall on your right side. At the light blue sign, turn right into the driveway.

You are drawn to **Casey Farm** (295–1030) by the circa 1750 farmhouse and the promise of fresh eggs and produce, but even better are the parts of the farm you don't immediately notice.

The farmers who still live and work at Casey Farm raise a variety of crops and livestock, much as farmers here have done for generations. Tours of the farmhouse are conducted regularly when the farm is open to the public, but Casey Farm also functions as a working museum, where visitors can explore the fields, barns, and pens while they actually are being used.

Situated between Narragansett Bay and the Pettaquamscutt (Narrow) River, Casey Farm flourished because goods could be moved easily to either waterway for transportation. Fortunately, the Society for the Preservation of New England Antiquities, which manages the farm, was able to obtain the property intact, so visitors can follow trails well beyond the cultivated fields. One such trail leads past the overgrown stone walls that mark the path of an old road to the riverbank, while another (across Route 1A) leads down to the rocky shoreline of the bay. In all, there are 300 acres of Casey Farm to enjoy.

There's a lot of history to this old farm, as well: Silas Casey was a general during the Civil War, and Thomas Lincoln Casey was an architect who helped design the Washington Monument and Grant's Tomb. Casey Farm is located on Route 1A in Saunderstown, 1 mile south of the intersection with Route 138. The farm is open to visitors from June 1 to October 15 on Tuesday, Thursday, and Saturday 1:00 to 5:00 P.M. Admission is $3.00 for adults, $2.50 for seniors, and $1.50 for children ages six to twelve.

A detour is necessary in order to see some of North Kingstown's other points of interest. Route 102, known locally as Ten Rod Road, connects with both Route 1A (at the southern end of Brown Street in Wickford village) and Route 1/Post Road (south of the Route 1A turnoff). Taking Route 102 west from Wickford, you'll pass though the old village of *Lafayette,* with its restored brick mill (now used for offices) and fine old homes. If you make the left turn onto Lafayette Road, you'll be rewarded by a fine view of the *old mill pond;* pause for a breath of fresh air or a photo before continuing to the entrance to the new *Ryan Park,* which follows the railbed of the old New York, New Haven, and Hartford Railroad line into Wickford.

Park in the lot on the left side of the road, and you have a choice of following the old railroad right-of-way west to Wickford Junction or heading east on one of two trails. Closer to the Lafayette mill and mill pond is the graded railbed, where you will still find the occasional arched stone bridge, old ties, and spikes in the woods. If you walk directly east from the parking lot, there's a sunnier dirt path that meanders over open fields and into the woods. Both pass by secluded *Belleville Pond* and are ideal for hiking or mountain biking.

Returning to Route 102, continue west and pass under the railroad tunnel that marks Wickford Junction. On your right you'll see a new shopping center with a string of stores on the west side of a roundabout. This is the home of *Martino's Pizzeria* (1051 Ten Rod Road, #7; 295–9382), the best place to get thin-crust, brick-oven-baked New York–style pizza in South County. The storefront locale is belied by a spacious, bistrolike dining room adorned with frescoes that look good enough to eat. A full menu of pasta dishes and other Italian specialties also is served. Open 11:30 A.M. to 9:00 P.M. Monday to Thursday and till 10:00 P.M. on Friday and Saturday.

Another $1/2$-mile drive will bring you to the intersection with Route 2

A Trio of Hatcheries

Besides the Lafayette Trout Hatchery, the state of Rhode Island maintains two other fish hatcheries that you can visit: the Perryville Trout Hatchery (783–5358) in South Kingstown, off Old Post Road just west of the terminus of Route 110/Ministerial Road (783–5358); and one in Richmond in the Arcadia Management Area (539–7333), off Arcadia Road, where salmon are raised.

All three hatcheries are open Monday to Friday 9:00 A.M. to 3:00 P.M., and admission is free.

north, known here as Quaker Lane. Make the right onto Route 2 and proceed for about a mile to our next stop, which is on your left.

Rhode Islanders love their donuts. In fact, the state seems to have a donut obsession, and it's hard to drive too far on any major road without passing a donut shop of one kind or another. But the undisputed champion of Rhode Island donutry is **Allie's Donuts** at 3661 Quaker Lane (295–8036).

Rhode Islanders, who as a rule don't like to drive anywhere, will make the trip from Providence and beyond to pick up donuts from Allie's. If you have never had anything other than franchise-type donuts, then you're in for a treat. Unlike those other shops, which tend to pile a lot of sugar onto rather lightweight donuts full of air pockets, Allie's donuts are dense and heavy, with less emphasis on the sweet and more on the cake. The effect is a much more subtle experience. Crunchy on the outside, soft on the inside, the donuts are like the ones your grandmother used to make. It says something about the quality of Allie's donuts when one of the most popular varieties is the plain, unglazed Old Fashioned.

Allie's is open 5:00 A.M. to 3:00 P.M. Monday through Friday and 6:00 A.M. to 1:00 P.M. on Saturday and Sunday.

Doubling back to Route 102/Ten Rod Road, travel another mile west, passing the interchange for Route 4. Soon you'll reach the intersection with Route 2, also known as the South County Trail. Make the left turn onto Route 2 south, and the first major landmark you'll come to is **Schartner's Farms** (1 Arnold Place, Exeter, 885–5510), on your right. Schartner's is the place where many South County residents come for their fresh produce, and their fruit pies are also top-notch. Schartner's does it all: berry picking in the summer, pumpkin picking in the fall, and cut-your-own Christmas trees in the winter. They also have a large greenhouse and a stand out front selling fresh-cut and deep-fried french fries, made from red potatoes pulled from Schartner's own fields. Open daily 8:00 A.M. to 6:00 P.M. and till 7:00 P.M. in summer; closed the months of January and February.

Just south of Schartner's Farms is Hatchery Road (on your left), which twists through the woods for about a half-mile before reaching the access road for the *Lafayette Trout Hatchery.*

Established in the 1920s, the trout hatchery is the main supplier of brook trout and rainbow trout for local ponds and rivers, which are stocked each year for sport fishing and to try to repopulate the species. The hatchery includes pools and a mesh-covered raceway teeming with trout fry of varying sizes, more than 60,000 in all. (The enclosures keep raccoons and birds from eating the fish.)

The kids will love this place, and the staff at the state-owned facility can explain how the hatchery works; there's an organized tour for children if you call ahead and make an appointment (294–4662).

Exeter

Although the owners certainly would prefer otherwise, the *Yawgoo Valley Ski Area and Water Park* (294–3802) remains one of Rhode Island's most overlooked attractions. Even many local skiers don't realize that there's a ski area right in their own backyard. With two chairlifts and a vertical drop of just a couple of hundred feet, Yawgoo won't be drawing any comparisons with Vail or Stowe. But as they like to say around here, it's not the height of the mountain, it's how many times you go up and down that counts.

The truth is that Yawgoo, with four main trails, makes a nice, affordable afternoon or evening of winter fun, either on its own merits or as a tune-up for a trip to the big mountains up north. It's also a good place to learn to ski, especially for kids, who also can try out the new snow-tubing hill on the south side of the park. Yawgoo has a base lodge restaurant and bar—just like the big ski resorts—and has recently added snow-tubing to its winter-fun activities.

During the summer Yawgoo operates a twin-tube water slide that's a lot of fun on a hot day. There's also a kiddie pool, a golf course, and a beach volleyball court. To get to Yawgoo Valley, take Route 2/South County Trail south of the intersection with Route 102/Ten Rod Road for approximately 4 miles, then make a left on Yawgoo Valley Road; drive for 1 mile, and the park will be on your right.

Running from Voluntown, Connecticut, to Wickford, Rhode Island, *Ten Rod Road*'s name refers to its width. Constructed in the early eighteenth century, the road was built 10 rods (165 feet) wide to allow farmers to drive herds of cattle down to the seaport in Wickford. Exploring the rest of rural Exeter is relatively easy, since nearly everything is located on or near scenic Ten Rod Road.

As you head west from the intersection of Ten Rod Road/Route 102 and South County Trail/Route 2, you pass through some lovely countryside, especially where the road dips into a small valley that is partially filled by the golf course at the **Exeter Country Club.** After passing the town grange, look for Widow Sweets Road on your right. (The town clerk's office is on this corner.) Turn onto Widow Sweets Road, then make the right on Pardon Joslin Road and follow the signs to the parking area of the **Fisherville Brook Wildlife Refuge** (949–5454).

This small (seventy-acre) refuge has 5 miles of trails that cross bridges over the Fisherville Brook, cut through stands of white pine, and skirt a historic cemetery. There's also a small dam and waterfall from an artificial pond on the property. The refuge is maintained by the Audubon Society and is open daily from dawn to dusk.

As you continue west on Route 102 past Tripps Corner Road, the paved road suddenly veers off to the north, while a smaller, wooded road continues straight ahead in a westerly direction. This actually is the continuation of Ten Rod Road (hereafter known alternatively as Route 165), so make sure you get off the main road at this point.

Almost immediately you'll come to an intersection with Gardiner Road. Make the left turn here and proceed south to the **Spring Hill Sugar House** (522 Gardiner Road, 295–7273).

You'll see the sign for Spring Hill Sugar House on the right side of the road; pull in the driveway, and the combination shop and maple syrup factory is at the bottom of the hill. Don't worry if nobody is behind the counter; you're welcome to walk in and look around, and there's an honor box if you decide to buy anything.

There's a lot to consider buying, too. Maple syrup, tapped from trees on the farm, is available in sizes ranging from a tiny sampler ($2.50) to a half-gallon ($20.00) for those Paul Bunyan types. If you want to wean the youngsters off the store-brand pancake syrups (which contain little or no maple syrup), give them a maple lollipop to suck on ($1.25).

The back of the shop building is filled with the evaporators that are used to distill the raw syrup that comes out of the maple trees each spring. If you visit on weekends between March and mid-April, you can see a demonstration of the whole sap-boiling process, from tapping the trees to the finished product. In September and October, owners Gibby Fountain and Brian Tefft start pressing apples for cider, also for sale in the shop. Fountain also breeds llamas and Sicilian donkeys, which the kids can visit in a pen just a few steps away.

When you're writing a book about out-of-the-way places in Rhode Island, there's no way you can resist including the **Middle of Nowhere Diner** (222 Nooseneck Hill Road/Route 3, 397–8855). It's tiny, but the friendly staff will treat you like locals and serve up great diner burgers and yummy fish and chips on Friday night. After returning to Ten Rod Road from the Sugar House, continue west to the intersection with Route 3. Make a right, and this short detour will bring you to the diner. The name says it all. Stop here if you're wandering the boondocks and need a bite to eat. Open daily 5:00 A.M. to 8:00 P.M.

After crossing Route 3 and going under Route 95, Ten Rod Road/Route 165 reverts back from dirt to pavement. Drive for $1/2$ mile, and on your right you'll see a sign for **The Christmas House** (1557 Ten Rod Road, 397–4255).

If you come to The Christmas House during the weeks leading up to Christmas, you might wonder whether "madhouse" would have been a more appropriate name. This old three-story farmhouse is crammed

Biking Arcadia

*O*ne of the many ways that you can enjoy the Arcadia Management Area is on a mountain bike. The huge park has miles and miles of narrow trails (known to mountain bikers as "singletrack"), fire roads, and graded dirt roads for both hiking and biking, with tracks suitable for novice riders as well as those that should be tackled only by experts.

One of the things mountain bikers like best about Arcadia is that there are very few people crowding the trails; it's also something you need to be aware of if you decide to hike or bike in Arcadia. While it may not be comparable to the backcountry at Yellowstone, Arcadia is about as wild as Rhode Island gets. Bring plenty of water and a compass.

Many of the Arcadia trails can be accessed on the north and south sides of Ten Rod Road; you can simply park your car and go, but stopping beforehand for a trail map from the Arcadia park ranger's office (539–2356—another significant trailhead, with ample parking) on Arcadia Road is highly recommended. You can also request a trail map by sending a self-addressed, stamped envelope to the Northeast Mountain Bikers Association, Rhode Island Chapter, 245 Old Coach Road, Charlestown 02813.

Tooling Down the Back Roads of Exeter

If you've got one of those rugged-looking SUVs that's never left the comfort of pavement, here's your big chance to get some mud under the fenders. Rural Exeter has a great network of dirt roads to explore, cutting through thick forests, past Colonial-style farmhouses and an old Quaker meetinghouse, and up and down challenging hills.

Often rutted, always bumpy, and sometimes treacherous after a hard rain, graded dirt tracks like Frosty Hollow Road, Skunk Hill Road, and Plain Road can put your driving skills and dental work to the test. Exeter also is crossed by the New London Turnpike, perhaps the longest dirt road in Southern New England. This dusty, ancient byway runs all the way from Richmond through Exeter and West Greenwich before reverting to blacktop in Coventry.

with every type of Christmas ornament and decoration you can imagine, many hanging on the dozens of Christmas trees located throughout the store. One room is filled with crystal, another with Christmas bears, and another with angels and cherubs. There are nutcrackers from Germany, music boxes and candles, and a wide variety of lighted villages and collectible dolls.

During the holidays, cars line the local roads as shoppers flock to The Christmas House to find that perfect gift or finishing touch for their trim-a-tree, but the store is open year-round, so you really can celebrate Christmas in August. On the other hand, this quaint place is best appreciated when the snow covers the ground, especially when you take a ride on the horse-drawn sleigh that follows a path in the woods behind the store. Sleigh rides are offered after Columbus Day on Saturday and Sunday noon to 5:00 P.M. and every night from 6:00 to 8:00 P.M. during the holiday season. It costs $4.00 to ride.

The Christmas House is open Monday through Saturday 10:00 A.M. to 5:00 P.M. and Sunday noon to 5:00 P.M. After Labor Day the store opens at 11:00 A.M. on Sunday, and on Thursday it stays open until 9:00 P.M. There are extended hours during the Christmas season.

Continuing west, Ten Rod Road soon enters the dense forest of the **Arcadia Management Area,** a 13,000-acre, state-managed wilderness of woodland, ponds, and trees with numerous hiking trails and places to swim. One of the park's best beaches is the **Browning Mill Pond Recreation Area** (539–2356), where you can swim in the pond or in a stream-fed pool that is perfect for children. Reach the park by making a left off Ten Rod Road onto Arcadia Road.

Continuing a bit farther west on Ten Rod Road, take the left turn for Summit Road and proceed to the **Tomaquag Indian Memorial Museum** (386 Summit Road, 539–7213).

Part of the purpose of the Tomaquag Museum, says caretaker and board member Loren Spears, is to remind visitors that the local Native

American tribes did not vanish in the seventeenth century, as some school textbooks assert, but remain a vital part of Rhode Island culture. Spears, Dawn Dove, and many other Native Americans, including members of the Narragansett tribe, help to run the museum, which for forty years has been collecting and displaying artifacts from New England tribes and others from as far away as Alaska.

Particularly significant are the museum's collection of handmade dolls and baskets, the latter woven by Northeastern tribes from birch bark and porcupine quills. There also are arrowheads, ax heads, and beadwork on display, as well as photos of Narragansett tribal leaders of the past.

The Tomaquag Indian Memorial Museum is open on Wednesday and Sunday during the summer from 10:00 A.M. to 2:00 P.M. and other times by appointment. Admission is $2.00 for adults and children over age twelve.

Step Stone Falls technically is just across the town line in *West Greenwich,* but the best way to get there is off Ten Rod Road. From the Tomaquag Museum, double back to Route 165, then make a left and head west to Escoheag Hill Road (approximately $2^3/_{10}$ miles). Make a right and head north past *Stepping Stone Ranch* (201 Escoheag Hill Road, 397–3725; www.steppingstoneranch.com), an oddball mix of horse farm and concert venue in the tiny village of Escoheag. Each fall Stepping Stone Ranch hosts a huge outdoor *Cajun and Bluegrass Festival,* touted as the largest outside New Orleans.

On a more everyday basis, the ranch offers horseback rides and hayrides, and there's a snack bar on the grounds, too. For a unique experience, saddle up for one of the ranch's overnight trail rides, which include a five-hour ride, dinner, breakfast, and a stay in a lakefront cabin. Overnight rides are offered for groups of eight persons from May to October and cost about $110 per person.

Leaving the few houses of Escoheag behind, continue north to Falls River Road and make a right. From here you'll have a slow (15 mph) half-mile drive over a bumpy dirt road to the parking lot for Step Stone Falls, located just before a small concrete bridge that spans the Falls River. (Look for a sign marking the nature trails.)

Not only is this one of Rhode Island's most obscure attractions, it is also one of the most lovely. The Step Stone Falls get their name from the series of rock ledges that the rushing water pours over on its way downhill; the ledges, only partially covered by water, make an excellent spot for sunbathing or picnicking. (*Note:* If you want to see the falls at their peak, come in the springtime; it's still a pretty spot in midsummer, but the water flow does tend to slacken in the warmest part of the year.) On the west side of the falls is a nature trail that follows the river downstream, passing near an abandoned campground and the remains of an old sawmill and gristmill along the way.

Hopkinton

Toddlers and younger children will love the **Enchanted Forest of Rhode Island** (539–7711), located on Route 3 off exit 2 on I–95 in Hope Valley. Calling the park a forest is no marketing gimmick: This kiddie amusement park is spread over a couple of acres of woodland, with shady paths leading from one attraction to the next. The park has a fairy-tale theme, with trails leading to the kid-sized Three Little Pigs House and the crooked House That Jack Built. Farm animals wander the grounds, and there also are a petting zoo, hayrides, and a nature trail, all on a small enough scale that the little ones won't feel overwhelmed.

The nice thing about the Enchanted Forest is the way the staff caters to children. Ride attendants constantly ask young guests if they are having a good time, and if a little boy or girl gets scared on the carousel, rollercoaster, or Ferris wheel, the ride is stopped so the child can get off. Older children and adults tend to gravitate to the miniature golf course, go-karts, and batting cages. The park also has a restaurant and numerous snack stands, although many families take advantage of the ample picnic areas found throughout the forest.

The Enchanted Forest is open 10:00 A.M. to 5:00 P.M. seven days a week from June 20 to Labor Day and on weekends from mid-May to mid-June and in September. Admission of $9.95 for everyone age two and up includes most rides and minigolf. (Batting cages and go-karts are a small extra fee.)

Richmond

Off Route 112 is the Washington County Fairgrounds, which is nothing more than a big field, unless you happen to come by in mid-August, when it comes to life with the opening of the annual **Washington County Fair.**

With its country music, livestock exhibits, truck pulls, and rodeo, the Washington County Fair may seem somewhat incongruous to visitors who think of New England in terms of colonial-era homes and lobster-in-the-rough. But the truth is that many parts of Rhode Island are fiercely proud of their agrarian past and present, and the fair fits right into the semirural, small-town patina evident in most of the state.

Even for city slickers, the Washington County Fair is a great time. Each year a giant midway with food booths, rides, and games is created, and special events include tractor pulls, pie-eating contests, and, yes, a dung-throwing contest. Special events for children include a cow-milking contest, costume parade, three-legged race, and pedal tractor pull, though they'll probably have as much fun walking around the fairgrounds meeting the cows, sheep, and pigs competing for the blue ribbons for best-of-show. Entertainment includes performances by country acts like Confederate Railroad and Ricky Skaggs, and the crowning of the Washington County Fair Queen and Princess is always a highlight.

Every year the fair starts on a Wednesday in mid-August and runs through the following Sunday. Admission is a bargain at $6.00 for adults, $5.00 for seniors, and free for children under twelve. For information, call 783–2070 or 783–2801.

For a glimpse of an authentic nineteenth-century mill village, make a turn off Route 2 onto Old Shannock Road, which leads to the small hamlet of *Shannock*. On the road into town, you'll cross a narrow white-fenced bridge next to an unusual horseshoe-shaped waterfall, the landmark for which the town is best known (to those few people who know about Shannock at all). You can stop here for a moment of peaceful relaxation or continue into town.

With ample waterpower and the railroad running right through town, it's not hard to imagine Shannock's past as a thriving mill town during the Industrial Revolution. Now the mill that once supported the town is in ruins, adding to the feeling that Shannock is the Place That Time Forgot.

PLACES TO STAY IN SOUTH COUNTY—NORTH KINGSTOWN AND INLAND

(ALL AREA CODES 401)

NORTH KINGSTOWN
Best Western Monte Vista Inn,
7075 Post Road,
884–8000

Country House B&B,
10 Kent Street,
294–4688 or 841–2083

The Haddie Pierce House,
146 Boston Neck Road,
294–7674

The Kingstown Motel,
6530 Post Road, 884–1160

Mount Maple of Wickford,
730 Annaquatucket Road,
295–4373

The Welcome Inn,
6481 Post Road,
884–9153 or 884–9300

The Wickford House,
68 Main Street, 294–6479

HOPKINTON
The General Thurston House 1763 B&B,
496 Main Street, 377–9049

RICHMOND
Country Acres B&B,
176 Townhouse Road,
Route 112, 364–9134

WEST GREENWICH
Best Western Inn,
101 Nooseneck Hill Road,
397–5494

Classic Motor Lodge,
859 Victory Highway,
397–6280

The Congress Inn,
101 Nooseneck Hill Road,
397–3381

**PLACES TO EAT IN
SOUTH COUNTY—NORTH
KINGSTOWN AND INLAND**

(All Area Codes 401)

NORTH KINGSTOWN
Allie's Donuts,
3661 Quaker Lane,
295–8036

The Breakfast Nook,
6130 Post Road, 884–6108

The Carriage Inn,
1065 Tower Hill Road,
884–6242

Duffy's Tavern,
235 Tower Hill Road,
295–0073

Selected Chamber of Commerce in South County— North Kingstown and Inland

Chamber of Commerce North Kingstown,
245 Tower Hill Road, North Kingstown 02852–4811;
295–5566

Oak Hill Tavern,
565 Tower Hill Road,
294–3282

Red Rooster Tavern,
7385 Post Road,
884–1987

A Taste of China,
6188 Post Road, 885–2216

Wickford Gourmet Foods,
21 West Main Street,
295–8190

EXETER
The Homestead Restaurant,
750 South County Trail,
294–7810

Middle of
Nowhere Diner,
222 Nooseneck Hill Road,
397–8855

HOPKINTON
The Wood River Inn,
1139 Main Street,
539–2009

WICKFORD
The Harborside Grill,
68 Brown Street,
295–0444

**OTHER ATTRACTIONS
WORTH SEEING IN
SOUTH COUNTY—
NORTH KINGSTOWN
AND INLAND**

Carolina Management
Area, *Richmond*

Fiddlesticks Miniature Golf
and Driving Range,
North Kingstown

Locustville Pond Public
Fishing Area, *Hopkinton*

Rhode Island Veteran's
Cemetery, *Exeter*

Rockville Management and
Public Fishing Area,
Hopkinton

**HELPFUL WEB SITES ABOUT
SOUTH COUNTY—NORTH
KINGSTOWN AND INLAND**

South County Fun,
users.ids.net/%7Escfun/

North Kingstown Chamber
of Commerce,
http://cshell.com/nkcc

South County— The Ocean Shore and Block Island

Narragansett

Unnoticed by most tourists—who naturally are drawn to Narragansett's fine bay beaches—the *Narrow (Pettaquamscutt) River* flows quietly from a series of inland ponds down to Pettaquamscutt Cove and, eventually, Narragansett Bay. In doing so, the river passes through undeveloped watershed lands and past historic homes as well as a pond whose steep sides give the impression of a fjord.

One of the best ways to stir the secret waters of the Narrow River is to use a kayak or canoe. *Narrow River Kayaks,* located riverside next to the bridge on Middletown Road, rents boats and offers lessons to novice paddlers. For beginners they even have special, easy-to-handle "kiwi kayaks." With a guide or solo, you can paddle upriver or down to the bay beaches, and there are pleasant spots along the way to stop for lunch.

Narrow River Kayaks is located at 94 Middlebridge Road, which connects Route 4 to the west and Boston Neck Road/Route 1A to the east. Prices start at $18 for two hours, or $25 for a half-day; for rates and information call Rob Ryder at 789–0334 or (800) 443–0334.

Before doubling back to Boston Neck Road/Route 1A, you can sample the fruit of these local waters at *Wiley's at Middlebridge* (95 Middlebridge Road, 782–3830), where fresh fish is the specialty. This small riverside restaurant is open May to January for lunch Tuesday through Saturday and for dinner on Friday and Saturday.

Proceeding south on Boston Neck Road (Route 1A from the intersection with Middlebridge Road), you soon will come upon the pavilion for the *Narragansett Town Beach.* Though the sand and surf may call out to you, proceed a little farther and look for a small road, cutting through the tall marsh grass on your right. You've found the entrance to the *South County Museum* (783–5400; www.southcountymuseum.org).

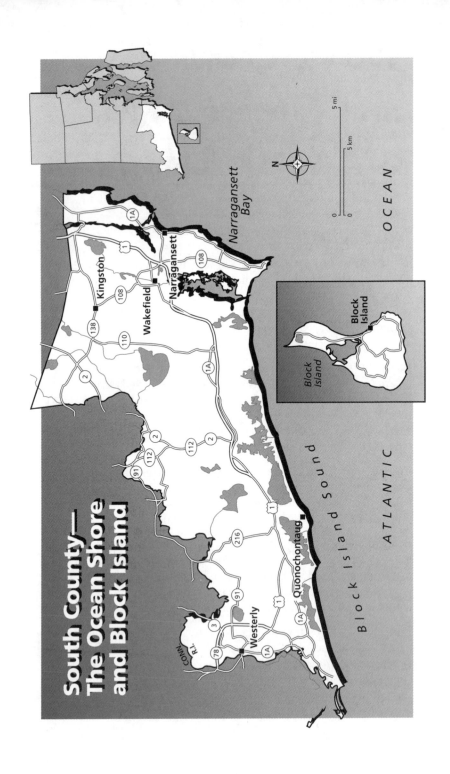

South County—
The Ocean Shore
and Block Island

Kingston

Narragansett

Wakefield

Narragansett Bay

Kingston

108

110

138

2

1A

1

108

1A

112

112

2

2

91

91

1

216

Quonochontaug

3

78

Westerly

1A

1A

11

11

CONN.

R.I.

Block Island Sound

ATLANTIC

OCEAN

Block Island

Block
Island

N

5 mi

5 km

0

0

(Beachgoers are charged for parking here in the summer, so don't be surprised if the attendant stops your car and asks for money. Simply explain that you're going to the museum, where parking is free.)

The South County Museum is an excellent assemblage of artifacts and information on the history of this area and the lives of the people who have lived here. The exhibits are varied and imaginative and are presented in an airy, high-ceilinged wooden building. One display features items that might have appeared in an early-twentieth-century country kitchen, while another reproduces an old country store. When we first visited, a collection of bathing costumes from Narragansett Pier's resort heyday were on display in a section reserved for revolving exhibits; recently, the museum added a new collection representing the items sold at Kenyon's Department Store, a South County institution that closed down a few years back.

Children are drawn to the active beehive that sits by one of the museum's windows; it has clear plastic sides that let you look into the honeycomb and an enclosed landing strip for bees flying in and out of the nest. Adjacent to the main museum building is a barn that contains horse-drawn carriages, a hearse, a milk wagon, and a mail wagon once used in the area; neighboring **Canonchet Farm** includes hiking trails. The museum is open from May through the end of October daily (except Tuesday) from 10:00 A.M. to 5:00 P.M. Admission is $3.50 for adults and $1.75 for children ages six to sixteen, with a maximum per-family fee of $10.00.

Soon after you pass the town beach, Route 1A becomes Kingstown Road and heads off to the west, but you'll want to continue straight toward the stone towers you see in front of you. This is all that remains of the **Narragansett Casino,** built by Stanford White (of the famed architectural firm McKim, Mead & White) in 1883 and destroyed by a fire in 1900. Just after you pass under the arch on Ocean Road, you'll see a stone building set beyond the breakwater. Once the headquarters of the Narragansett Pier Coast Guard Station, it now houses the **Coast Guard House** restaurant (40 Ocean Road, 789–0700).

The Coast Guard House was heavily damaged in a hurricane a few years ago—not surprising, given its exposed location—but was rebuilt and has come back strong as one of South County's best restaurants. Seafood, of course, is always on the menu, but steaks and other continental fare are also available. Whether you choose to dine indoors or on the outside deck, awesome views of the pounding surf are a constant dinner companion. Open 11:30 A.M. to 3:00 P.M. Monday to Friday for lunch and 5:00 to 9:00

P.M. for dinner; 11:00 A.M. to 10:00 P.M. on Saturday (an hour later daily during summertime). Sunday brunch is served 10:00 A.M. to 2:00 P.M.

From the pier it's a very pretty waterfront drive down Ocean Avenue to *Point Judith,* where you can walk around the *Point Judith Lighthouse* (1816) or catch the *ferry to Block Island* (783– 4613). First, though, consider a stop at *Aunt Carrie's Seafood Restaurant (*1240 Ocean Road, 783–7930), for more than seventy-five years a Rhode Island landmark at the corner of Ocean Road and Route 108.

Aunt Carrie's is one of those places that expends less effort on outward appearances than on delivering fresh, inexpensive seafood to its customers. Its many devotees will tell you that the best clams in the state

Victorian Vistas in Narragansett

*I*n its Victorian heyday, Narragansett was one of the most popular resorts on the East Coast. Drawn by the beautiful beaches and cool ocean breezes, visitors flocked to Narragansett by rail from around New England and New York during the late nineteenth century. The prosperity of this time was reflected in the great Narragansett Casino, built in 1883 by the famous architectural firm of McKim, Mead & White.

The fire that swept through the casino in 1900 coincided with a decline in Narragansett's fortunes. But like the great stone casino towers on Ocean Road, Narragansett survived the fire and remains a popular summer destination. Although many of the grand Victorian hotels are gone, they have been replaced by an excellent selection of small inns and bed-and-breakfasts.

Like the Casino, the cliffside 1883 Victorian that is home to the Stone Lea Bed & Breakfast (40 Newton Avenue, 783–9546) was designed by McKim, Mead & White. Another B&B that is reminiscent of Narragansett's illustrious past is The Richards B&B (144 Gibson Avenue, 789–7746), an 1884 stone mansion with a distinctive front gable, which has four guest rooms with working fireplaces. The gardens and spacious grounds are reminders that this once was the centerpiece of a sprawling country estate.

One of the most architecturally interesting B&Bs in town is Dunmere (560 Ocean Road, 783–3797), a turreted, fortresslike stone house that sits on a ledge overlooking the ocean. There's only one guest room, so you'll have the clay tennis court and lovely grounds—which include a pond with a small bridge and an inviting gazebo—all to yourselves. For a completely different experience, try the Old Clerk House (49 Narragansett Avenue, 783–8008), a simple wood-frame Victorian surrounded by rose gardens and a white picket fence, or the Pleasant Cottage B&B (104 Robinson Street, 783–6895), hosted by Fred and Terry Sepp and within easy walking distance of Narragansett Pier and the beach.

can be found here. You can also enjoy traditional Rhode Island shore dinners and a hearty chowder. In Narragansett, Aunt Carrie's is what summer is all about. Open noon to 9:00 P.M. Memorial Day to Labor Day; closed Tuesday. Also open April 1 to Memorial Day and Labor Day through the end of September, 4:00 to 8:00 P.M. on Friday and noon to 8:00 P.M. on Saturday and Sunday.

A brief drive north on Route 108, followed by a left turn on Galilee Escape Road, will land you at the seaport of **Galilee,** Rhode Island's leading fishing port, both commercial and recreational, and home to a variety of fine seafood restaurants. Take a seat in the deck at **Champlin's** (256 Great Island Road, 783–3152) for fresh ocean breezes and great harbor views, or drop in at **George's of Galilee** (250 Sand Hill Cove Road, 783–2306 or 800–399–8477) and learn why Rhode Islanders have been coming here for lobster and fish since 1948. Among the boats in this busy harbor are those belonging to the **Frances Fleet,** including the 105-foot yacht *Lady Frances,* which six days a week departs for the open ocean on whale-watching tours.

AUTHOR'S FAVORITE ATTRACTIONS/ EVENTS IN SOUTH COUNTY—THE OCEAN SHORE AND BLOCK ISLAND

Napatree Point

Theatre by the Sea

Aunt Carrie's Seafood Restaurant

Wilcox Park

Charlestown Seafood Festival, Charlestown; August

Swamp Yankee Days, Charlestown; September

Narragansett Indian Powwow, Charlestown; August

Shakespeare in the Park, Westerly; July

Virtu Art Festival, Westerly; May

Narragansett Art Festival, Narragansett; June

South County Hot Air Balloon Festival, Kingston; July

Aided by state-of-the-art sonar equipment and reports from other boats, the *Lady Frances* cruises up to 35 miles out to sea to chase down humpback, finback, right, and minke whales. Among the most commonly spotted are the 80-foot-long finbacks, which are seen speeding around their summer feeding grounds off Block Island each year. Rarest are the right whales, which were hunted nearly to extinction during the latter half of the nineteenth century and the early part of the twentieth century.

You'll get to see whales on most days, but even when the whales are shy the *Lady Frances* gives you a bird's-eye view of fish, Portuguese man-of-wars, and an abundance of waterfowl. The ship has a large outdoor observation deck as well as an air-conditioned cabin and a galley stocked with food and beverages.

The *Lady Frances* departs on five-hour whale-watching cruises Monday through Saturday at 1:00 P.M., weather permitting, from July 1 through Labor Day. Tickets are $30 for adults, $27 for seniors, and $20

The *Lady Frances*

for children. Reservations are recommended and can be made by calling 783–4988 or (800) 662–2824. From Route 1 south, get off at the Point Judith/ Galilee exit, then take Route 108/Point Judith Road south to Galilee, making a right onto Galilee Escape Road. At the end of the road make a right, then turn left at the Captain's Table Restaurant. The Frances Fleet ticket office is located at the Capt.'s Tackle store.

For a less ambitious but no less enjoyable boat ride, check out the ***Southland*** (783–2954), a sight-seeing riverboat that cruises around Point Judith and the Great Salt Pond, offering a unique perspective on such landmarks as the Point Judith Lighthouse, sheltered Great Island and Harbor Island, and the tiny fishing hamlet of Jerusalem, not to mention numerous clammers and quahoggers at work. You'll also get a close-up look at the massive stone breakwaters that create the Point Judith Harbor of Refuge. One and three-quarter-hour narrated cruises are $8.00 for adults and $4.00 for children ages three to twelve, Two-and-a-half hour sunset cruises are $12.00 for adults and $6.00 for kids and include snacks and live entertainment. The boat sails Memorial Day to Columbus Day.

South Kingstown

Start your exploration of South Kingstown at the northeast corner of Route 1/Tower Hill Road and Route 138, where you will see a tall ***wooden observation tower.*** A popular misconception is that the tower was used to spot forest fires. Actually, it was built in 1937 as a military lookout to keep watch over the waters of the lower bay; frequent U-boat activity around this region a few years later justified the concerns of the builders.

Park in the small lot at the base of the 100-foot tower and make the climb to the top to enjoy a commanding view of the new ***Jamestown***

Bridge and the rusting span of its abandoned predecessor, as well as the western shoreline of Jamestown itself. In the foreground is the valley cut by the Pettaquamscutt (Narrow) River.

Beside the tower is *Hannah Robinson's Rock*. The stone recalls the classic South County romance about young Hannah and her lover, an older man who was her French tutor. Hannah's father disapproved of the romance, so the lovers would secretly meet at this rock. Later, Hannah ran off and got married, only to be abandoned by her husband. Sick and heartbroken, she eventually returned to her family, passing by the rock she had visited so many times in her younger days.

From this point, head west on Route 138, which takes you over a hilly, rather desolate landscape until you reach the village of *Kingston.* There is at least one good reason to stop along the way, however: the *King's Rose* bed-and-breakfast (1747 Mooresfield Road/Route 138, 783–5222 or 888–230–ROSE). A country estate built in Colonial style in 1933, the property is highlighted by lovely grounds that include a formal English garden, a goldfish pool and rose arbor, and a pair of tennis courts. The gardens make a peaceful backdrop both for the guest bedrooms and the full breakfast served in the sunroom, on the patio, or in the formal dining room. Innkeeper Perry Viles's Quaker family helped settle the area in the seventeenth century; Perry maintains the gardens, while wife Barbara, a retired nursing supervisor, does the cooking. Room rates range from $80 to $145.

Home to the main campus of the University of Rhode Island, Kingston also has a cluster of historic homes centered on the crossroads of Kingstown Road (Route 138) and the Old North and Old South Roads. The *Kingston Free Library* (2605 Kingstown Road) dates from 1775; the *First Congregational Church* (2601 Kingstown Road) was built in 1820.

Owing partly to its proximity to one of the state's centers for the arts and education, Kingston also is a center for South County's creative minds. The *Helm House Gallery,* located in another historic home at 2587 Kingstown Road (783–2195), is the headquarters of the South County Art Association, which holds regular exhibits of artwork by local residents and students. The *Fayerweather Craft Center* (1859 Moorsefield Road/Route 138, 789–9072), occupies the 1820 home of the town blacksmith and holds workshops every Tuesday in July and August. The center is open on Tuesday, Thursday, and Saturday 10:00 A.M. to 4:00 P.M.

Idyllic as Kingston may sound, the community had its share of trou-blemakers like any other town. For many years, running afoul of the law in this part of the state could land you in a dark cell at the **Old Washington County Jail** (2636 Kingstown Road, 783–1328). Built in 1792, the jail had separate but equal cells for men and women, and neither had windows. Visitors can see for themselves how eighteenth- and nineteenth-century justice was meted out thanks to the Pet-taquamscutt Historical Society, which maintains the jail and opens the building for tours three days a week.

Besides the old jail cells, the historical society has created exhibits illus-trating different aspects of the lives of South County residents during the past 300 years. Some rooms and former prison cells are furnished to rep-resent a typical home in the area, and central to the collection is a large eighteenth-century clock that once belonged to John Raleigh Ellard, a Kingston artist who graduated from the College of Agriculture and Mechanical Arts (now URI) in 1900. Another room depicts a school classroom, and there also are displays of locally made textiles, tools used by local farmers and artisans, antique toys, and Indian artifacts. An exten-sive historical and genealogical library also is housed in the building.

The Old Washington County Jail is open from May to October on Tues-day, Thursday, and Saturday from 1:00 to 4:00 P.M.

Leaving Kingston and heading west, you travel only about a mile and a half on Route 138 before reaching the village of **West Kingston.** As you approach town, you cross a small bridge, and immediately there is a fork in the road. If you turn left off Route 138 into Liberty Lane, a short drive will bring you to Great Neck Road; a left turn here will bring you to the parking lot for the **Great Swamp Wildlife Reservation,** a huge nature park with a swamp that drains Wordens Pond. It was on an island fortress in the Great Swamp that the Narragansett Indians were attacked and defeated during King Philip's War. A **memorial** to the peo-ple who died in that 1675 battle stands in the swamp and is reached by the aptly named Great Swamp Monument Road, located on the left side of Route 2 about $1\frac{1}{4}$ miles south of the intersection with Route 138.

Just before the rairoad bridge on Route 138 is the turnoff for the **Kingston Station** parking lot. This quiet Amtrak station, with its lov-ingly restored 1875 depot building, also serves as the northern termi-nus of the new **South County Bicycle Path.** The 4-mile ribbon of paved path skirts the Great Swamp Management Area and leads bikers, skaters, and walkers through quiet woodlands to the village of Peace Dale (see page 183).

Ride the South County Trail

*R*oute 2, also known as the South County Trail, has an excellent bike route that officially begins at the intersection with Route 138 in South Kingstown. With wide shoulders and a moderate traffic flow, Route 2 gives riders a great opportunity to get a taste of rural Rhode Island without leaving civilization entirely.

The official bike trail stretches north from Route 138 to the intersection of Routes 2 and 102 in North Kingstown, a distance of about 6 miles that features a few challenging hills but also stretches of nice, flat cruising. Along the way, you'll pass such landmarks as the Rhode Island Veterans' Cemetery, Schartner's Farms, the Homestead Restaurant, and Barber's Pond—a beautiful spot to pull over and enjoy a picnic lunch. If you reach the halfway point and need some replenishment, Oatley's Junction at the intersection of Routes 2 and 102 has a convenience store and a restaurant.

Although Route 2 south of the Route 138 intersection is not officially marked as a bike route, the shoulders here are equally wide and inviting. The hills, however, are steeper and longer, but your exertion is rewarded by more beautiful countryside, as you cross over cold-running streams and pass by turf farms that look like the world's largest front lawn. If you're riding a mountain bike, you might want to pull off at Great Swamp Monument Road to visit the memorial to the Narragansett tribe.

For more information on organized rides and bicycling throughout Rhode Island, contact Narragansett Bay Wheelmen (www.aljian.com/ nbw/) at 435–4012, or write NBW, P.O. Box 41177, Providence 02940-1177.

Just past the Route 2 intersection on Route 138 is the tiny **Queen's River Baptist Church,** a simple white building hugging a bend in the road. This is one of my favorite places in Rhode Island, a quintessential country church with an old cemetery, completely surrounded by open farmland. Pull over to the right just past the church to park, and take a few moments to walk through the rows of ancient headstones. Besides the occasional passing car, there is nothing to disturb your silent contemplation but the muted sounds of a tractor in the nearby fields toiling at that endless cycle of sowing and harvesting that is a metaphor for life itself.

Back in the car, a short drive farther west on Route 138 brings you to Old Usquepaugh Road; turn right here, then right onto Glen Rock Road, and on your right you'll see **Kenyon's Grist Mill** (783–4054).

For centuries, gristmills occupied an important place in New England village life. The grains harvested by local farmers were not of much use until they were taken to the miller, who would crack the grain with huge grindstones powered by wind or water and make flour and meal. In the modern age, most of these old mills have been demolished, abandoned, or turned into museums.

Part of what makes Kenyon's Grist Mill such an interesting place to visit is the fact that it remains a viable business. Built in 1886, the mill still produces a variety of products, including Kenyon's Jonny Cake Corn Meal and flours made of whole wheat, rye, and buckwheat. Sold in small, turn-of-the-century-style bags, Kenyon's products can be found in specialty stores throughout Rhode Island, as well as in the Grist Mill Store located across the street from the mill.

Behind the mill you can walk out onto an old dam and see the millrace that carries water under the mill. The Queen's River no longer powers the mill, but the original grindstones are still in use, and the miller is always happy to show visitors how the raw grains are turned into edible products. Tours of the gristmill are given year-round by appointment. The Grist Mill Store, which also sells jams and jellies, relishes, mincemeat, syrup, pancake mix, and homemade soap, is open weekends year-round from noon to 5:00 P.M. and on weekdays, Memorial Day to Labor Day, from 10:00 A.M. to 5:00 P.M.

Glen Rock Road leads north into one of the quietest, most scenic back-road areas in the state. In a scant $2^{1}/_{2}$-mile loop from Glen Rock Road to Dugway Bridge Road back down to Route 138, you cross three bridges over Glen Rock Brook and other small streams, drive past a towering stand of pine trees, and see pastoral country homes. Along the way you also pass the entrance to the **Marion Eppley Wildlife Sanctuary** (505 Dugway Bridge Road, 949–5454), another Audubon Society property.

One stop you definitely should make on Glen Rock Road is at **Peter Pots Pottery** (494 Glen Rock Road, 783–2350). Peter Pots's fine stoneware pottery is produced at the historic 1779 Glen Rock Mill. Lamps, pitchers, vases, and tea sets are just some of the handcrafted items fired in the kilns of this old gristmill and offered for sale in the mill shop. By tradition, most of Peter Pots's pottery is glazed in either mahogany brown or seagull blue.

Besides pottery, the Peter Pots store also has an assortment of antiques on display. It's a fun place to poke around in, and the view out the side window, where the river rushes under and past the mill's old waterwheel, is in itself worth the visit. Open Monday through Saturday from 10:00 A.M. to 4:00 P.M. and Sunday 1:00 to 4:00 P.M.

Peace Dale, located off Route 108 in the most populous part of South Kingstown, is one of Rhode Island's prettiest mill villages. (Route 108, also known as Ministerial Road, connects with Route 138 in Kingston to the north and with Route 1 in Wakefield to the south.) At the center of the village, on Kingstown Road (Route 108) next to the Saugatucket River, is the mill complex that formerly housed the *Peace Dale Manufacturing Company.* From 1802 on, the Hazard family built a succession of cotton and textile mills that were the lifeblood of Peace Dale. During the Civil War the Peace Dale mill made blankets for Union soldiers; during World War I khaki was woven for uniforms.

Today a group of smaller companies lease the mill buildings, but you can still walk around the courtyard and admire the mill's nineteenth-century architecture and gaze down upon the river waters rushing through the sunken, well-preserved raceways. Across the street from the mill is the 1856 Peace Dale Office Building, home of the *Museum of Primitive Art and Culture* (1058 Kingstown Road, 783–5711), which houses a collection of tools, weapons, and artifacts of Native American tribes and other native cultures from around the world. The museum is open Labor

The Peace Dale Manufacturing Company

*T**he history of the Peace Dale Manufacturing Company includes many of the touchstones of the American Industrial Revolution. The company founded by the Hazard family in 1802 began as a mixture of manufacturing mill and cottage industry: Rhode Island's first carding machine separated the tough cotton fibers at the mill, but the bundles of processed wool were then turned over to local families to spin on hand looms. Power looms were installed in 1814, and the company became known for its shawls and blankets.*

Like mills all over the United States, the Peace Dale Manufacturing Company was built with the sweat of immigrant labor. More than a hundred Irish immigrants worked at the mill by 1857, driven out of their homeland by the great potato famine. The latter half of the nineteenth century saw improvements in work conditions and the rise of unionism: The workday was shortened in 1887, and a noon recess was established. In 1906 weavers at the mill went on strike, and a train full of Italian strikebreakers were brought in from Lowell, Massachusetts.

After World War II, the Peace Dale mill began to experience the same problems as many other New England textile firms: high labor costs and aging facilities. By 1947 the owners had shuttered the mill and moved the operation to North Carolina in search of cheap labor and lower transportation costs. The mill, which once employed 40 percent of Peace Dale's residents, was relegated to the shadows of its former importance, and the town gradually made the shift from mill village to suburb.

Day through Memorial Day, Tuesday, Wednesday, and Thursday 10:00 A.M. to 2:00 P.M. and by appointment and the first Saturday of each month from 10:00 A.M. to noon; $1.00 donation suggested.

Behind the office building is a small park that runs along the riverbank, with a big playground and a pretty footbridge that spans the stream. Across Columbia Street is the *Hazard Memorial Library,* built in 1891.

Just north on Route 108 (Kingstown Road) is an 1888 pumping station that provided water to Peace Dale until 1946, when it was abandoned. The fieldstone building was renovated in the 1960s, however, and once again is serving the residents of Peace Dale as *The Pump House* restaurant (1464 Kingstown Road, 789–4944). The towering, peaked ceiling in the dining room is one visible reminder of the building's history, and the restaurant is nicely decorated with plants and lots of polished wood. The fish and chips is a menu favorite, but The Pump House also serves a variety of fresh seafood dishes, chicken, roast duckling, and top cuts of steak. Open Monday 4:00 to 9:00 P.M., Tuesday to Thursday 11:30 A.M. to 10:00 P.M., Friday 11:30 A.M. to 11:00 P.M., Saturday 4:00 to 11:00 P.M., and Sunday noon to 9:00 P.M.

If you're one of those people who believe that the best flavor enhancer for seafood is a mild salt breeze, proceed south on Route 108 to Route 1 south, then take the South County Hospital/Salt Pond Road exit to find *Hanson's Landing* (210 Salt Pond Road, Wakefield, 782–0210). Located between a pair of picturesque marinas, Hanson's offers everything from pub sandwiches to entrees like the sinfully delicious Lobster Cheesecake and a charbroiled tuna steak marinated in sesame oil, soy sauce, garlic, and scallions. Mr. Joe's Chicken, a boneless breast in a white-wine sauce served over pasta with sausage, spinach, tomatoes, garlic, and shallots, is another favorite.

The pub at Hanson's is small, local, and friendly, and both the indoor dining rooms and the outdoor deck offer great views of Salt Pond. Thanks to the miracle of portable propane heaters, the deck and outdoor bar are even open in winter, and there's live music year-round on the weekends.

Our final stops in South Kingstown take us down to the town's shore area, popular for such ocean beaches as Moonstone, East Matunuck, Green Hill, and Roy Carpenter's. Another famous shoreline attraction for more than sixty years has been the *Theatre by the Sea,* located on Card's Pond Road in Matunuck.

Listed on the National Register, the Theatre by the Sea looks decidedly untheaterlike from the outside, resembling a rambling seaside cottage.

Perryville's Most Famous Son

"We have met the enemy, and he is ours."

*T*he tiny South Kingstown community known as Perryville has one very big claim to fame: It's the birthplace of Commodore Oliver Hazard Perry, hero of the Battle of Lake Erie in the War of 1812.

Born here in 1785, Perry became a Navy midshipman at the tender age of fourteen and served in the West Indies and in the Tripoli wars in the Mediterranean. He received his first command in 1811, and in 1812 he was sent to Lake Erie to take on a large British fleet that threatened that critical waterway.

During the ensuing battle, Perry's flagship, the brig Lawrence, *was battered by the British and nearly sunk. But Perry transferred his flag to the* Niagara, *and fifteen minutes of pounding cannon fire later he had defeated a squadron of British ships. Perry's victory and his famous message back to Washington—"We have met the enemy, and he is ours"—made national heroes of him and his crew, and the battle ultimately turned the tide of the war.*

Once the actors take the stage in this big old barn, however, the work is strictly professional. The Theatre by the Sea hauls in the best of the Broadway musicals, such as *My Fair Lady, Funny Girl, The Sound of Music, Grease,* and *42nd Street,* as well as hosting an annual children's festival.

After the show, you can step outside for a walk in the gardens or follow the path to the **SeaHorse Grill,** which serves sandwiches and pizza in a casual atmosphere and also has a special cabaret room where performances run late into the night.

The theater season runs from May to September; cabaret performances are held June to August. The Theatre by the Sea is located at 364 Card's Pond Road; phone 782–8587 (box office) or 789–3030 (restaurant, after 3:00 P.M.). To get to Card's Pond Road, take Route 1 south to the Matunuck Beach Road exit, then follow Matunuck Beach Road for approximately 1 mile to Card's Pond Road and make a left.

There are myriad summer rentals, motels, and small inns and bed-and-breakfasts to choose from around Matunuck, but one of the best is the **Admiral Dewey Inn** (668 Matunuck Beach Road, 783–2090 or 800–457–2090; www.admiraldeweyinn.com). Named one of Rhode Island's top seashore inns by *Rhode Island Monthly* magazine, the Admiral Dewey is a National Register Victorian home with a big running porch and ten guest rooms, many with ocean views. Once a boardinghouse for beachgoers, the inn is now dressed in high Victorian style, with brass beds, big overstuffed chairs, and fine antiques collected by innkeeper Joan LeBel. Room rates are $90 to $120, year-round, including a "continental-plus" breakfast.

South County's best venue for live music is located right on the beach in Matunuck: the **Ocean Mist** (895 Matunuck Beach Road, 782–3740). More an oversized bar than a concert hall, the Ocean Mist gets you within arm's-length of local and nationally known reggae, rock, punk, ska, and hip-hop bands. Plus there's an amazing variety of drink and food specials, from taco night to wing night to the Tuesday Power Hour, when the drinks are on the house from 9:30 to 10:30 P.M. If you need a breath of fresh air, you can duck outside on the deck overlooking the ocean. Even when there's no band playing, the Ocean Mist can be a fun place to hang around with friends. The food is reasonably priced and good—even breakfast is served on the weekends—and on Sunday there's free pool and $2.00 burgers from 6:00 to 11:00 P.M.

Charlestown

You have to be hungry to find the **Nordic Lodge** (178 East Pasquiset Trail, 783–4515; www.nordic-lodge.com): first because it probably is the most out-of-the-way restaurant in Rhode Island, and second because it serves an incredible all-you-can-eat buffet that includes unlimited lobster and filet mignon.

The Narragansetts

Central Charlestown is dominated by the 2,500-acre Narragansett Indian Reservation, home of the native people who once controlled the entire West Bay side of Rhode Island. Called "the people of the small point," about 10,000 Narragansett once lived here, but the plagues, wars, and enslavement associated with the arrival of European settlers in the seventeenth century reduced the population to about 500 by 1682.

The survivors settled on the Charlestown reservation, where they saw their land whittled down from 15,000 acres to just 2 acres in 1880; a 1978 court decision restored the current reservation land to the tribe. In recent years the tribe has fought unsuccessfully to establish a gambling casino or high-stakes bingo operation on its reservation.

You can get a taste of Narragansett history by visiting the tribe's Royal Indian Burial Ground, located on Narrow Lane off Route 2/112 near Post Road, or by attending the annual Narragansett Indian Powwow, held on the reservation in August; call 364–1100 for information.

Ninigret Park's Hidden Charms

*T*he charms of Charlestown's Ninigret Park (364–1222) are not immediately apparent; at first glance, you're likely to notice grassy fields and long stretches of pavement (actually the remains of runways from the old Charlestown Naval Airfield), but little else.

But give the 1,172-acre park a chance, and you'll be rewarded. As you drive on the main access road, one of the first things you'll see is the Frosty Drew Observatory (364–9508 or 596– 7688), open to the public for stargazing at dusk every Friday night. With its lack of lights and distance from any major city, the park is an ideal place to explore the heavens, as our family found when we brought our telescope down to view the Hale-Bopp comet in 1997.

Push on, and you'll find a quiet, spring-fed swimming pond that's great for families with small children, a bicycle racing course, playing fields, and walking trails. Keep your eye out for herds of wild deer and the occasional vestiges of the old airfield, where future President George Bush and other naval aviators honed their skills during World War II.

Ninigret Park also hosts an annual visit by the Big Apple Circus in July , the taste-tempting Charlestown Seafood Festival each August, and the down-home Swamp Yankee Days in September. For information on any of these events, call 364–0890 or 364–3878.

Getting to the **Nordic Lodge** is part of the fun: "If you find us, you'll like us" is the restaurant's motto. From Route 2 in Charlestown, turn onto Maple Lake Farm Road at the NORDIC LODGE sign, then proceed $1^7/_{10}$ miles to Old Coach Road. Make a right, then follow this twisting rural road until you start wondering why in the heck anyone would put a restaurant up here. About this time you'll see a sign for the Nordic Lodge entrance. A narrow road will eventually bring you to the restaurant parking lot.

The Nordic Lodge is set in a pretty location by the side of sparsely developed Pasquiset Pond. Operated by the Persson family since 1963, the restaurant's modest exterior and brick-lined dining room belie the fantastic spread laid out for the buffet. What sets the Nordic Lodge apart from your average buffet is not the *quantity* of food but its *quality*. There are trays full of oriental spare ribs, chicken cordon bleu, and baked mushrooms. Filet mignon, prime rib, and marinated teriyaki steak tips are served from a charcoal grill. And there are mounds of jumbo shrimp and hot lobsters, fresh from a 200-gallon cooking pot. If somehow you make it to dessert, the Nordic Lodge has a Haagen Dazs ice cream bar and a wide variety of cakes and pastries. If you want to at least make a nod to sensible eating, there's also a selection of fresh fruit and nuts.

Such wild indulgence does have its price, and at the Nordic Lodge that price is $44.95 per person for the unlimited buffet. The restaurant is open Friday 5:00 to 9:00 P.M., Saturday 3:00 to 9:00 P.M., and Sunday 1:00 to 7:00 P.M. Also open Thursday 5:00 to 9:00 P.M. during summer, and hours are sometimes extended to accommodate bus tours.

The Nordic Lodge gets very busy on weekends, so come early. While you wait for your table, you can amuse yourself by visiting the Welsh pony, Australian emu, or other animals in the pens outside. Or prepare for the coming feast by reviewing the buffet map over a cold one at the Nordic Lodge's spacious bar.

Back out on Old Coach Road, and practically across the street from the Nordic Lodge entrance, is another offbeat local attraction: the **Rathskeller** restaurant and bar (783–7839). Reputed to be a former speakeasy, the Rathskeller retains much of its Roaring Twenties decor, from separate gentlemen's and ladies' entrances to interior walls adorned with murals depicting flappers and early film stars. The menu is straightforward comfort food, and the bar is tiny but inviting, making the Rathskeller a neat little place hidden away in the woods of Charlestown.

The **Fantastic Umbrella Factory** is like a time capsule from the 1960s, an artists' cooperative that over the years has transformed an abandoned eighteenth-century farm into a minivillage of small shops surrounding a wonderful wildflower garden.

What's nice about the Fantastic Umbrella Factory is its utter lack of pretense. Narrow dirt paths, sometimes covered by a tin-roofed arbor, lead from one shop to the next through overgrown gardens and past the rusted hulks of old cars. A sign by the garden notes, CLOTHING OPTIONAL; SHOES REQUIRED.

Vines and creepers hang from the ramshackle buildings, but inside the stores are surprisingly neat. The main building, known formally as the **International Bazaar** (364–6616), is filled with an eclectic array of unusual toys, windsocks, posters, bath accessories, jewelry, and, yes, umbrellas. Blown-glass and handmade pottery are the centerpieces at **Small Axe Gallery** (364–1060), where the artists often are working before your eyes. The **Mazzone Gallery** (364–0591) has a split personality: one half devoted to antiques, the other to original watercolors and oil paintings by owners Betty and Mike Mazzone. **Dave's Den** sells Native American jewelry and dreamcatchers as well as incense, tapestries, and funky rugs.

The tie-dyed atmosphere continues in the **Spice of Life Cafe** (364–

2030), which offers free-range chicken sandwiches, hummus pockets, and some great chocolate chip cookies. Order some organic espresso or fresh-squeezed lemonade to go with your meal. (Open Thursday to Sunday 11:00 A.M. to 5:00 P.M.) After lunch, why not take the children over to the barnyard, filled with peacocks, hens, and crowing roosters.

If your lasting impressions of the Fantastic Umbrella Factory are images of those flower gardens, fear not. The *Greenhouse* (364–6616), open in the spring and early fall, sells a variety of traditional perennials and unusual daylilies like those found growing around the property.

The Fantastic Umbrella Factory is located on Scenic Route 1A; take the Ninigret Park/Tourist Information exit off Route 1 and proceed past the tourist information center and the entrance to Ninigret Park. Drive slowly or you'll miss the dirt road leading to the Umbrella Factory parking lot, which is a short distance farther on your right. Open daily 10:00 A.M. to 6:00 P.M. during the summer; 10:00 A.M. to 5:00 P.M. after Labor Day.

Returning to Route 1 south, you quickly will come to the turnoff for East Beach Road. Like all of South County's ocean beaches, *East Beach* is popular with sun lovers from Connecticut, Massachusetts, and Rhode Island. What makes East Beach unique, however, is the combination of a small parking lot (maximum capacity of ninety-five cars) and a 3-mile-long expanse of undeveloped beachfront.

If you crave solitude, this is your place. Down by the parking lot at the west end of the beach are lifeguards and crowds, but there are fewer and fewer people as you walk east along the shoreline until, in many places, you have the beach pretty much to yourself. In front of you are the ocean and the shadowy outline of Block Island; behind you are Ninigret Pond and the dunes of the Ninigret Conservation Area. If you keep walking east, you will eventually reach the Charlestown Breach-way, marked by huge boulders piled on each side of the inlet.

Parking at East Beach is $10.00 on the weekend and $8.00 during the week for nonresidents; the lot fills up quickly during the summer, so get there early.

Westerly

The town of *Westerly* has two main communities, and neither should be missed. First is the village of Westerly itself, an early center of commerce on the old Lower Road (part of the Boston Post Road, later Route 1) and famous from the mid-nineteenth century on for the blue granite produced in local quarries. To reach downtown Westerly, take exit 1 in Rhode Island on Interstate 95, then proceed south on Route 3, which will eventually bring you to the heart of downtown.

The largest town in South County, Westerly nonetheless retains a small-town feel. Much of the credit is due to beautiful *Wilcox Park* (596–8590), eighteen acres of gardens, statues, and serene pathways located on High Street in the heart of downtown. Besides being a nice place to walk around or relax under a shady tree, Wilcox Park also is home to a free summer Shakespeare festival on July evenings. Designed by a student of Frederick Law Olmsted, who created New York's Central Park, Wilcox Park features a wide variety of interesting plants and trees, with a unique garden that includes braille descriptions for the visually impaired.

Directly across from the park entrance is *Kismet on the Park* bed-and-breakfast, located in a stately 1845 former private home at 71 High Street (596–3237). The locale has dual benefits: Not only do many of the rooms have lovely views of the park, but guests can settle into chairs on the terrace to enjoy park concerts and performances. Innkeeper Cindy Slay has four rooms available with private baths, including a suite that can accommodate up to four people. Rates range from $65 to $125, depending on the season.

Downtown Westerly features a number of impressive and historic public buildings, including the Westerly Town Hall at the corner of Broad Street and Union Street, the Washington Trust Bank building on Broad Street, Christ Church at Broad and Elm, and the distinctive, yellow-brick Westerly Public Library, also on Broad Street. Next door to the library, fronted by massive columns, is the town post office.

Adding to Westerly's charm are the presence of the Pawcatuck River, which defines the boundary between Westerly and Pawcatuck, Connecticut; a quaint Victorian train station that marks the passage of the railroad through the heart of downtown; and a fine assortment of well-maintained old homes. Preeminent among the latter is the *Babcock-Smith House* (124 Granite Street, 596–4424), a restored circa 1732 Georgian mansion that welcomes visitors by appointment on Sunday afternoons (2:00 to 5:00 P.M.) May to October (also Wednesday in July and August). The house belonged to Dr. Joshua Babcock, a physician who served as a member of the general assembly and Chief Justice of the Rhode Island Supreme Court. Babcock also was a friend of Benjamin Franklin, who often visited Babcock's home. Orlando Smith, who owned the house in the mid-nineteenth century, was the man who discovered the granite deposits that made Westerly world famous.

The Babcock-Smith House is fully furnished and decorated, including authentic eighteenth-century wall and floor treatments and fine antique furniture, with many eighteenth- and nineteenth-century pieces belonging to the Smith family, who lived here until 1972. Admission is $3.00 for adults and 50 cents for children.

Also on Granite Street is the brooding Greek Revival building that houses the **Colonial Theatre** (3 Granite Street, 596–0810). This professional theater group, which annually produces the free Shakespeare in the Park Festival, also presents a full schedule of contemporary musicals, comedies, and dramas. The Colonial Theatre's presentation of *A Christmas Carol* has become an annual tradition.

The Colonial Theatre's performances are enhanced by the ambience of the setting, Westerly's 150-year-old former First Congregational Church building, which is listed on the National Register. Ticket prices typically range from $15 to $25 for adults, $18 for adults and $10 for children on Wednesday and Sunday, and $10 for all performances of *A Christmas Carol*. The season runs from April through December.

Straddling the Pawcatuck River on Main Street is the celebrated **Three Fish** (37 Main Street, 348–9700). The restaurant's name honors the Westerly town crest, which pictures three swimming salmon (the Westerly area was known to the Native tribes as Misquamicut, or "place of salmon"). This upscale eatery literally sits over the river: At the time the cotton mill housing the restaurant was built, the Westerly waterfront already was crowded with buildings, so this was the only space left to build on.

Owner Nick Gumprecht has retained much of the mill's natural beauty, including the wide plank floors and stone walls composed of rocks that once traveled the world as ballast on old sailing ships. Similarly, the chefs at Three Fish have made an international culinary journey, featuring Asian, French, Southwestern, and traditional American influences in their cooking. Specialties include a tender filet mignon, rack of lamb, and a hugely popular dessert menu. Open Tuesday to Friday 11:30 A.M. to 2:30 P.M. for lunch; dinner is served Tuesday through Thursday 5:30 to 9:00 P.M. and Friday and Saturday until 9:30 P.M. On Wednesday, Thursday, and Friday there is live music, and selections from the bar menu are available until 1:00 A.M.

One of the roads that intersect in downtown Westerly is Beach Street/Route 1A, which also happens to be your southern passage to Westerly's other major community, **Watch Hill.**

A right turn from Beach Street onto Watch Hill Road brings you onto a winding, hilly road that meanders toward the southwestern corner of Rhode Island. Along the way, you'll pass the **Sun-Up Gallery** (95 Watch Hill Road, 596–3430) in the village of Avondale, which has won a strong regional following for its unique American-made clothing, crafts, and jewelry. Open Monday to Saturday 10:00 A.M. to 6:00 P.M.; Sunday noon to 5:00 P.M.

Watch Hill's name derives from the fact that it was used during the Revolutionary War as a lookout for British privateers, who made a habit of raiding coastal New England villages. Like Newport and Narragansett, Watch Hill became a fashionable vacation resort in the latter half of the nineteenth century, as evidenced by the many fine homes that sit along the road and up on the hills as you drive into town. For a real step back in time, book a room at the **Ocean House** (2 Bluff Avenue, 348–8161), a grand old oceanfront hotel built in 1868. Within walking distance to the village of Watch Hill, the Ocean House also has its own private beach.

Watch Hill is almost entirely residential with the exception of the length of Bay Street, facing Watch Hill Cove, which is lined with small specialty shops and eateries, most of which are open April through December. Some of the stores run to the T-shirt and snow globe variety, but most still exude the feel of an upscale New England seaside town.

Nowhere is the atmosphere more traditional than at the **Olympia Tea Room** (74 Bay Street, 348–8211), where waitresses in ruffled, black-and-white Victorian uniforms serve a simple but excellent variety of seafood and other dishes. Still going strong after eighty-four years, the Olympia Tea Room has an Art Deco look about it, with salmon walls contrasting with dark wood trim on the high-backed booths and large, mirrored bar.

An etching on the bay windows (aptly named, since they offer a great view of the water) eloquently understates a good dinner served here, although the restaurant is open for breakfast and lunch, too. Try a long-time favorite like a lobster salad roll or the fried local flounder sandwich, or go with the littleneck clams and fresh sausage steamed in marinara sauce—so good that it's still on the ever-changing dinner menu after twenty-three years. The restaurant is open for breakfast, lunch, and dinner daily from Memorial Day to Labor Day, and for lunch and dinner daily and for breakfast Sunday during the winter.

The **St. Clair Annex** (141 Bay Street, 348–8407) has been serving homemade ice cream to summer visitors as long as they have been coming to Watch Hill—the business started in 1880. In a nod to more modern tastes, frozen yogurt has been added to the menu, and a small restaurant serves breakfast and lunch Memorial Day to Labor Day, 7:00 A.M. to 10:00 P.M.

If you needed one reason and one reason only to visit Watch Hill, look no farther than the corner of Bay Street and Fort Street. The *Flying Horse Carousel* (596–7761) is the oldest continually operating merry-go-round in the United States. Built in 1867, the open-air carousel doesn't look like much when it is not in operation. The simple structure, which consists of a round, peaked, wooden roof supported by stone pillars and surrounded by a white picket fence, sits right by the roadside on a small lot. But when the old wooden horses are rehung each spring and the joyful sounds of children are added, something magical occurs.

Each 100-year-old, intricately carved horse is made from a single piece of wood and decorated with manes of real horsehair. Unlike more modern carousels, where the horses are attached by poles to the floor as well as the roof, the horses on the Flying Horse Carousel are attached only at the top, so when the carousel is in motion the horses swing outward and really do "fly." No adults are permitted to ride the carousel, and children must be able to sit without their feet touching the ground. The carousel operates from June 15 to Labor Day, Monday through Friday 1:00 to 9:00 P.M. and Saturday and Sunday 11:00 A.M. to 9:00 P.M. It costs $1.00 to ride.

One of the best things about Watch Hill is the variety of things there are to do in a small area. Striking out from the heart of town, you can explore two areas where history competes with great natural beauty for your attention. From the Flying Horse Carousel, walk down Larkin Road until you reach Lighthouse Road, which you follow to the end. Here stands the *Watch Hill Lighthouse*, a white brick and granite tower built in 1856 to guard the east entrance to Fisher's Island Sound. You can walk around the outside of the lighthouse or simply relax and enjoy the sensation of being surrounded on three sides by ocean. To the southwest you can see Fisher's Island, an isolated outpost of New York State.

Not only does *Napatree Point* offer a panoramic view of the Atlantic Ocean, but if you hike out to the end you can tell your grandchildren that you stood on the *westernmost spot in Rhode Island*. At the end of Fort Road begins a nature trail that takes you along the privately owned Nap-atree Beach out to the tip of Napatree Point, about a mile-and-a-half walk. While you're walking, you can reflect on what it must have been like to be living on this narrow strip of land when the hurricane of 1938

Birding on Block Island

*N*early a third of Block Island has been preserved as open space— some in its original, pristine state, some as reclaimed farmers' fields that are slowly returning to nature. Thanks to local conservation efforts and the island's location on a major migratory route, a wide variety of birds make stopovers here, including shorebirds, waterfowl, raptors, and songbirds. Others, like the rare northern harrier, make Block Island their home, patrolling the grassy scrubland prevalent over much of the island in search of food.

Block Island's beaches also provide a sanctuary for nesting birds, although some have been driven out by human activity along the shoreline. The best time to do some serious birding on Block Island is during the fall, when migration is at its peak. For more information contact the Block Island Nature Conservancy at 466–2129.

struck. Not only were most of the houses on Napatree Point destroyed, but the tip of the point was literally washed away by the storm.

The *Napatree Point Conservation Area* offers some great opportunities for bird-watching, with a nesting area set aside for ospreys and terns. When you reach the end of the point, you are rewarded by the ruins of *Fort Mansfield*, a stone-walled fort built in 1898 to defend the shoreline during the Spanish-American War. Look for the overgrown walls of the fort a few yards inland, up a path that climbs a ridge at the tip of the point.

The Villa (190 Shore Road/Route 1A, 596–1054 or 800–722–9240 out of state) is not your ordinary bed-and-breakfast. Here, in the land of Victorian and Colonial-era inns and homes, is an Italian villa surrounding a beautiful pool, with market umbrellas shading small tables by the water. Steps away is an outdoor hot tub, and a flight of stairs leads from the patio up to a deck belonging to the inn's La Sala di Verona suite, where Romeo and Juliet would have felt right at home. Four of the six suites have Jacuzzi tubs, two have fireplaces.

Innkeepers Angela Craig and Peter Gagnon serve breakfast poolside in the summertime and offer personalized service and friendly dining and touring advice year-round.

This mini-resort occupies a sheltered spot amid flowering gardens, off a gravel drive on Route 1A/Shore Road. In-season rates range from $130 to $245 for the inn's six suites; off-season rates range from $85 to $185.

If you simply must stay by the water, find your way to the *Weekapaug Inn* (25 Spring Avenue, 322–0301), a traditional New England seashore hotel.

Simple but elegant, the hundred-year-old Weekapaug Inn is a throwback to a time when vacation resorts were expected to provide three meals a day, enough activities to keep you busy for as long as you stayed, and a certain sense of decorum.

All this, the Weekapaug does admirably, with fresh local produce and seafood featured prominently in the formal dining room (jacket and tie required for gentlemen) and the weekly Thursday cookout on the lawn. The resort's 2-mile-long private beach is ideal for swimming and sailing, and lawn bowling, tennis, croquet, shuffleboard, and an indoor game room are all available on-site. Join in a game—there are no phones or TV to distract you.

All rates are Full American Plan and charged per-person; double occupancy is $175 to $225 per person, with children's rates from $35 to $125 per day, depending on age and which part of the inn they'll be staying in. The Weekapaug Inn is open from mid-June to Labor Day. It's at the end of Weekapaug Avenue off Route 1A; stay on the paved road until you reach the hotel.

Block Island

Block Island is a study in contradiction: Just 12 miles from the coast of Rhode Island, it feels so much farther away; just 11 square miles in area, it feels so much bigger. It's a bustling harbor and village, and its long stretches of road are best navigated by bicycle to take in the full sweep of the island's beauty. With the ocean all around and a pristine sanctuary at its center, it's no wonder that Block Island has been called one of the last great places on earth.

Visitors flock to the island by the thousands in the summer, mostly via the ferries that depart from the State Pier in Galilee. (The Interstate Navigation Company, 783–4613, operates ferries year-round to Block Island.) With so many people on such a small island, it's natural that most of the popular sites—the Southeast Lighthouse; the Mohegan Bluffs; the charming shops, restaurants, and old hotels of the Old Harbor and New Harbor—have been explored pretty thoroughly. Still, Block Island retains hidden places and new experiences for you to discover.

One way to enjoy Block Island is to come during the off-season. Although a good number of the businesses on the island close down after Labor Day, many stay open through September and even year-round. In fact, September is a great time to visit: The summer crowds are gone, but the warm weather and warm water remain through the end of the month.

There is a *harvest festival* on Columbus Day weekend, and the annual *shopper's stroll* is a highlight of the Christmas season. Call the Block Island Chamber of Commerce at 466–2982 for more information.

A few unusual attractions await you as you step off the ferry. Just a two-minute walk from the ferry dock is the *Hotel Manisses* (Spring Street in the Old Harbor, 466–2063), built in 1872 and perhaps the most beautiful of all the Victorian inns on the island. Surprisingly small, the Manisses sits close to Spring Street yet maintains an impeccable, quiet charm and elegance. It's a wonderful place to stay (room rates range from $50 to $350, depending on the season), and the restaurant is one of the island's best. For a special treat, take a seat in the Manisses's dessert parlor, located on the main floor of the hotel (upstairs from the restaurant). If you love sweets, this could be the highlight of your trip. Relax in quiet elegance while being served such tantalizing treats as Joan's Delight—delicious sour cream pie filled with blueberries and pineapple in a cracker crust—and the Manisses's chocolate silk pie with mousse filling and a chocolate cookie crust. Flaming coffees are served tableside, the 151-proof liquor set alight before your eyes. A selection of cinnamon, sugar, whipped cream, and assorted liqueurs is brought on a tray for you to choose from.

In a somewhat jarring contrast to the elegant surroundings, the Hotel Manisses also maintains a small *animal farm* with exotic creatures sure to delight children and adults alike. Llamas, emus, geese, pygmy goats, black swans, and a Scottish highland steer named Mr. MacDuff are among the beasts roaming the grounds behind the hotel. Recent additions include a zebu, the oldest type of cattle in the Northern Hemisphere, and another type of cattle, a Brahmin heifer.

Another sign that relaxed elegance is what Block Island is all about is the *farmers' market* held at the Manisses each Wednesday morning. Here island farmers and gardeners gather to sell their produce, fresh flowers, herbs, and other homemade products to summer visitors and residents alike. The farmers' market also is held on Saturday at Negus Park on Ocean Avenue. For information call 466–5364.

A short walk farther up the hill on Spring Street in the Old Harbor brings you to the driveway of *The Spring House* (Spring Street, 466–5844 or 800–234–9263), another of Block Island's grand old Victorians. Set on a fifteen-acre hilltop, this beautiful hotel has a magnificent red-and-white porch running the length of the building and offering ocean views that couldn't be any better unless they were from the top of the hotel. In fact, The Spring House offers a romantic dinner for two in the cupola that sits above the roof line of the hotel. For $100 plus the cost of whatever you order off the menu, you and that special someone can spend an evening in the glass-enclosed cupola enjoying a gourmet dinner from the hotel's restaurant. From your secluded perch you have a panoramic view of the whole island from the windows on all four sides of the cupola, and your private waiter will bring appetizers, entrees, dessert, and drinks (alcohol included) to your table. For another $225 to $315 (depending on the season), you can rent the honeymoon suite, complete with Jacuzzi, private deck with French doors, and another great ocean view. In the summer schedule your visit to coincide with the Spring House's jazz concerts, held out on the lawn Sundays in July and August.

Over in the New Harbor on Ocean Avenue, the 1905 **Narragansett Inn** (466–2626) has a tiny bar with an awesome view of the harbor. Most island visitors never find it; you should. Sit at one of the handful of tables inside, or take your drink outside on the deck or onto the lawn to admire the scenery. Of all the island's old hotels, by the way, the Narragansett is the only one to retain its original floor plan. Room rates range from $65 to $140, double occupancy; open May 1 to November 1.

To really get a feel for the "different" side of Block Island, however, you need to get out of town and explore the rest of the island, particularly the north end—accessible only via Corn Neck Road—and the southwestern corner, where many of the sites are reached only by traveling over bumpy dirt roads. If you need to commune alone with the sea, you usually can get your wish at such isolated stretches of sand as **North Light Beach** and **Mansion Beach** on the north end and **Black Rock Beach** (home of the island's unofficial "clothing optional" beach), **Charlestown Beach,** and **Grace's Cove** on the west side. Charlestown Beach and Black Rock Beach lure surfcasters with the promise of biting striped bass—a 75-pound striper was taken from the beaches here in 1984. To get the lowdown on local fishing, stop by **Twin Maples** on Beach Avenue (466–5547) and let Mack Swentor, the island's fishing guru, bend your ear for a while.

The North Light Beach is located past the eponymous lighthouse. From the end of Corn Neck Road, walk along the shoreline past the lighthouse and around Sandy Point to the beach. While you're here, stop at the **North Light Interpretive Center,** open daily 10:00 A.M. to 5:00 P.M. from June 18 to Labor Day and 11:00 A.M. to 4:00 P.M. from September 6 to October 10; weekends 11:00 A.M. to 4:00 P.M. from May 28 to June 12, and 11:00 A.M. to 3:00 P.M. from October 15 to November 27. Admission is $2.00 and free for children under six.

Mansion Beach is at the end of Mansion Road, a dirt path on the east side of Corn Neck Road just north of the Great Salt Pond. Black Rock

Beach is at the end of a very long dirt path off Cooneymus Road. Charlestown Beach is at the end of Coast Guard Road, and Grace's Cove is at the end of Grace's Cove Road; both are off West Side Road.

In order to explore the island, you first need to choose a mode of transportation. Cars, expensive to bring over on the ferry and useless on many of the island's smaller roads, are a poor choice. Ditto for mopeds, which can be dangerous in the hands of novices and a source of irritation for island residents. The best choice, if you can brave Block Island's many hills, is to ride a bicycle. Either bring your own or rent one on the island.

For a change of pace, though, why not try a carriage ride? Joe and Lisa Sprague have fifteen Percheron draft horses and a wagon and surrey that you can rent by the hour for a ride around the island. For romance, choose the surrey (and yes, there is fringe on top), which can seat up to three passengers; if you have a big group, go for the twelve-passenger wagon. *Sprague Farms* (West Side Road, 466–2885) offers charter rates of $60 for the first hour, $50 for each additional hour; for weddings, they will decorate the surrey and groom the horses especially for the big event.

Continuing the equestrian theme, horseback riding at *Rustic Rides Stables* (West Side Road, 466–5060) is another way to enjoy the western side of Block Island. The expert trail guides will lead your well-mannered mounts through seventy acres of countryside and right down to the shore for a ride on the beach between the cliffs and the sea. The one-hour trail rides are offered every day during the summer between 9:00 A.M. and 6:00 P.M. and cost $35 to $45. There are ponies for the children, too.

Closer to town on West Side Road is the *Island Cemetery,* an interesting place to walk around and a great spot for gravestone etchings. Almost any old New England cemetery holds its fascinations, but Block Island's graveyard is notable for the nautical themes on the markers and the numerous stones with family names like Ball and Dodge—descendants of the sixteen original white settlers who landed on the island in 1661. The oldest headstone, remarkably well preserved after three centuries of salt water and wind, is that of Margaret Guthry, who died in 1687.

The *Mohegan Bluffs,* 200-foot-tall cliffs carved out of the island by the relentless Atlantic, arguably make up the most famous spot on Block Island. Nearly everyone who visits the island goes to see the bluffs and the adjacent *Southeast Light,* the 1875 lighthouse that is equipped with the East Coast's most powerful beacon. Relatively few, however, climb down the seemingly endless stairs that lead to the narrow beach at the foot of the cliffs. Once you descend, there are more than 3 miles of secluded shore to explore, but keep in mind that what goes down must, of necessity, come back up again. It's a workout, but worth it.

One of Block Island's prettiest buildings also is home to a bed-and-breakfast. The **Weather Bureau Inn** (Beach Avenue, New Harbor, 466–9977 or 800–633–8624) really was a U.S. weather station from 1903 to 1950, but the inn is the furthest thing from a typical cinder-block government building. Sitting on top of a hill that backs onto a pond, the symmetrical white Federal-style building is fronted by a Greek Revival porch. A huge flag flies from a flagpole on the roof, which also has a deck and chairs for guests. Innkeeper Brian Wright welcomes guests year-round to stay in the inn's four rooms, each with high ceilings and decorated in light colors, and one of which has a fireplace that is popular with winter visitors.

Breakfast includes fresh fruit and coffee cake made right on the island, portobello mushroom quiche, and blueberry biscuits. Chocolate chip cookies are on the table all day long, and at night guests can relax with a glass of wine or cognac and nibble on some cheese. If you feel like working off that food in the morning, the inn has free 15-speed mountain bikes and kayaks you can borrow. Room rates are $95 to $345 in the summer and $95 to $169 after Columbus Day.

We won't say that a stay at the **Sasafrash** bed-and-breakfast (Center Road, 466–5486) will be a religious experience, but one of the charms of this island B&B is that it's located in a turn-of-the-century church.

Bloody Bluffs

*T*he natives of Block Island were called the Manisseans, and they called their home Manisses—The Island of the Little God. So why is the island's most prominent natural feature named after a mainland tribe, the Mohegans?

According to Manissean legend, island natives were preparing for a raid on nearby Long Island when they spied a war party of Mohegans approaching Block Island on a raid of their own. The Manissean warriors quickly turned back to shore and set an ambush for the Mohegans. Taken by surprise, the Mohegan war party was driven to the edge of the cliffs at the southern end of the island, where they threw up an earthen defensive berm in a last-ditch attempt to stave off annihilation.

During the pitched battle that followed the Mohegans were wiped out. But long after their fortifications faded away and the Manisseans slipped away into history, the battle is remembered in the name of the Mohegan Bluffs.

Southeast Light

The building, which also houses an antiques shop, retains many vestiges of its former use, including stained-glass windows, a choir loft, and a raised pulpit. Guests often come away enraptured by the large, clean rooms and the hospitality of inn-keepers Shirley and Sanford Kessler. Each morning is welcomed with a continental breakfast served in the former church sanctuary.

The circa 1870 **Woonsocket House,** standing at the corner of Old Town Road and Ocean Avenue, is home to the **Block Island Historical Society** (466–2481), which has a museum that's open to the public. Part of the exhibit depicts the interior of a typical island home of the late nineteenth century, with antique furnishings, dishes, and an old loom. An upstairs gallery is devoted to changing exhibits on different aspects of the island's history and heritage. The museum and gift shop are open daily 10:00 A.M. to 5:00 P.M. from the end of June to Labor Day and on weekends through Columbus Day.

Because Block Island is surrounded by the Atlantic Ocean, most visitors naturally think about activities centered on the open sea rather than the island's more than one hundred ponds. Renting a kayak is a great way to explore these inland waterways, and **Oceans & Ponds** at the Orvis Store rents single or double kayaks by the hour, half-day, and full day. After a short instruction period, Bruce Johnson and his staff will drive you and your kayak to the town dock in New Harbor, where you can launch into the waters of Trims Pond, Harbor Pond, and the expansive Great Salt Pond. Trims Pond and Harbor Pond are free of boat traffic and are full of geese and ducks; you get to paddle under two bridges and can slow to admire the cottages along the shore or cruise around tiny coves. There are plenty of big boats in the Great Salt Pond, including the ferries from Long Island and the huge yachts cluttering the local marinas, but there also are quiet spots like Cormorant Point Cove and Skipper's Island, which sits offshore of the beach at the end of Andy's Way.

If you have children with you, you can forgo the windy Great Salt Pond and head north to Sachem's Pond at the end of Corn Neck Road. Located in the middle of a nature preserve, Sachem's Pond teems with wildlife and has a small, sandy beach and virtually no waves. Across the parking lot is *Settler's Rock,* marking the spot where the original European settlers and their cows came ashore in 1661. For a taste of adventure, rent one of the ocean kayaks at the Town Beach and spend a few hours riding the waves back into shore. Oceans & Ponds rents single kayaks for $25 per half-day; doubles are $35 per half-day. Rates include instruction and transportation. The Town Beach rents ocean kayaks for $15 per hour.

The Orvis store is located on Ocean Avenue (466–5131). The staff also run charter boats that go for stripers, bluefish, and bonito; excursion boats to Newport; and guided beach fly-fishing trips.

Finally, don't forget to take the time to explore the *Greenway,* the network of trails that link a series of properties preserved by the Nature Conservancy and other island residents—more than 600 acres in all. There are access points for the Greenway off many of the island's main

The Happy Accident of Block Island

*B**lock Island as we know it today probably wouldn't exist if not for a couple of unfortunate turns of fate that befell this small community.*

Like most of New England, big chunks of Block Island were cleared for farming during the eighteenth and nineteenth centuries. And as on the mainland, the local farming industry went into near-terminal decline in the middle of the twentieth century, as big Midwestern farms and modern shipping and preservation techniques undercut the region's produce market. This only added to the problems of an island economy already battered by the decline of the tourist trade after World War I, which had left many of the island's big Victorian-era inns shuttered and empty.

When preservationists and the tourist industry rediscovered Block Island in the 1970s, both found a diamond in the rough. Groups like the Nature Conservancy began working to preserve all of those old farmers' fields that had grown wild again, as well as tracts of land that had never been developed. At the same time, work began on restoring the big hotels—many of which still remained despite years of neglect, partly because no one could afford to tear them down.

So, whenever you look at Block Island's beautiful artificial and natural wonders, it's appropriate to remember the old adage: When life hands you lemons, make lemonade. They've sure made some sweet stuff here.

roads, and paths take you from **Rodman's Hollow,** carved by an ancient glacier and overlooking Black Rock, and north through a pretty vale called the **Enchanted Forest** to the shores of the Great Salt Pond. Across the street from Littlefield's Bee Farm on Corn Neck Road is the entrance to the Nature Conservancy's **Clay Head** nature preserve, which features hiking trails down to a secluded beach edged by clay bluffs. A highlight of any visit to Block Island should be a walk through The Maze, a unique pine forest crisscrossed by trails off the main path at Clay Head.

Call the Nature Conservancy's Block Island headquarters (466–2129) for more information, or you can get a Greenway map at the group's office on Ocean Avenue, in New Harbor across the street from Deadeye Dick's. The Nature Conservancy also runs four weekly guided nature walks in the spring and fall and ten weekly walks in the summer; staff members and volunteers also do a guided winter walk for groups if you call ahead; the suggested donation is $2.00 per person and is well worth it.

PLACES TO STAY IN SOUTH COUNTY—THE OCEAN SHORE AND BLOCK ISLAND

(ALL AREA CODES 401)

NARRAGANSETT
The Atlantic House,
85 Ocean Road, 783–6400

Dunmere,
560 Ocean Road, 783–3797

The Lighthouse Inn
307 Great Island Road,
Galilee, 789–9341 or
(800) 336–6662

The Four Gables,
12 South Pier Road,
789–6948

1900 House B&B,
59 Kingstown Road,
789–7971

Old Clerk House,
49 Narragansett Avenue,
783–8008

The Ocean Rose Inn,
113 Ocean Road, 783–4704

The Pleasant Cottage B&B,
104 Robinson Street,
783–6895

The Richards B&B,
144 Gibson Avenue,
789–7746

Stone Lea B&B,
40 Newton Avenue,
783–9546

The Village Inn,
One Beach Street,
783–6767 or
(800) THE–PIER

SOUTH KINGSTOWN
The Admiral Dewey Inn,
668 Matunuck Beach Road,
789–2090 or
(800) 457–2090

Almost Heaven in Snug
Harbor B&B,
49 West Street, 783–9272

Selected Chambers of Commerce in South County—The Ocean Shore and Block Island

Block Island Chamber of Commerce,
234 Water Street, Block Island 02807; 466-2982

Narragansett Chamber of Commerce,
P.O. Box 742, Narragansett 02882-3612; 783-7121

South Kingstown Chamber of Commerce,
328 Main Street, Wakefield 02879-7404; 783-2801

Westerly-Pawcatuck Chamber of Commerce,
One Chamber Way, Westerly 02891-2600; 596-7761

The Applewood Greene
B&B, 841 East Mooresfield
Road, 789–1937

The Captain's B&B,
2 Heather Hollow,
782–3445

The Coachman Motor Inn,
3199 Tower Hill Road,
Routes 1 and 138,
783–2516

Green Hill Beach Motel,
Green Hill Beach Road,
789–9153

The Kings' Rose, 1747
Mooresfield Road,
783–5222 or
(800) 230–ROSE

The Larchwood Inn,
521 Main Street, Wakefield,
783–5454

Matunuck Breakers,
955 Matunuck Beach Road,
789–3801 or 273–9849

CHARLESTOWN
The General Stanton Inn,
Route 1A, 364–8888 or
364–0100

Hathaway's B&B,
4470 Old Post Road,
364–6665

The Ocean View Motor Inn,
5407B Post Road, Route 1,
364–0080

One Willow by the Sea, One
Willow Road, 364–0802

The Summer House,
2231 Schoolhouse/
Charlestown Beach Road,
364–6926

The Willows Motel-Resort,
5310 Post Road,
364–7727 or
(800) 842–2181

WESTERLY
The Country Club Inn,
164 Shore Road, 348–8216

Grandview B&B,
212 Shore Road, 596–6384
or (800) 447–6384

The Inn at Watch Hill,
118 Bay Street, Watch Hill,
596–0665

Kismet on the Park,
71 High Street, 596–3237

The Ocean House,
2 Bluff Avenue, Watch Hill,
348–8161

Pine Lodge Motel,
92 Old Post Road,
322–0333

Pleasant View Inn,
65 Atlantic Avenue,
Misquamicut, 348–8200 or
(800) 782–3224

The Shelter Harbor Inn,
10 Wagner Road, 322–8883

The Villa,
190 Shore Road,
596–1054 or
(800) 722–9240

The Watch Hill Inn,
38 Bay Street, Watch Hill,
348–6300 or
(800) 356–9314

The Weekapaug Inn,
25 Spring Avenue,
Weekapaug, 322–0301

The Winnapaug Inn,
169 Shore Road, Scenic
Route 1A, 348–8350 or
(800) 288–9906

Woody Hill B&B,
149 South Woody Hill Road,
322–0452

BLOCK ISLAND
The Atlantic Inn, High
Street, 466–5883

Ballard's Inn, Water Street,
466–2231

Blueberry Hill Guest
House, West Side Road,
466–2159

The Blue Dory Inn, Dodge
Street, 466–5891 or
(800) 992–7290

Calico Hill B&B, Old Town
Road, 466–2136

Champlin's Hotel, West Side
Road, 466–2641 or
(800) 762–4541

The Fagan Cottage B&B,
Beacon Hill Road,
466–5383

The Gables Inn, Dodge
Street, 466–2213

The Gothic Inn, 440 Dodge
Street, 466–2918

The Harborside Inn, Water
Street, 466–5504 or
(800) 892–2022

The Hotel Manisses, Spring
Street, 466–2063 or
466–2421

The Island Manor Resort,
Chapel Street, 466–5567 or
466–2431

Maple Leaf Cottage, Off Beacon Hill Road, 466–2065

The Narragansett Inn, Ocean Avenue, 466–2626

The National Hotel, Water Street, 466–2901

The Weather Bureau Inn, Beach Avenue, (800) OFF–TO–BI

The Pondview B&B, Mitchell Lane, 466–2937

The Rose Farm Inn, Roslyn Road, 466–2034

The Sasafrash B&B, Center Road, 466–5486

The Seacrest Inn B&B, High Street, 466–2882

The Sheffield House, High Street, 466–2494

The 1661 Inn, Spring Street, 466–2421 or 466–2063

The Spring House, 52 Spring Street, 466–5844, 466–2633, or (800) 234–9263

The Sullivan House, 416 Corn Neck Road, 466–5020

The Water Street Inn, Water Street, 466–2605 or (800) 825–6254

The White House, Spring Street, 466–2653

PLACES TO EAT IN SOUTH COUNTY—THE OCEAN SHORE AND BLOCK ISLAND

(ALL AREA CODES 401)

NARRAGANSETT

Aunt Carrie's Seafood Restaurant, 1240 Ocean Road, 783–7930

Casa Rossi, 90 Point Judith Road, 789–6385

Charlie O's Tavern on the Point, 2 Sand Hill Cove Road, 782–2002

George's of Galilee, 250 Sand Hill Cove Road, 783–2306

The Spanish Tavern, 1 Beach Street, 783–3550

Spain Restaurant, 1144 Ocean Road, 783–9770

Terms Restaurant, 135 Boon Street, 782–4242

Twin Willows, 865 Boston Neck Road, 789–8153

SOUTH KINGSTOWN

The Italian Village, 195 Main Street, 783–3777

The Larchwood Inn, 521 Main Street, 783–5454

The Mews Tavern, 456 Main Street, 783–9370

The Pump House, 1464 Kingstown Road, 789–4944

CHARLESTOWN

Charlestown Lobster Pot, Route 1, 322–7686

The Nordic Lodge, 178 East Passquiset Trail, 783–4515

Spice of Life Cafe, Fantastic Umbrella Factory, Scenic Route 1A, 364–2030

The Wilcox Tavern, 5153 Old Post Road, 322–1829

WESTERLY

Mary's Italian Restaurant, Route 1, Haversham Corners, 322–0444

Olympia Tea Room, 74 Bay Street, 348–8211

Rafters, 55 Beach Street, 596–5709

The Shelter Harbor Inn, 10 Wagner Road, 322–8883

Three Fish, 37 Main Street, 348–9700

BLOCK ISLAND

Aldo's Place, 130 Chapel Street, 466–5871

The Atlantic Inn, High Street, 466–5883

Ballard's Inn, Water Street, Old Harbor, 466–2231

The Beachhead, Corn Neck Road, 466–2249

Bethany's Airport Diner, 466–3100

Champlin's Marina Restaurant, New Harbor, 466–2760

Dead Eye Dick's,
218 Ocean Avenue,
466–2654

The Hotel Manisses, Spring
Street, 466–2063 or
466–2421

McGovern's Yellow Kittens,
Corn Neck Road, 466–5855

Mohegan Cafe,
Water Street, 466–5911

The Oar, New Harbor,
466–8820

Samuel Peckham Tavern,
New Harbor, 466–5458

The Spring House,
Spring Street, 466–5844

Water Street Cafe,
Water Street, 466–5540

Winfield's, Corn Neck
Road, 466–5856

**OTHER ATTRACTIONS WORTH
SEEING IN SOUTH COUNTY—
THE OCEAN SHORE
AND BLOCK ISLAND**

Adventureland,
Narragansett

Atlantic Beach Amusement
Park, *Westerly*

Burlingame Management
Area, *Charlestown*

Kimball Wildlife Refuge,
Charlestown

Narragansett Indian
Monument, *Narragansett*

Point Judith Lighthouse,
Narragansett

Water Wizz, *Westerly*

**HELPFUL WEB SITES ABOUT
SOUTH COUNTY—
THE OCEAN SHORE
AND BLOCK ISLAND**

Block Island, Rhode Island,
www.blockisland.com

Charlestown Home Page,
www.charlestown.com

Narragansett, Rhode
Island, cshell.com/ncc/

South County, cshell.com/

South County Fun,
users.ids.net/%7
Escfun/

South County,
Rhode Island,
www.southcounty.com/

South Kingstown,
http://cshell.com/skcc

Town of Westerly,
www.watchhill.com/townof
westerly/

Unofficial South Kingstown
Home Page, users.ids.
net/~garyc/skri.htm

Westerly Visitor's Guide,
cshell.com/wcc/

Index

A

AS220, 12
Aardvark Antiques, 121
Abigail and Magnolia's, 143
Abraham Manchester
   Restaurant, 147
Adamsville, 147
Admiral Dewey Inn, 185
Aidan's Pub, 93
Alaimo Gallery, 3
Alanjays Music and Gift Shop, 86
Allen House, 45
Allie's Donuts, 164
America's Cup Hall Of Fame, 95
Ancients & Horribles Parade, 66
Angelo's Civita Farnese, 6
Animation Art Gallery, 120
Ann & Hope, 70
Antiques and Artifacts, 3
Appleland, 71
Apponaug, 34
Aquidneck Lobster, 107
Arcadia Management Area, 168
Armory of the Kentish Guards, 42
Arnold Mills, 68
Artillery Company of Newport
   Museum, 115
Artrolley, 13
Ashland Causeway, 42
Atomic Grill, 4
Audubon Society of Rhode Island, 71
Audra's Cafe, 44
Aunt Carrie's Seafood
   Restaurant, 176
Avon Cinema, 1

B

Babcock–Smith House, 190
Baptist Church in Warren, 83
Barn, The, 148

Barrington, 81–82
Barrington Town Hall, 82
Battery Park, 104
Bay Queen Cruises, 85
Bay Voyage Inn, 128
Beavertail Lighthouse, 129
Beavertail Lighthouse Museum, 129
Beavertail State Park, 129
Belcourt Castle, 109
Belleville Pond, 163
Ben and Jerry's Folk Festival, 115
Benefit Street, 10
Black Hut Management Area, 62
Black Marble, 86
Black Rock Beach, 197
Black Ships Festival, 115
Blackstone Boulevard, 10
Blackstone Gorge Bi-State Park, 58
Blackstone River State Park, 55, 73
Blackstone Valley Explorer, 53
Blithewold Mansion
   and Gardens, 96
Block Island, 195–202
Block Island Ferry, 176
Block Island Historical Society, 200
Blue Grotto, The, 6
Borden Mill, 145
Boston Paintball South, 26
Boston–Providence
   Skydiving Center, 75
Boyd's Windmill, 134
Bradford-Dimond-Norris
   House, 90
Brandaris, 160
Brenton Point State Park, 119
Brickyard Pond, 79
Bristol, 87–93
Bristol Cinema, 90
Brown & Hopkins Country
   Store, 63

Browning Mill Pond
   Recreation Area, 168
Buck Hill Managament Area, 61
Burnside Memorial, 81
Burrillville, 60–63
Byfield School, 92

C

CAV, 3
C. R. Wilbur General Store, 149
Cable Car Cinema, 10
Cafe Dolce Vita, 5
Cafe Nuovo, 8
Cajun and Bluegrass Festival, 169
Call, The, 4
Callegaro's Old Depot Deli, 16
Camden Passage, 9
Camille's Roman Garden, 6
Canonchet Farm, 175
Cardines Field, 105–06
Casa Christine, 6
Caserta's, 6
Casey Farm, 162
Casimir Pulaski State Park, 62
Castique, Inc., 37
Castle Hill Inn and Resort, 119
Castle Hill Light, 120
Castle Luncheonette, 57
C. C. Ledbetter, 15
Century Lounge, 5
Chace Farm, 75
Champlins, 177
Chan's Fine Oriental Dining, 57
Charlestown, 186–89
Charlestown Beach, 197
Chase Cory House, 144
Chepachet, 63
Cherry Valley Herb Farm, 67
Chocolate Delicacy, The, 43
Christmas House, The, 167–68
Church of Saint John the
   Evangelist, 103

City Nights Dinner Theatre, 19
Clay Head, 202
Clemence-Irons House, 26
Cliffside Inn, The, 110
Coast Guard House, 175
Coffee Exchange, 1
Coggeshall Farm Museum, 89
Cogswell Tower, 23
Colonial Theatre, 191
Colt State Park, 79
Comedy Connection, 15
Comina, 9
Commons Restaurant, 149
Commons, The, 148–49
Conimicut Point Lighthouse, 33
Conimicut Point Park, 33
Conklin Limestone Quarry, 72
Copper Wave, 38
Cottage at Four Corners, The, 143
Courtyards, 144
Coventry, 47–50
Cranston, 22–25
Crescent Park Looff Carousel, 17
Croquet Hall of Fame, 112
Crossroads Coffeehouse, 39
Crow's Nest, 35
Culinary Archives and
   Museum, 14
Cumberland, 67–70

D

Daggett House, 22
Dame Farm, 25
Dari-Bee Soft Serve, 16
Dave's Den, 188
Davisville Memorial
   Wildlife Refuge, 47
Decorum, 38
Delekta Pharmacy, 83
Depasquale Square, 5
Diamond Hill State Park, 69
Diamond Hill Vineyards, 68

INDEX

Dino's General Store, 94
Diva's Palace, 36
Doll Museum, 116
Donovan Gallery, 143
Dorr, Thomas, 65
Duffy's Tavern, 158
Dunmere, 176
Dutch Island, 131

E

East Bay B&B, The, 128–29
East Bay Bike Path, 16, 79
East Beach, 189
East Greenwich, 42–47
East Greenwich Town Hall, 45
East Providence, 15–17
Easton's Point, 101
Edgewood Manor, 25
Eight Rod Way, 145
1880 Town Hall, 91
1890 Town Hall, 82
1873 House, 45
1817 Bristol County Courthouse, 92
Eleazer Arnold House, 74
Emile Reuker Wildlife
    Refuge, 142
Enchanted Cottage B&B Inn, 33
Enchanted Forest, 202
Enchanted Forest of
    Rhode Island, 170
Evelyn's Drive-In, 142
Exeter, 165–70
Exeter Country Club, 166

F

Fantastic Umbrella Factory, 188
Fayerweather Craft
    Center, 179
Feast of Saint Joseph, 7
Federal Hill, 5
Fellini Pizzeria, 1
Festival of Lights, 161

15 Point Road, 138
First Baptist Church, 92
First Congregational
    Church, 179
First Methodist Church, 84
Fisherville Brook Wildlife
    Refuge, 166
Florentine Grill, 17
Flo's Clam Shack, 138
Flying Horse Carousel, 193
Fogland Beach, 145
Fort Adams, 114
Fort Barton, 141
Fort Getty, 131
Fort Mansfield, 194
Fort Wetherill State Park, 130
Foster, 49–51
Four Corners Grille, 143
Frances Fleet, 177
Frank and John from Italy, 44
Freeman's Farm Bed and
    Breakfast, 66
Fuller Rock Lighthouse, 16

G

Galilee, 177
Ganier Memorial Dam, 42
Garden Grille, 20
Gardiner Jackson Park, 9
Gaspee Days Celebration, 31
Gatehouse Restaurant, 10
Gator's Pub and Restaurant, 60
General James Mitchell Varnum
    House, 42
General Prescott's guardhouse, 131
George Hail Library, 82
George B. Parker Woodland, 48
George's of Galilee, 177
George Washington
    Management Area, 62
Gilbert Stuart Birthplace and
    Museum, 161–62

Gloucester, 63–67
Goat Island, 104
Governor Sprague Mansion, 23
Grace-fully Yours, 43
Grace's Cove, 197
Gray's Ice Cream, 142
Gray's Store, 148
Great Swamp Wildlife
    Reservation, 180
Green Animals Topiary
    Gardens, 137
Green Door, 43
Greenhouse, 189
Greenvale Vineyards, 140
Greenway, 201
Greenwich Odeum, 45
Grille on Main, The, 44

H

Haddie Pierce House, The, 161
Haffenreffer Museum of
    Anthropology, 96
Haines Memorial State Park, 79
Hanging Rock, 136
Hannah Robinson's Rock, 179
Hannaway Blacksmith Shop, 75
Hanson's Landing, 184,
Harbourside Lobstermania, 46
Harmony House B&B, 150
Haunted Newport Week, 110
Haven Bros. Diner, 13
Hazard Memorial Library, 184
Helm House Gallery, 179
Hemenway's, 9
Heritage Foundation of
    Rhode Island, 94
Herreshoff Marine
    Museum, 95
Hilltop Creamery, 46
Historic Pontiac Mills, 36
Hopkinton, 170
Horsefeathers Antiques, 86

Horseshoe Dam, 41
Hotel Manisses, 196
Houle Pianos, 38
Hunter House, 101

I

Ice Cream Machine, 69
Independence Park, 81
Indian Club, 44
Inn at Shadow Lawn, The, 135
International Bazaar, 188
Island Cemetery, 198
Island Park, 138
Island Park Beach, 139

J

Jack's Island Beach, 142
Jailhouse Inn, 116
Jamestown, 125–31
Jamestown B&B, 129
Jamestown Bridges, 178–79
Jamestown & Newport Ferry
    Company, 127
Jedediah Smith Homestead, 72
Jewelry District, 3
Jigger's Diner, 43
Job Armstrong Store, 64
Johnston, 25–27
Joseph Reynolds House, 88
Julia's, 45
JVC Jazz Festival, 115

K

Keep Providence Beautiful
    Pasta Challenge, 8
Kelly House, 74
Kennedy Plaza, 8
Kent Restaurant, 44
Kenyon's Grist Mill, 181
King Philip's Chair, 98
King's Rose, 179
Kingston, 179

Kingston Free Library, 179
Kismet on the Park, 190
Kountry Kitchen, 72

L

La Gondola, 8
L'Elizabeth, 9
Lady Next Door, The, 86
Lafayette, 163
Lafayette Trout Hatchery, 165
Land's End B&B, 149
Lighthouse Bed and Breakfast, 94
Lincoln, 72–76
Linden Place, 90
Little Compton, 146
Little Compton Historical
    Society, 150
Little Purls, 144
Living Room, 12
Llama Farma, 69
Lobster Pot Restaurant and
    Gallery, 95
Looff Carousel, 22
Lupo's Heartbreak Hotel, 12

M

Madiera, 17
Magic Garden of Tiverton, 144
Mansion Beach, 197
Marcie's General Store, 94
Marion Eppley Wildlife
    Sanctuary, 182
Market Square, 56
Martino'a Pizzeria, 163
Masonic Temple, 84
Massasoit Spring, 82
Maxmillian's, 10
Maxwell House, 84
Mazzone Art Gallery, 188
McCoy Stadium, 20
Met Cafe, 12
Mexico, 7

Mi Guatemala, 7
Middle of Nowhere
    Diner, 167
Middletown, 131–37
Mill Pond Shops, 144
Modern Diner, 20
Mohegan Bluffs, 198
Montego Bay on the Hill, 7
Morris Novelty, 19
Mount Hope Bridge, 99
Mount Hope Farm, 98
Mount Maple of Wickford, 161
Mowry's Tavern, 73
Mr. Doughboy, 63
Mr. Taco, 40
Mudville's Pub, 106–7
Museum of Rhode Island History at
    Aldrich House, 11
Museum of Primitive Art and
    Culture, 183
Museum of Work and Culture, 56

N

Napatree Point, 193
Napatree Point Conservation
    Area, 194
Narragansett, 173–78
Narragansett Casino, 175
Narragansett Inn, 197
Narragansett Town Beach, 173
Narrow (Pettaquamsutt)
    River, 173
Narrow River Kayaks, 173
Nathaniel Greene
    Homestead, 47
Nathaniel Porter Inn, 84
Nature's Best Dairy World, 24
Naval War College Museum, 116
New England Architectural
    Center, 37
New England Wireless and Steam
    Museum, 46

New Tyler Point Grille, 82
Newport, 101–23
Newport Aquarium, 117
Newport Bridge, 104
Newport Butterfly Farm, 134
Newport Casino, 112
Newport Dinner Train, 121
Newport Vineyards and
    Winery, 137
Newport Visitor and Information
    Center, 105
Nordic Lodge, 186
Norman Bird Sanctuary, 136
North Central State Airport, 75
North Kingstown, 153–65
North Light Beach, 197
North Light Interpretive
    Center, 197
North Providence, 17–18
North Scituate, 40
North Smithfield, 58–60
North Tollgate House, 72

O

Observation Tower, 178
Ocean Avenue, 119
Ocean Coffee Roasters, 86
Ocean House, 192
Oceans & Ponds, 200
O-Cha Cafe, 3
Ochre Court, 110
Old Aaron Smith Farm, 62
Old Canteen, 6
Old Clerk House, 176
Old Colony & Newport
    Scenic Railway, 122
Old Court Bed and Breakfast,
    The, 15
Old Narragansett
    Church, 158–59
Old Post Office, The, 63
Old Washington County Jail, 180

Olympia Tea Room, 192
OOP!, 1
Osamequin Park, 81

P

Paddle Providence, 8
Paradise School, 134
Paradise Valley Park, 133
Parker Borden House, 90–91
Pawtucket, 18–22
Pawtucket Red Sox, 20
Pawtuxet Reservation
    Riverwalk, 25
Pawtuxet River, 38
Pawtuxet Village, 25
Peace Dale, 183
Peace Dale Manufacturing
    Company, 183
Pentimento, 68
Perishable Theatre, 12
Peter Pots Pottery, 182
Phantom Farms, 67
Pine Hill Point, 94
Pleasant Cottage B&B, 176
Point Judith, 176
Point Judith Lighthouse, 176
Pond Lilies, 144
Pontiac Mills' Young Actor's
    Theatre Company, 37
Portofino, 34
Portsmouth, 137–41
Post Office Cafe, 44
Post Road, 153
Powder Mill Ledges Wildlife
    Refuge, 70
Prescott Farm, 131
Prospect Terrace, 11
Provender, 143
Providence, 1–15
Providence Antique Center, 3
Providence Children's Museum, 5
Providence Point, 94

INDEX

Providence Riverwalk, 7
Prudence Island, 93
Pump House, The, 184
Purgatory Chasm, 136
Purple Cat, The, 64

Q

Queen's River Baptist Church, 181
Quonset Air Museum, 155
Quonset Point, 155
Quonset View Farm, 140

R

Redlefsen's Rotisserie and Grill, 93
Rathskeller, 188
Redwood Library and Athenaeum, 113
Renaissance Cafe, 39
Rhode Island Black Heritage
    Society Museum, 12
Rhode Island Fishermen and
    Whale Museum, 118
Rhode Island Red Monument, 147
Rhode Island Rock Gym, 19
Rhumb Line, The, 105
Richard Smith's Grove, 158
Richmond, 170–71
River Cafe, 57
River Island Park, 55
Riverside, 16
Robin's Nest Gift Shoppe, The, 43
Rockwell House Inn, 90
Rocky Point Chowder House, 33
Rod's Grill, 83
Rodman's Hollow, 202
Roost, The, 147
Rose Island Lighthouse, 104
Roseland Acres, 145
Rue de France, 120
Rumrunner II, 107
Rustic Drive-In, 60
Rustic Rides Stables, 198
Ryan Park, 163

S

S.S. Dion, 93
Sachuest Point Wildlife Refuge, 136
Sakonnet Light, 151
Sakonnet Point, 151
Sakonnet River Inn, 140
Sakonnet Vineyards, 146
St. Clair Annex, 192
St. Mark's Episcopal Church, 84
St. Mary's Catholic Church, 40
Samuel Whitehorne House, 108–9
Sandra Feinstein-Gamm Theatre, 4
Sandy Point Lighthouse, 94
Sanford-Covell Villa Marina, 103
Sasafrash B&B, 199
Schartner's Farms, 164
Schoolhouse Cafe, 127
Scialo Bros. Bakery, 6
Scituate, 40–42
Scituate Arts Festival, 41
Scituate Reservoir, 40
Sea Fare Inn, 139
Seagrave Memorial
    Observatory, 41
SeaHourse Grill, 185
Seamen's Church Institute, 118
Seaport Tavern, 159
Seapowet Marsh Wildlife
    Refuge, 142
Settler's Rock, 201
Shady Acres Restaurant and
    Dairy Bar, 50
Shannock, 171
Silvertop Diner, 13
Silverwood B&B, 46
Sin and Flesh Brook, 141
Slater Memorial Park, 22
Slater Mill National
    Historic Site, 18
Slatersville, 59
Small Axe Gallery, 188
Smith-Appleby House, 71

Smith's Castle at Cocumscussoc, 157
Smithfield, 70–72
Snake Den State Park, 26
Snookers, 4
South County Museum, 173
South End State Park, 94
South Kingstown, 178
South Main Street, 8
Southeast Light, 198
Southland, 178
Speaking Rocks, 145
Spice of Life Cafe, 188
Sprague Farms, 198
Spring Hill Sugar House, 166
Spring House, The, 196
Squantum Woods State Park, 16
Square Peg, The, 86
Stage Coach Tavern, The, 66
State House, 8
State House Inn, 15
Station, The, 40
Stella Maris Inn, 103
Step Stone Falls, 169
Stepping Stone Ranch, 169
Stone Bridge Dishes, 148
Stone House Club, 150
Stone Lea Bed and Breakast, 176
Stone Mill Antiques &
    Craft Center, 63
Stuart, Gilbert, 161
Summit, 49
Summit General Store, 49
Sunflower Cafe, The, 24
Sun-Up Gallery, 192
Swamp Meadow Covered Bridge, 50
Swan Point Cemetery, 10
Sydney L. Wright Museum, 125
Sylvanius–Brown House, 18

T
Tailored Crafts, 43
Tangy's Indoor Archery Lanes, 38

Ten Rod Road, 165
Thayer Street, 1
Theatre by the Sea, 184
Themes restaurant, 121
The Richards B&B, 176
Third and Elm Press, 105
Three Fish, 191
Tiverton, 141–46
Tiverton Four Corners, 142
Tiverton Historical Society, 144
Tiverton Town Hall, 141
Tomaquag Indian Memorial
    Museum, 168
Touisset Wildlife Refuge, 87
Touro Synagogue, 113
Trattoria Simpatico, 127
Tweet Balzano's Family
    Restaurant, 99
20 Water Street, 46
Twin Maples, 197
Twin Oaks, 23

U
United Congregational Church, 149

V
Valley Falls Heritage Park, 69
Vanderbilt Hall, 111
Varnum Military Museum, 43
Veteran's Memorial Parkway, 16
Villa, The, 194
Vincent House, 46

W
Walter's La Locanda del Coccio, 6
Warren, 82–87
Warren Antique Center, 86
Warren Fire Museum, 84
Warwick, 31–39
Warwick City Park, 35
Warwick Museum, 34
Washington County Fair, 170

Watch Hill, 191
Watch Hill Lighthouse, 193
Water Street, 84
Water Street Antiques, 86
Waterplace Park, 7
Watson Farm, 125
Weather Bureau Inn, 199
Weekapaug Inn, 194
Weetamoo Woods, 144
Wein-O-Rama, 24
West Greenwich, 169
West Kingston, 180
West Warwick, 40
Westerly, 189–95
Westin Hotel, 15
Wes's Rib House, 13
Whale Rock Lighthouse, 129
Wharf Tavern, 85
Whipple-Cullen Farmstead, 74
Whitehall, 133
White Mill Park, 62
Wickenden Street, 1
Wickford, 158

Wickford Art Festival, 160
Wickford Gourmet Foods, 159
Wilbor House, 150
Wilcox Park, 190
Wiley's at Middlebridge, 173
Wilkinson Mill, 18
William's Grant Inn, 92
Williams, Roger, 11, 71, 82, 157
Willingham Manor, 61
Woonsocket, 55–58
Woonsocket House, 200
Wright's Dairy Farm, 59
Wright's Farm Restaurant, 60

Y

Yankee Consignment, 86
Yawgoo Valley Ski Area
    and Water Park, 165
Ye Old English Fish and Chips
    Restaurant, 57

Z

Z Bar and Grille, 3

About the Author

A resident of Rhode Island since 1991, author Bob Curley is still finding new things to do and interesting places to visit in the Ocean State—often by accident, since well-marked roads and adequate street signs are not among the state's charms.

While not driving around visiting bed and breakfasts, museums, and Del's lemonade stands, Bob works out of his North Kingstown home as a full-time freelance writer and editor, covering such topics as travel, public policy, computers and technology, and health care. Bob shares office space with his wife, Christine, an attorney in private practice. The Curleys have two children, Christopher and Shannon, who are wise enough to occasionally drag their parents away from the office and out to play.

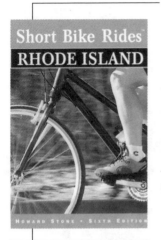

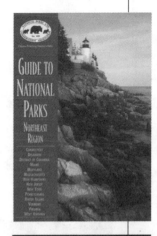